Rick and Morty

• presents •

AN ONI PRESS PUBLICATION

[adult swim]

THE VINDICATORS
WRITTEN BY **J. TORRES**
ILLUSTRATED BY **CJ CANNON**
COLORED BY **NICK FILARDI**
LETTERED BY **CRANK!**

KROMBOPULOS MICHAEL
WRITTEN BY **DANIEL MALLORY ORTBERG**
ILLUSTRATED BY **CJ CANNON**
COLORED BY **NICK FILARDI**
LETTERED BY **CRANK!**

Rick and Morty presents

SLEEPY GARY
WRITTEN BY **MAGDALENE VISAGGIO**
ILLUSTRATED BY **CJ CANNON**
COLORED BY **NICK FILARDI** AND **SARAH STERN**
LETTERED BY **CRANK!**

PICKLE RICK
WRITTEN BY **DELILAH S. DAWSON**
ILLUSTRATED BY **CJ CANNON**
COLORED BY **BRITTANY PEER**
LETTERED BY **CRANK!**

EDITED BY
ARI YARWOOD AND SARAH GAYDOS

DESIGNED BY
ANGIE KNOWLES

RETAIL COVER BY
CJ CANNON

ONI EXCLUSIVE COVER BY
JULIETA COLÁS

PUBLISHED BY ONI PRESS, INC.

JOE NOZEMACK, FOUNDER & CHIEF FINANCIAL OFFICER

JAMES LUCAS JONES, PUBLISHER

CHARLIE CHU, V.P. OF CREATIVE & BUSINESS DEVELOPMENT

BRAD ROOKS, DIRECTOR OF OPERATIONS

MELISSA MESZAROS, DIRECTOR OF PUBLICITY

MARGOT WOOD, DIRECTOR OF SALES

SANDY TANAKA, MARKETING DESIGN MANAGER

AMBER O'NEILL, SPECIAL PROJECTS MANAGER

TROY LOOK, DIRECTOR OF DESIGN & PRODUCTION

KATE Z. STONE, SENIOR GRAPHIC DESIGNER

SONJA SYNAK, GRAPHIC DESIGNER

ANGIE KNOWLES, DIGITAL PREPRESS LEAD

ARI YARWOOD, EXECUTIVE EDITOR

SARAH GAYDOS, EDITORIAL DIRECTOR OF LICENSED PUBLISHING

ROBIN HERRERA, SENIOR EDITOR

DESIREE WILSON, ASSOCIATE EDITOR

MICHELLE NGUYEN, EXECUTIVE ASSISTANT

JUNG LEE, LOGISTICS COORDINATOR

SCOTT SHARKEY, WAREHOUSE ASSISTANT

[adult swim]™

ONIPRESS.COM
FACEBOOK.COM/ONIPRESS
TWITTER.COM/ONIPRESS
ONIPRESS.TUMBLR.COM
INSTAGRAM.COM/ONIPRESS
ADULTSWIM.COM
FACEBOOK.COM/RICKANDMORTY
TWITTER.COM/RICKANDMORTY

THIS VOLUME COLLECTS ISSUES
RICK AND MORTY™ PRESENTS: THE VINDICATORS #1,
RICK AND MORTY™ PRESENTS: KROMBOPULOS MICHAEL #1,
RICK AND MORTY™ PRESENTS: SLEEPY GARY #1,
RICK AND MORTY™ PRESENTS: PICKLE RICK #1.

FIRST EDITION: MAY 2019
ISBN: 978-1-62010-552-8
EISBN: 978-1-62010-593-1
ONI EXCLUSIVE ISBN: 978-1-62010-592-4
LIBRARY OF CONGRESS CONTROL NUMBER: 2018962625

1 2 3 4 5 6 7 8 9 10

RICK AND MORTY™ CREATED BY JUSTIN ROILAND AND DAN HARMON

SPECIAL THANKS TO JUSTIN ROILAND, DAN HARMON, MARISA MARIONAKIS, ELYSE SALAZAR, MIKE MENDEL, MEAGAN BIRNEY AND JANET NO.

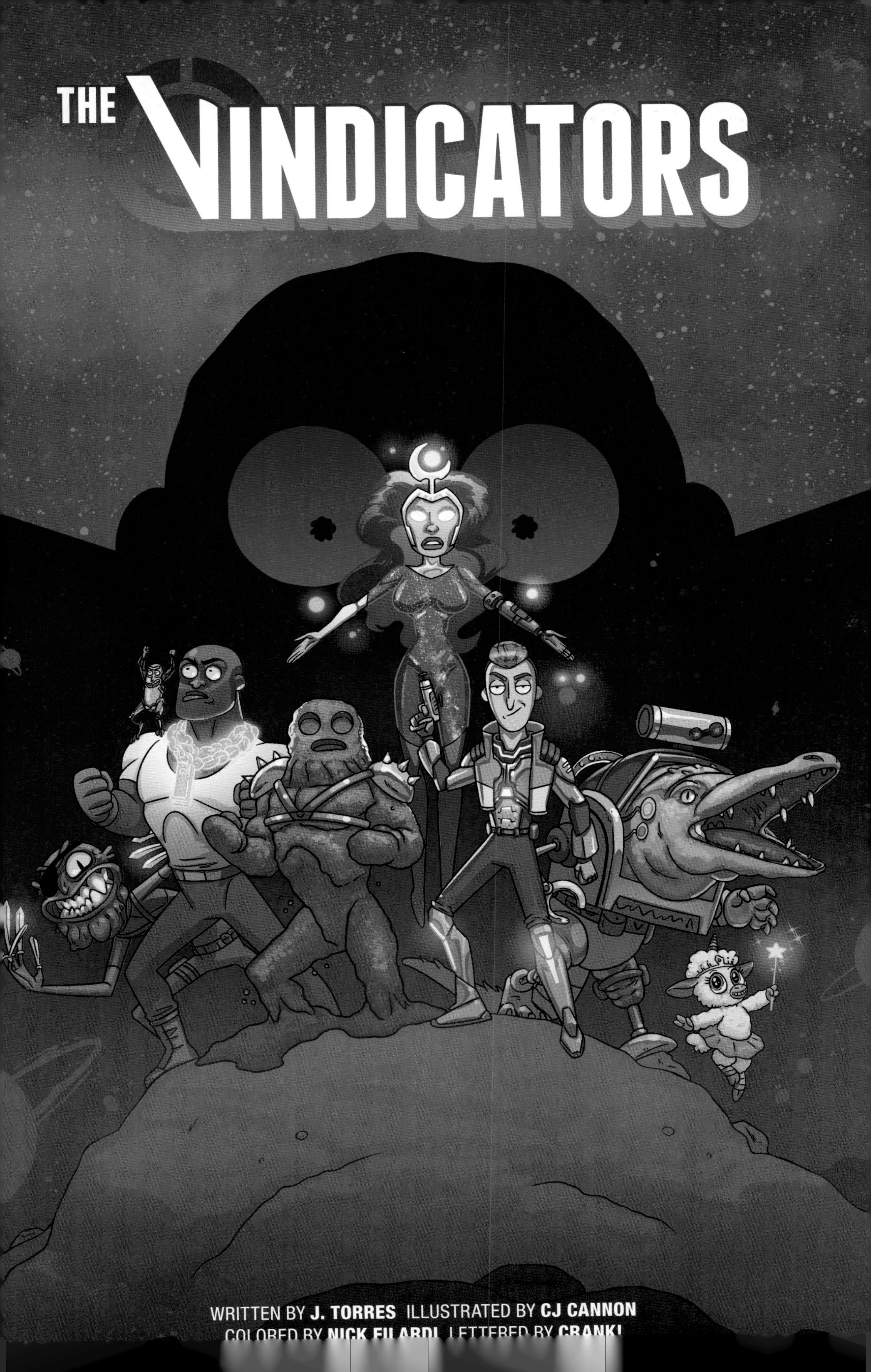
THE VINDICATORS
WRITTEN BY J. TORRES ILLUSTRATED BY CJ CANNON
COLORED BY NICK FILARDI LETTERED BY CRANK!

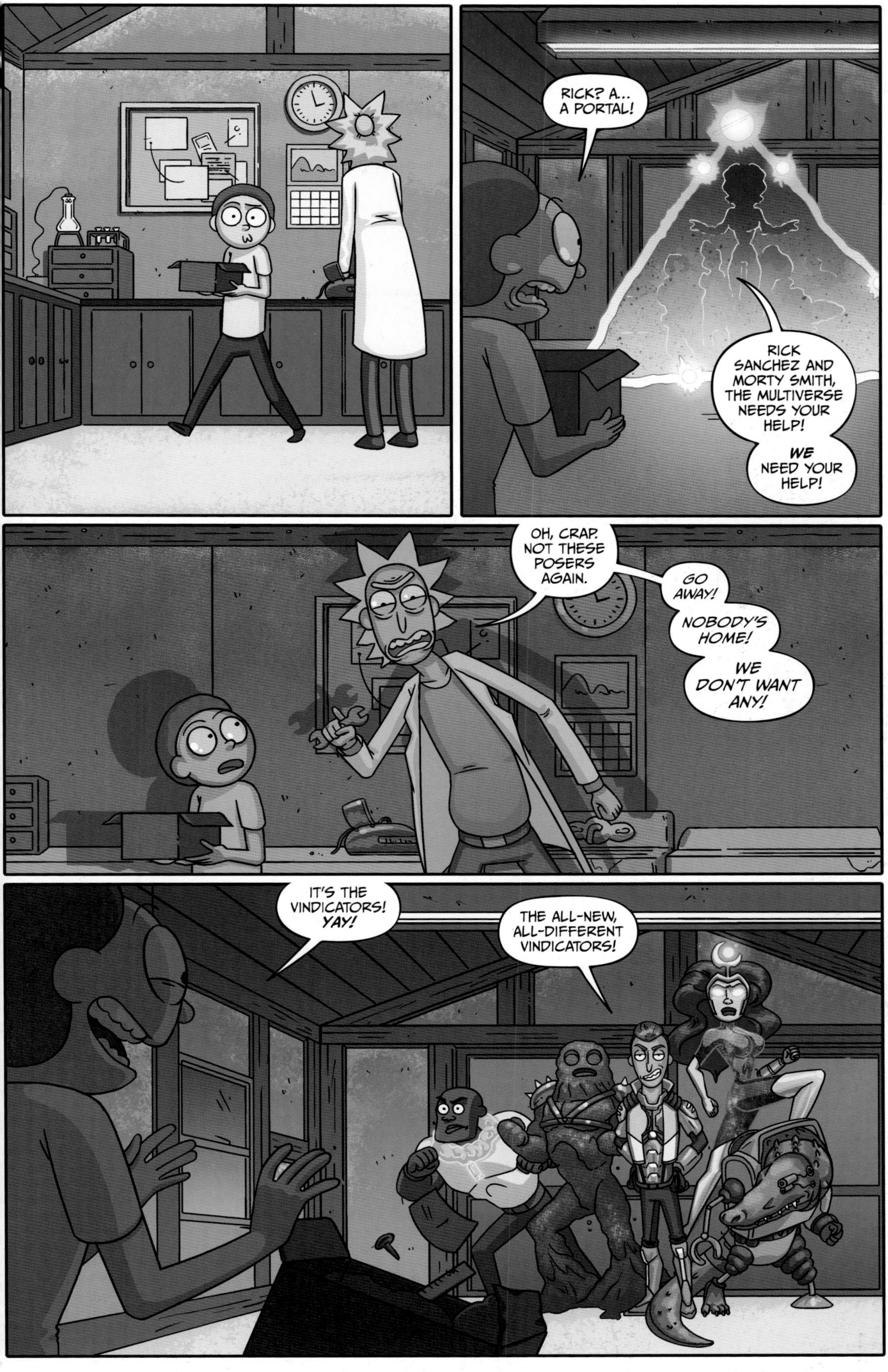

RICK? A... A PORTAL!
RICK SANCHEZ AND MORTY SMITH, THE MULTIVERSE NEEDS YOUR HELP!
WE NEED YOUR HELP!
OH, CRAP. NOT THESE POSERS AGAIN.
GO AWAY!
NOBODY'S HOME!
WE DON'T WANT ANY!
IT'S THE VINDICATORS! *YAY!*
THE ALL-NEW, ALL-DIFFERENT VINDICATORS!

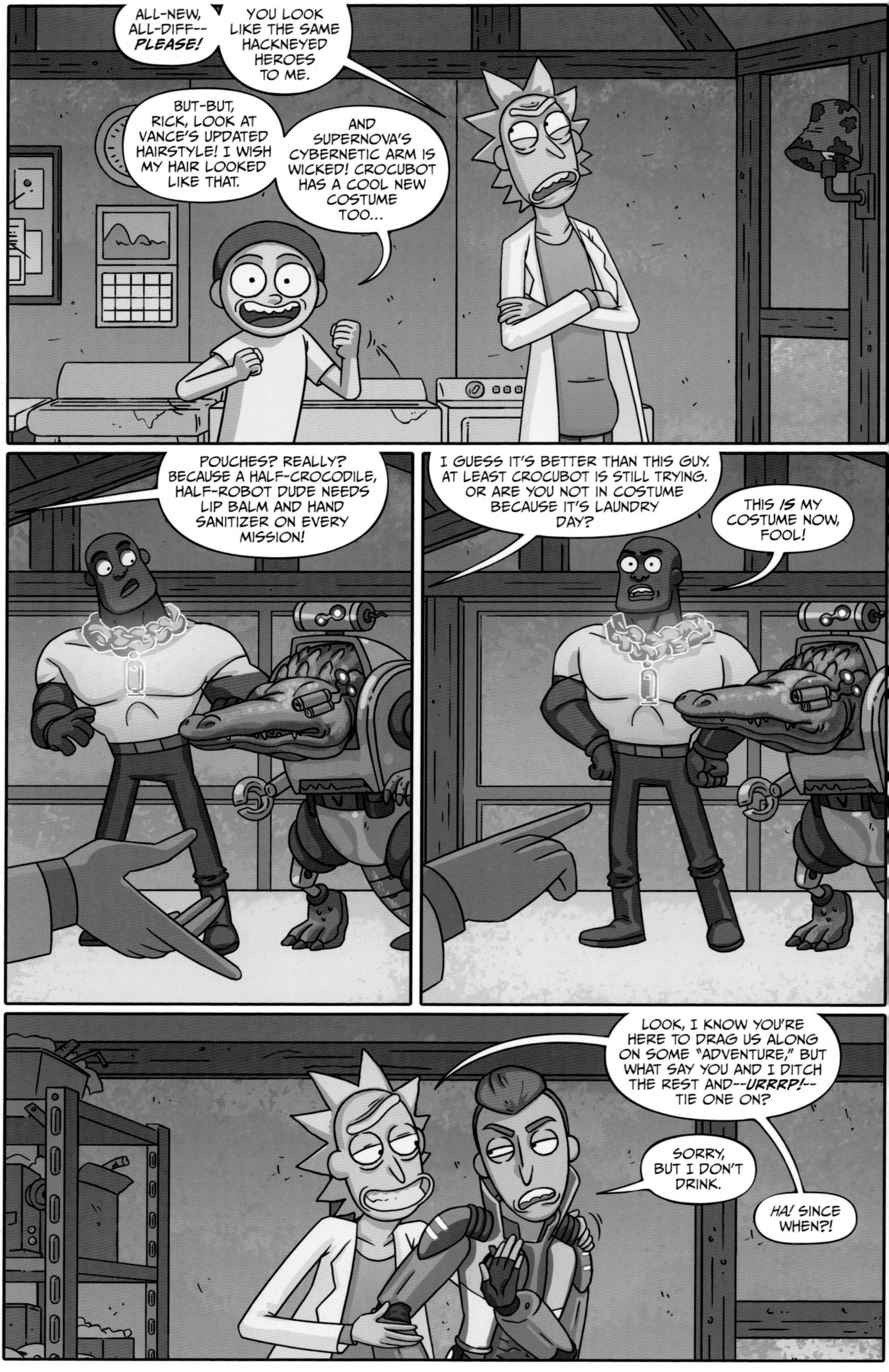
ALL-NEW, ALL-DIFF-- PLEASE!
YOU LOOK LIKE THE SAME HACKNEYED HEROES TO ME.
BUT-BUT, RICK, LOOK AT VANCE'S UPDATED HAIRSTYLE! I WISH MY HAIR LOOKED LIKE THAT.
AND SUPERNOVA'S CYBERNETIC ARM IS WICKED! CROCUBOT HAS A COOL NEW COSTUME TOO...
POUCHES? REALLY? BECAUSE A HALF-CROCODILE, HALF-ROBOT DUDE NEEDS LIP BALM AND HAND SANITIZER ON EVERY MISSION!
I GUESS IT'S BETTER THAN THIS GUY. AT LEAST CROCUBOT IS STILL TRYING. OR ARE YOU NOT IN COSTUME BECAUSE IT'S LAUNDRY DAY?
THIS IS MY COSTUME NOW, FOOL!
LOOK, I KNOW YOU'RE HERE TO DRAG US ALONG ON SOME "ADVENTURE," BUT WHAT SAY YOU AND I DITCH THE REST AND--URRRP!-- TIE ONE ON?
SORRY, BUT I DON'T DRINK.
HA! SINCE WHEN?!

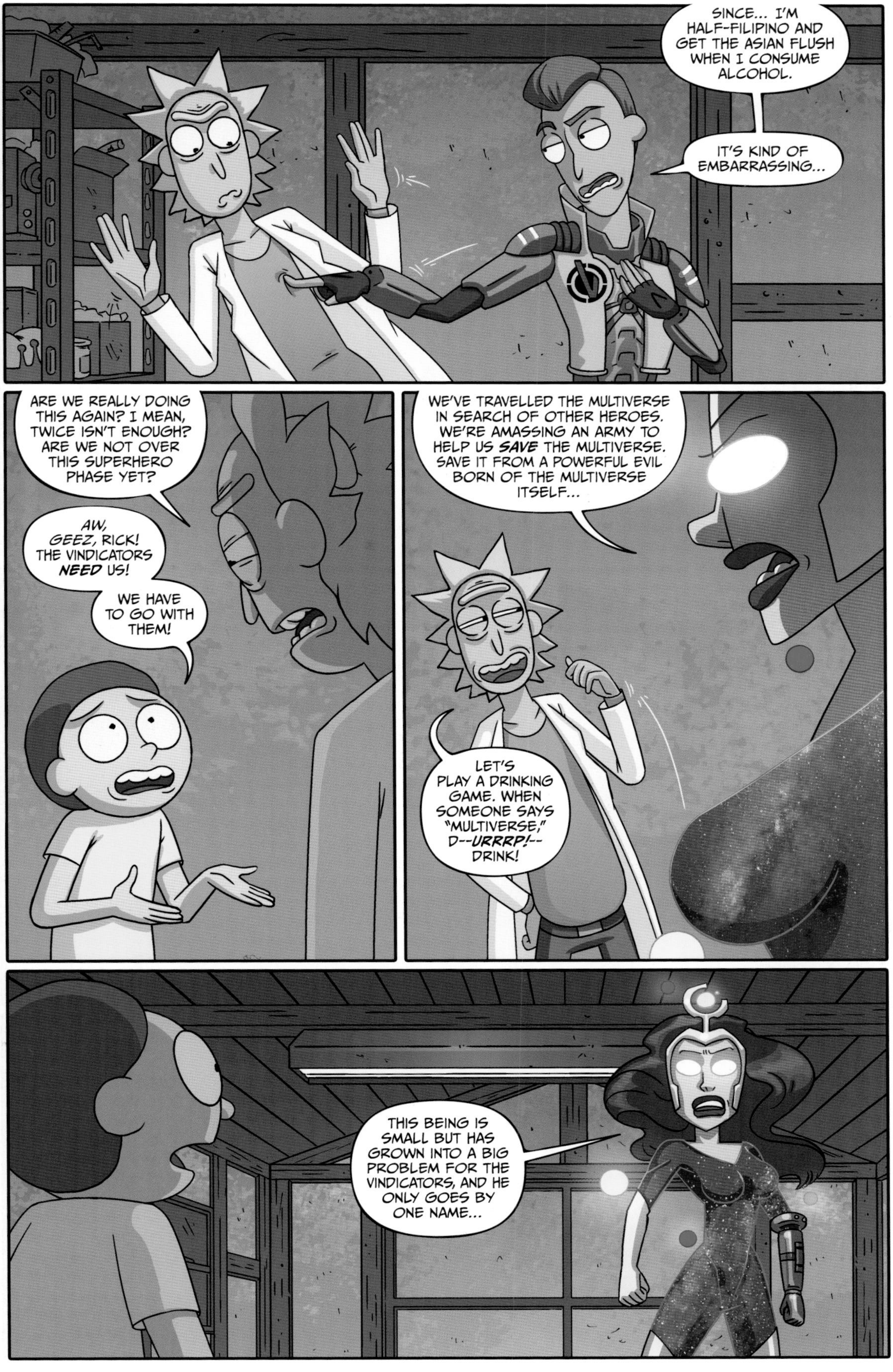
SINCE... I'M HALF-FILIPINO AND GET THE ASIAN FLUSH WHEN I CONSUME ALCOHOL.
IT'S KIND OF EMBARRASSING...
ARE WE REALLY DOING THIS AGAIN? I MEAN, TWICE ISN'T ENOUGH? ARE WE NOT OVER THIS SUPERHERO PHASE YET?
AW, GEEZ, RICK! THE VINDICATORS NEED US!
WE HAVE TO GO WITH THEM!
WE'VE TRAVELLED THE MULTIVERSE IN SEARCH OF OTHER HEROES. WE'RE AMASSING AN ARMY TO HELP US SAVE THE MULTIVERSE. SAVE IT FROM A POWERFUL EVIL BORN OF THE MULTIVERSE ITSELF...
LET'S PLAY A DRINKING GAME. WHEN SOMEONE SAYS "MULTIVERSE," D--URRRP!--DRINK!
THIS BEING IS SMALL BUT HAS GROWN INTO A BIG PROBLEM FOR THE VINDICATORS, AND HE ONLY GOES BY ONE NAME...

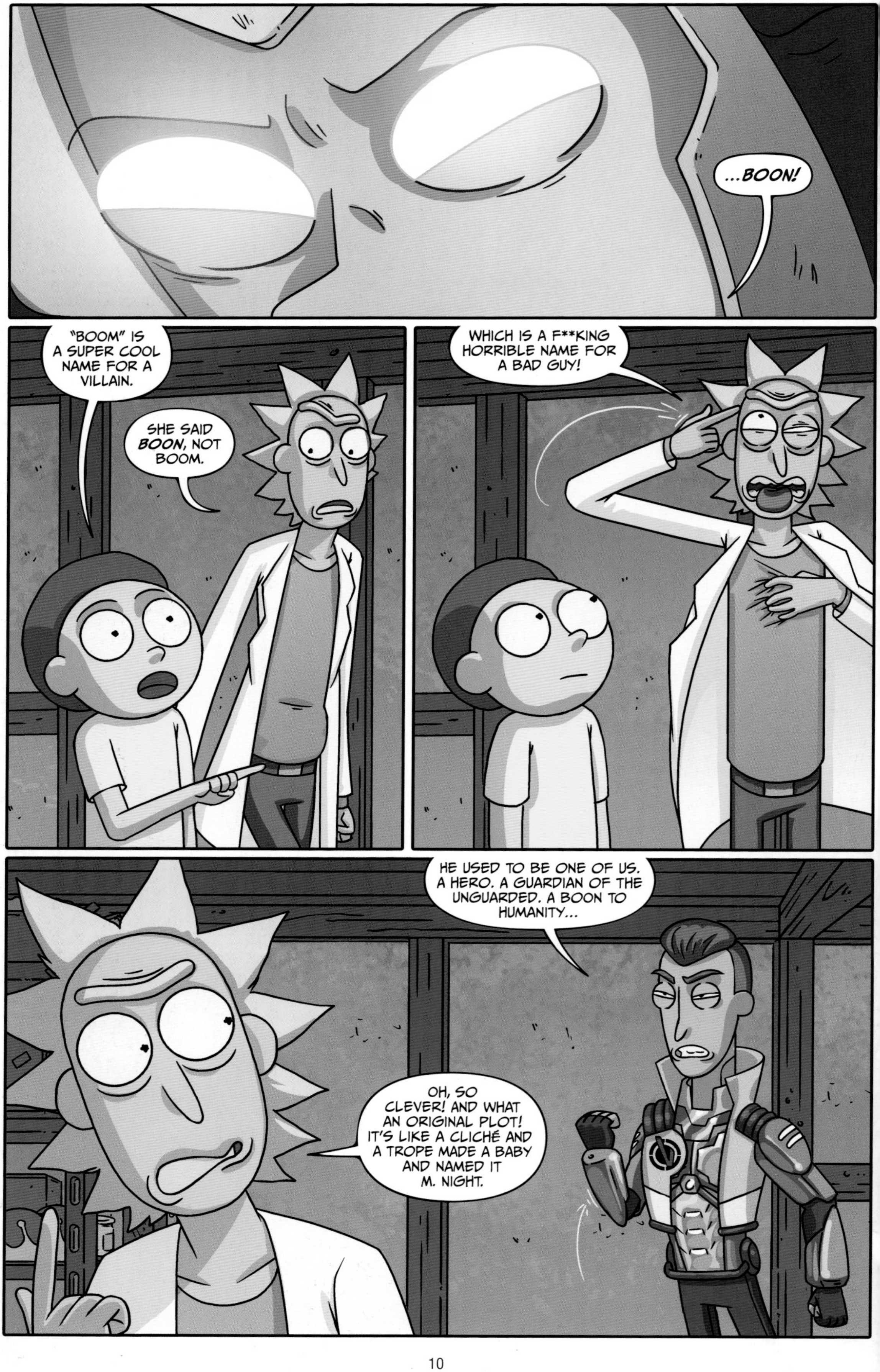
...BOON!
"BOOM" IS A SUPER COOL NAME FOR A VILLAIN.
SHE SAID BOON, NOT BOOM.
WHICH IS A F**KING HORRIBLE NAME FOR A BAD GUY!
HE USED TO BE ONE OF US. A HERO. A GUARDIAN OF THE UNGUARDED. A BOON TO HUMANITY...
OH, SO CLEVER! AND WHAT AN ORIGINAL PLOT! IT'S LIKE A CLICHÉ AND A TROPE MADE A BABY AND NAMED IT M. NIGHT.

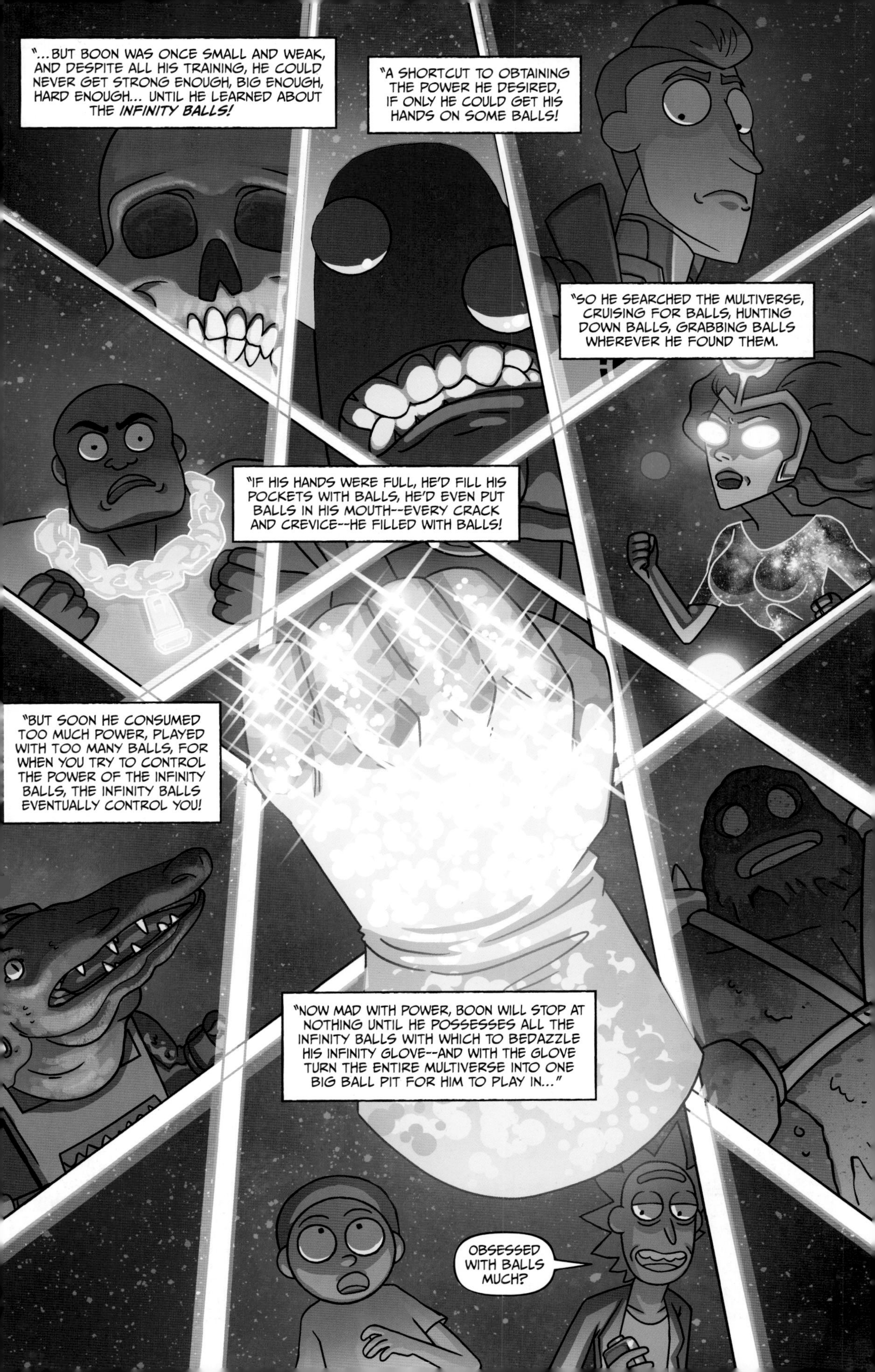
"...BUT BOON WAS ONCE SMALL AND WEAK, AND DESPITE ALL HIS TRAINING, HE COULD NEVER GET STRONG ENOUGH, BIG ENOUGH, HARD ENOUGH... UNTIL HE LEARNED ABOUT THE *INFINITY BALLS!*
"A SHORTCUT TO OBTAINING THE POWER HE DESIRED, IF ONLY HE COULD GET HIS HANDS ON SOME BALLS!
"SO HE SEARCHED THE MULTIVERSE, CRUISING FOR BALLS, HUNTING DOWN BALLS, GRABBING BALLS WHEREVER HE FOUND THEM.
"IF HIS HANDS WERE FULL, HE'D FILL HIS POCKETS WITH BALLS, HE'D EVEN PUT BALLS IN HIS MOUTH--EVERY CRACK AND CREVICE--HE FILLED WITH BALLS!
"BUT SOON HE CONSUMED TOO MUCH POWER, PLAYED WITH TOO MANY BALLS, FOR WHEN YOU TRY TO CONTROL THE POWER OF THE INFINITY BALLS, THE INFINITY BALLS EVENTUALLY CONTROL YOU!
"NOW MAD WITH POWER, BOON WILL STOP AT NOTHING UNTIL HE POSSESSES ALL THE INFINITY BALLS WITH WHICH TO BEDAZZLE HIS INFINITY GLOVE--AND WITH THE GLOVE TURN THE ENTIRE MULTIVERSE INTO ONE BIG BALL PIT FOR HIM TO PLAY IN..."
OBSESSED WITH BALLS MUCH?

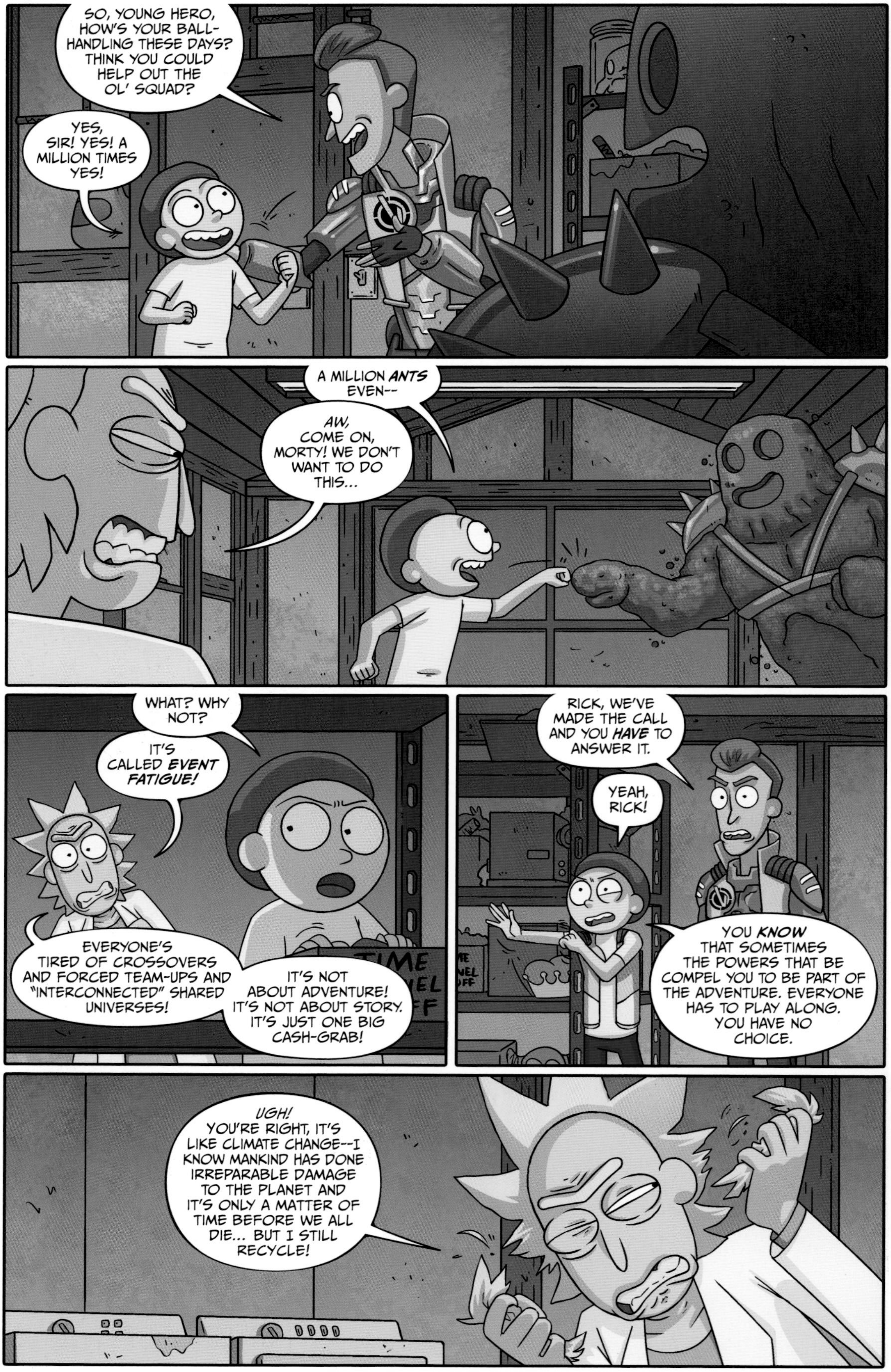
SO, YOUNG HERO, HOW'S YOUR BALL-HANDLING THESE DAYS? THINK YOU COULD HELP OUT THE OL' SQUAD?
YES, SIR! YES! A MILLION TIMES YES!
A MILLION ANTS EVEN--
AW, COME ON, MORTY! WE DON'T WANT TO DO THIS...
WHAT? WHY NOT?
IT'S CALLED EVENT FATIGUE!
EVERYONE'S TIRED OF CROSSOVERS AND FORCED TEAM-UPS AND "INTERCONNECTED" SHARED UNIVERSES!
IT'S NOT ABOUT ADVENTURE! IT'S NOT ABOUT STORY. IT'S JUST ONE BIG CASH-GRAB!
RICK, WE'VE MADE THE CALL AND YOU HAVE TO ANSWER IT.
YEAH, RICK!
YOU KNOW THAT SOMETIMES THE POWERS THAT BE COMPEL YOU TO BE PART OF THE ADVENTURE. EVERYONE HAS TO PLAY ALONG. YOU HAVE NO CHOICE.
UGH! YOU'RE RIGHT, IT'S LIKE CLIMATE CHANGE--I KNOW MANKIND HAS DONE IRREPARABLE DAMAGE TO THE PLANET AND IT'S ONLY A MATTER OF TIME BEFORE WE ALL DIE... BUT I STILL RECYCLE!

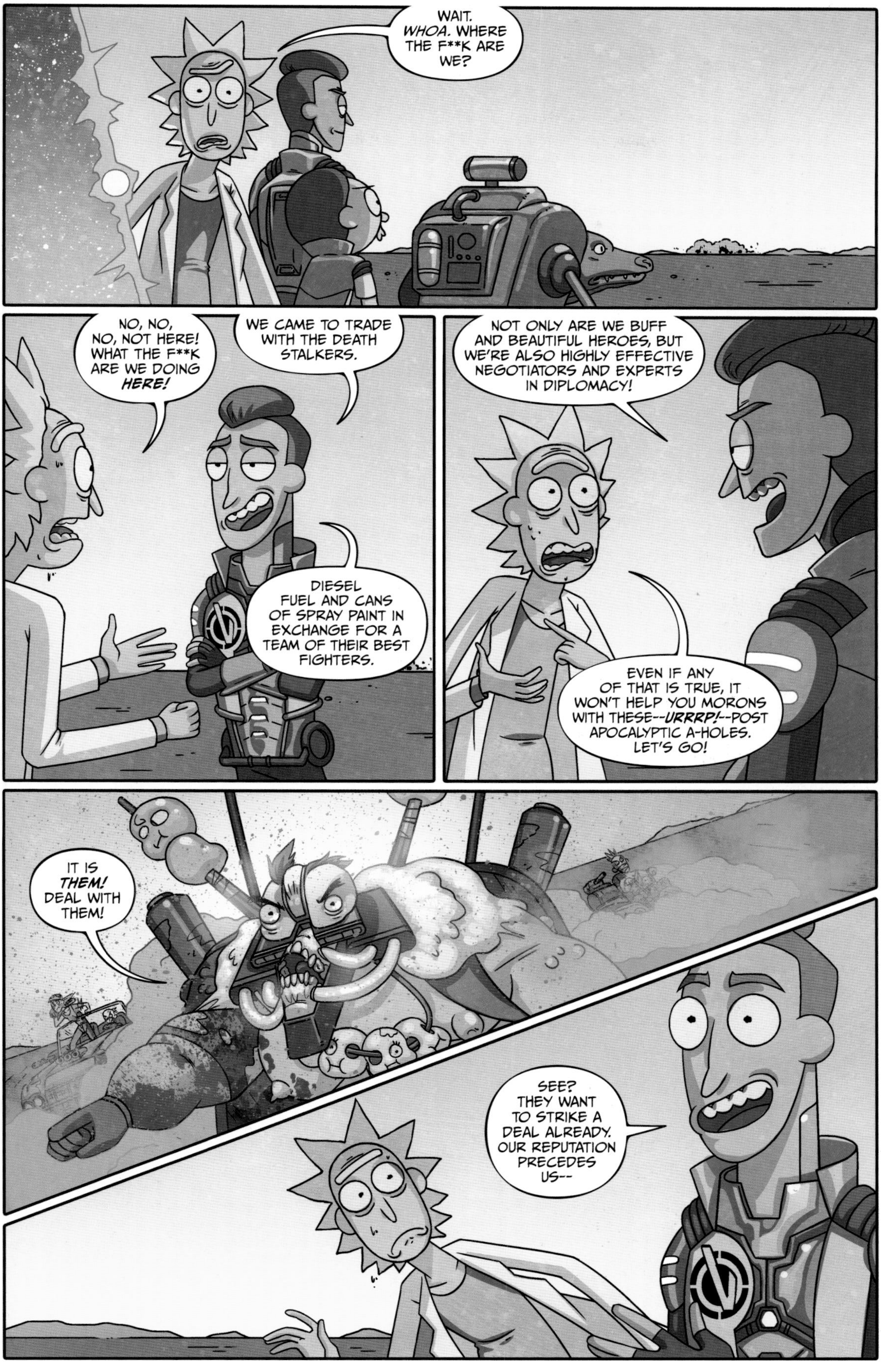
WAIT. *WHOA.* WHERE THE F**K ARE WE?
NO, NO, NO, NOT HERE! WHAT THE F**K ARE WE DOING *HERE!*
WE CAME TO TRADE WITH THE DEATH STALKERS.
DIESEL FUEL AND CANS OF SPRAY PAINT IN EXCHANGE FOR A TEAM OF THEIR BEST FIGHTERS.
NOT ONLY ARE WE BUFF AND BEAUTIFUL HEROES, BUT WE'RE ALSO HIGHLY EFFECTIVE NEGOTIATORS AND EXPERTS IN DIPLOMACY!
EVEN IF ANY OF THAT IS TRUE, IT WON'T HELP YOU MORONS WITH THESE--*URRRP!*--POST APOCALYPTIC A-HOLES. LET'S GO!
IT IS *THEM!* DEAL WITH THEM!
SEE? THEY WANT TO STRIKE A DEAL ALREADY. OUR REPUTATION PRECEDES US--

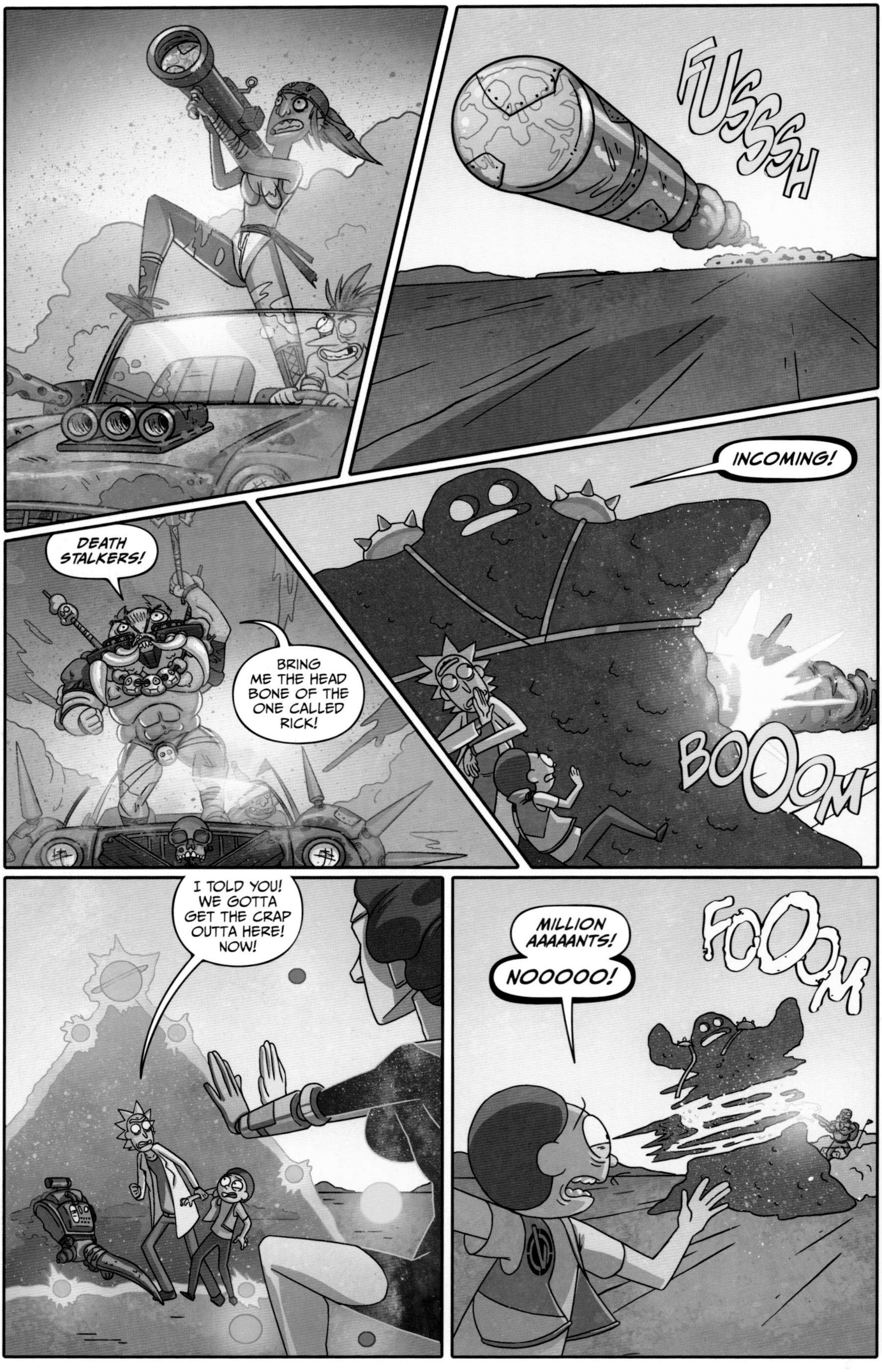
FUSSSH
INCOMING!
DEATH STALKERS!
BRING ME THE HEAD BONE OF THE ONE CALLED RICK!
BOOOOM
I TOLD YOU! WE GOTTA GET THE CRAP OUTTA HERE! NOW!
MILLION AAAAANTS!
NOOOOO!
FOOOOM

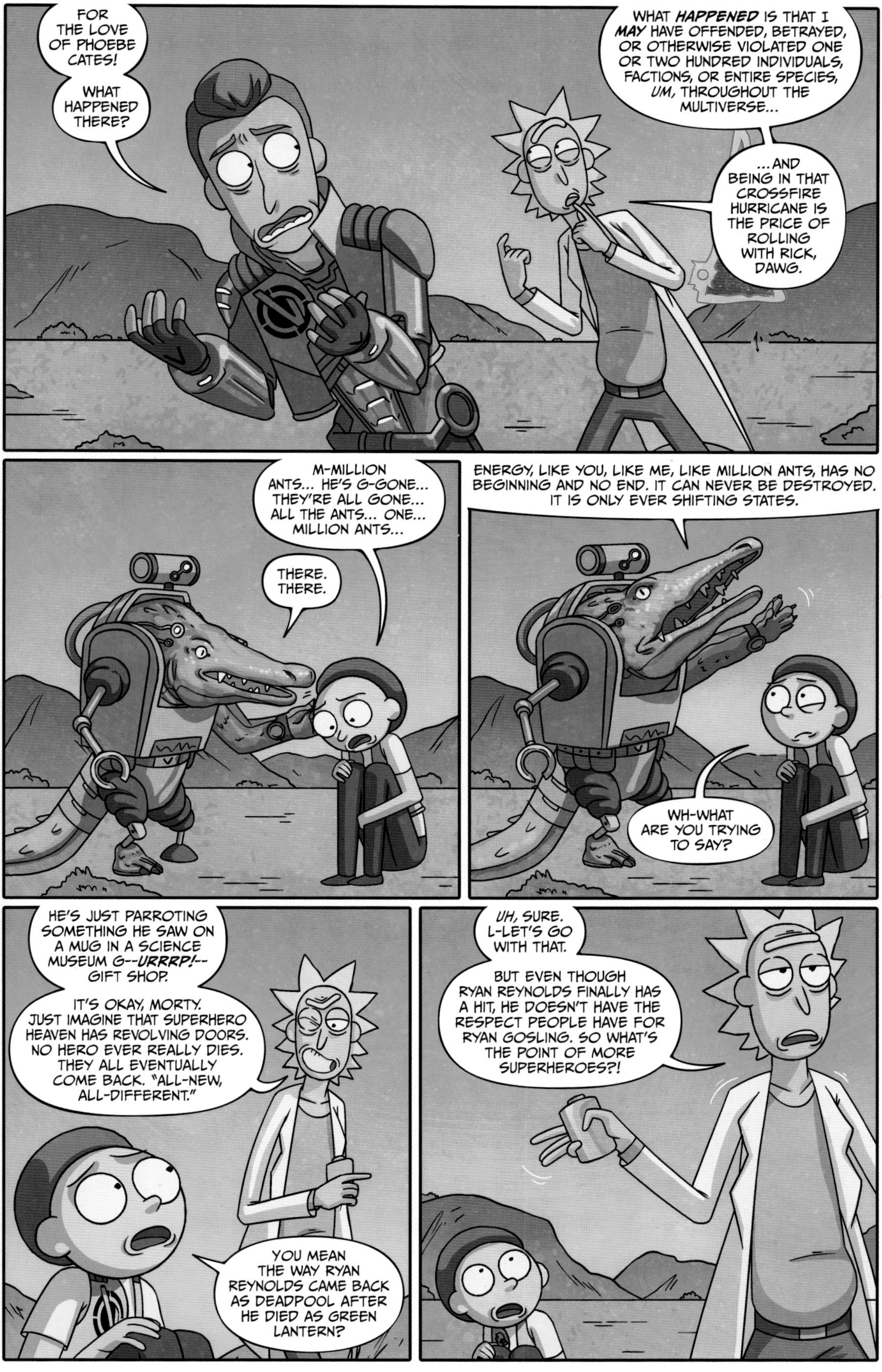
FOR THE LOVE OF PHOEBE CATES!
WHAT HAPPENED THERE?
WHAT ***HAPPENED*** IS THAT I ***MAY*** HAVE OFFENDED, BETRAYED, OR OTHERWISE VIOLATED ONE OR TWO HUNDRED INDIVIDUALS, FACTIONS, OR ENTIRE SPECIES, *UM,* THROUGHOUT THE MULTIVERSE...
...AND BEING IN THAT CROSSFIRE HURRICANE IS THE PRICE OF ROLLING WITH RICK, DAWG.
M-MILLION ANTS... HE'S G-GONE... THEY'RE ALL GONE... ALL THE ANTS... ONE... MILLION ANTS...
THERE. THERE.
ENERGY, LIKE YOU, LIKE ME, LIKE MILLION ANTS, HAS NO BEGINNING AND NO END. IT CAN NEVER BE DESTROYED. IT IS ONLY EVER SHIFTING STATES.
WH-WHAT ARE YOU TRYING TO SAY?
HE'S JUST PARROTING SOMETHING HE SAW ON A MUG IN A SCIENCE MUSEUM G--***URRRP!***--GIFT SHOP.
IT'S OKAY, MORTY. JUST IMAGINE THAT SUPERHERO HEAVEN HAS REVOLVING DOORS. NO HERO EVER REALLY DIES. THEY ALL EVENTUALLY COME BACK. "ALL-NEW, ALL-DIFFERENT."
YOU MEAN THE WAY RYAN REYNOLDS CAME BACK AS DEADPOOL AFTER HE DIED AS GREEN LANTERN?
UH, SURE. L-LET'S GO WITH THAT.
BUT EVEN THOUGH RYAN REYNOLDS FINALLY HAS A HIT, HE DOESN'T HAVE THE RESPECT PEOPLE HAVE FOR RYAN GOSLING. SO WHAT'S THE POINT OF MORE SUPERHEROES?!

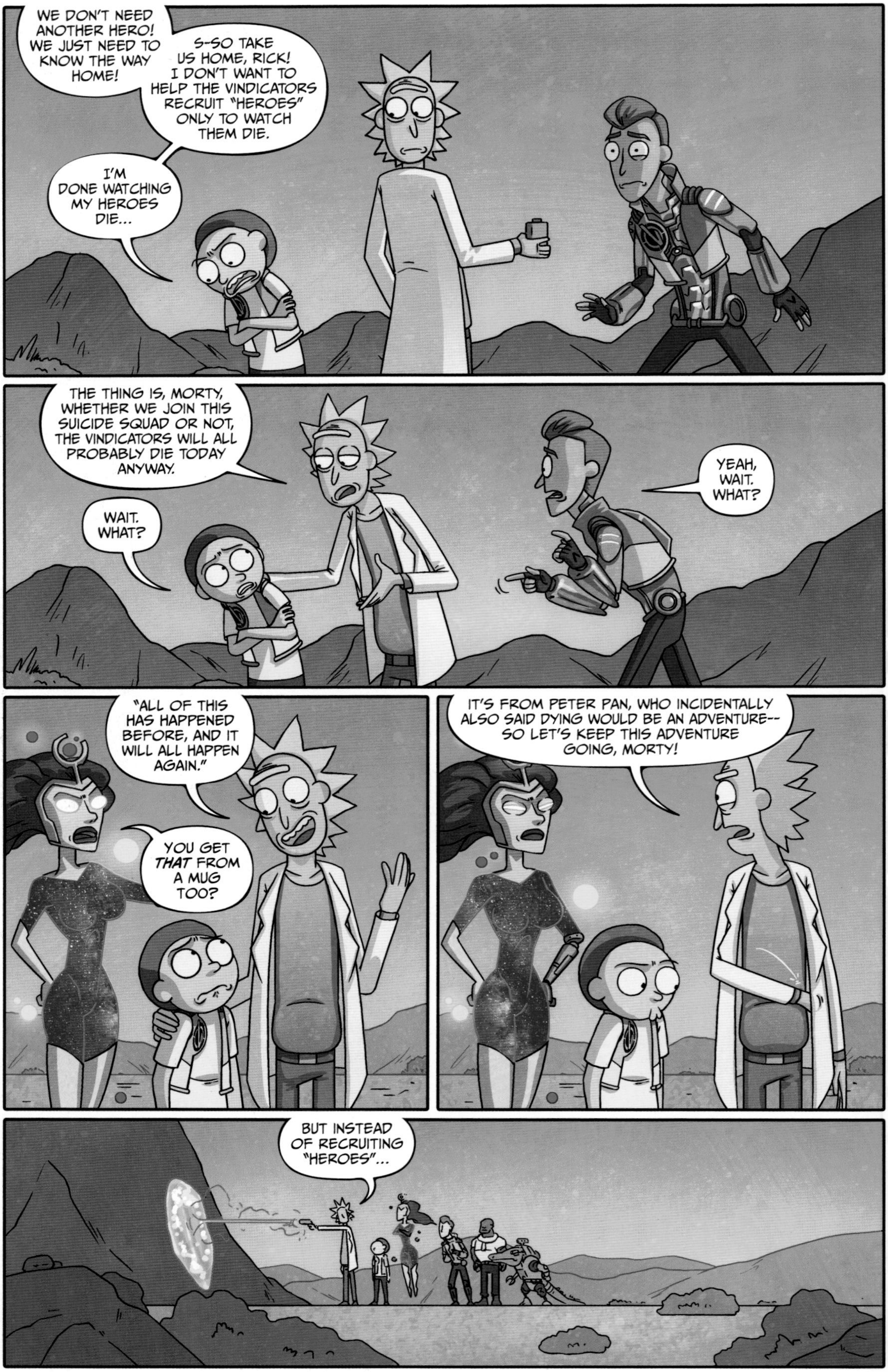
WE DON'T NEED ANOTHER HERO! WE JUST NEED TO KNOW THE WAY HOME!
S-SO TAKE US HOME, RICK! I DON'T WANT TO HELP THE VINDICATORS RECRUIT "HEROES" ONLY TO WATCH THEM DIE.
I'M DONE WATCHING MY HEROES DIE...
THE THING IS, MORTY, WHETHER WE JOIN THIS SUICIDE SQUAD OR NOT, THE VINDICATORS WILL ALL PROBABLY DIE TODAY ANYWAY.
WAIT. WHAT?
YEAH, WAIT. WHAT?
"ALL OF THIS HAS HAPPENED BEFORE, AND IT WILL ALL HAPPEN AGAIN."
YOU GET THAT FROM A MUG TOO?
IT'S FROM PETER PAN, WHO INCIDENTALLY ALSO SAID DYING WOULD BE AN ADVENTURE-- SO LET'S KEEP THIS ADVENTURE GOING, MORTY!
BUT INSTEAD OF RECRUITING "HEROES"...

...WHY DON'T WE TRY TEAMING UP WITH SOME LOVABLE "ANTI-HEROES"!

KRZAK

YIKES! L-LIGHTNING? INDOORS?

WHERE ARE WE, RICK?

YEAH, RICK. WHERE THE HELL ARE WE?

IF MY TIMING IS RIGHT, WHICH IT ALWAYS IS, WE ARE ABOUT TO WITNESS A REBIRTH.

THE REB-- URRRP!--BIRTH OF...

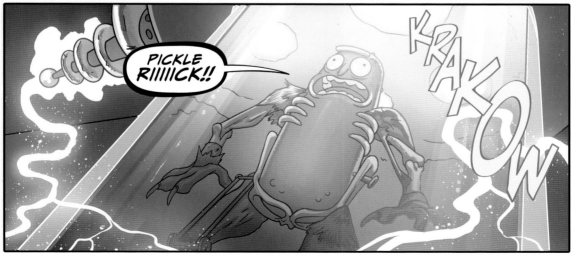

PICKLE RIIIIICK!!

KRAKOW

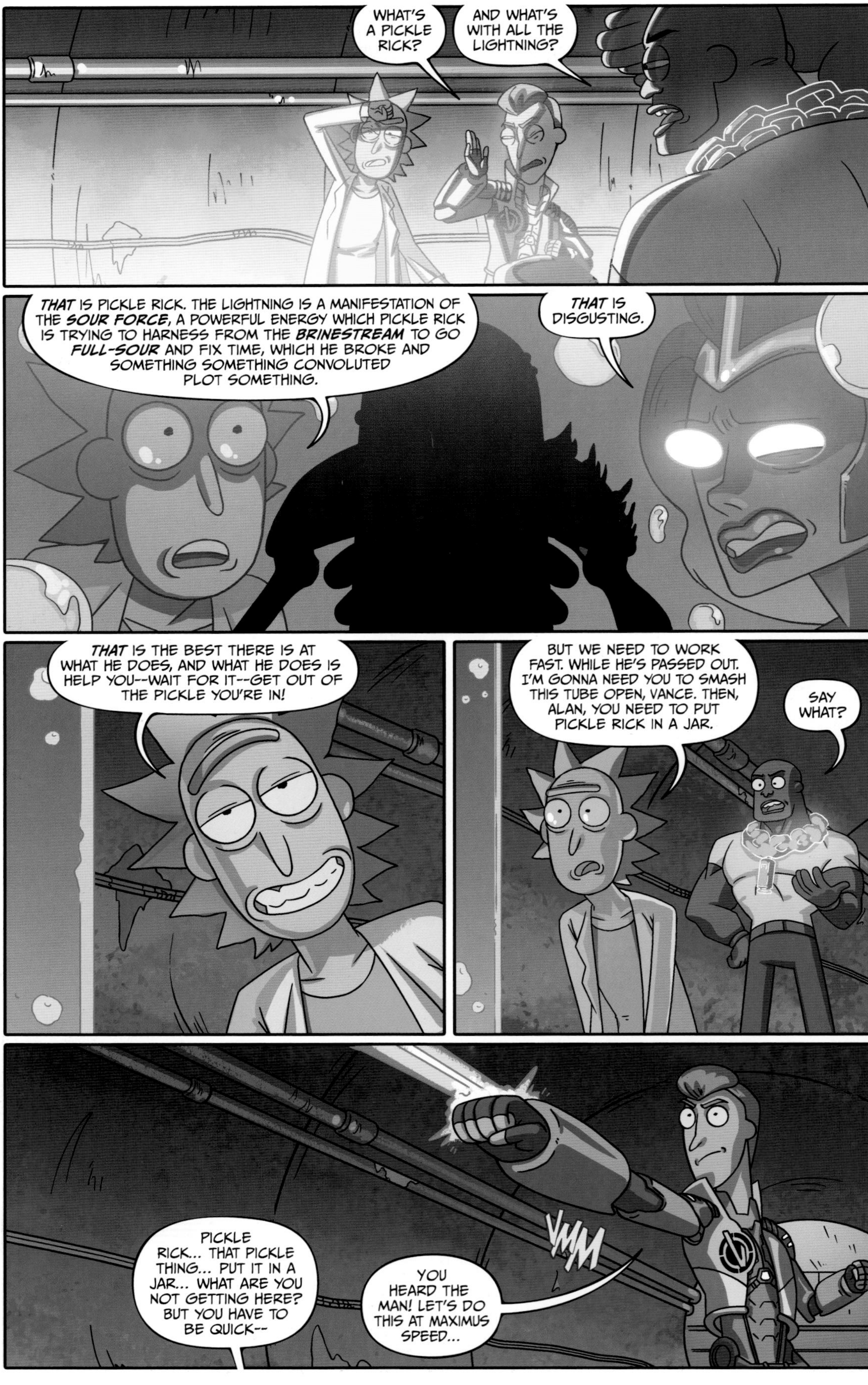
WHAT'S A PICKLE RICK?
AND WHAT'S WITH ALL THE LIGHTNING?
THAT IS PICKLE RICK. THE LIGHTNING IS A MANIFESTATION OF THE SOUR FORCE, A POWERFUL ENERGY WHICH PICKLE RICK IS TRYING TO HARNESS FROM THE BRINESTREAM TO GO FULL-SOUR AND FIX TIME, WHICH HE BROKE AND SOMETHING SOMETHING CONVOLUTED PLOT SOMETHING.
THAT IS DISGUSTING.
THAT IS THE BEST THERE IS AT WHAT HE DOES, AND WHAT HE DOES IS HELP YOU--WAIT FOR IT--GET OUT OF THE PICKLE YOU'RE IN!
BUT WE NEED TO WORK FAST. WHILE HE'S PASSED OUT. I'M GONNA NEED YOU TO SMASH THIS TUBE OPEN, VANCE. THEN, ALAN, YOU NEED TO PUT PICKLE RICK IN A JAR.
SAY WHAT?
VMM
PICKLE RICK... THAT PICKLE THING... PUT IT IN A JAR... WHAT ARE YOU NOT GETTING HERE? BUT YOU HAVE TO BE QUICK--
YOU HEARD THE MAN! LET'S DO THIS AT MAXIMUS SPEED...

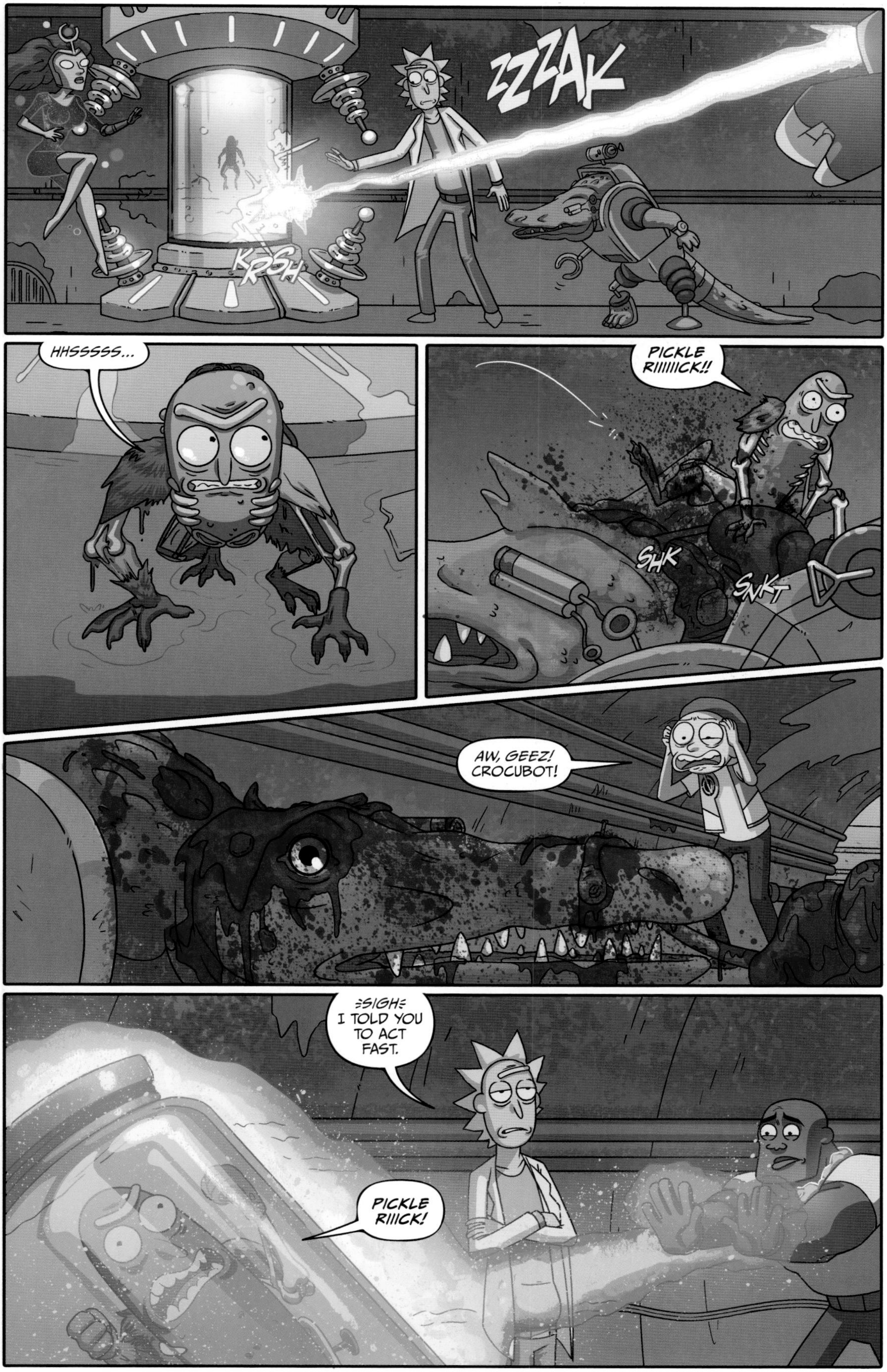
ZZZAK
KRSH
HHSSSSS...
PICKLE RIIIIICK!!
SHK
SNKT
AW, GEEZ! CROCUBOT!
=SIGH= I TOLD YOU TO ACT FAST.
PICKLE RIIICK!

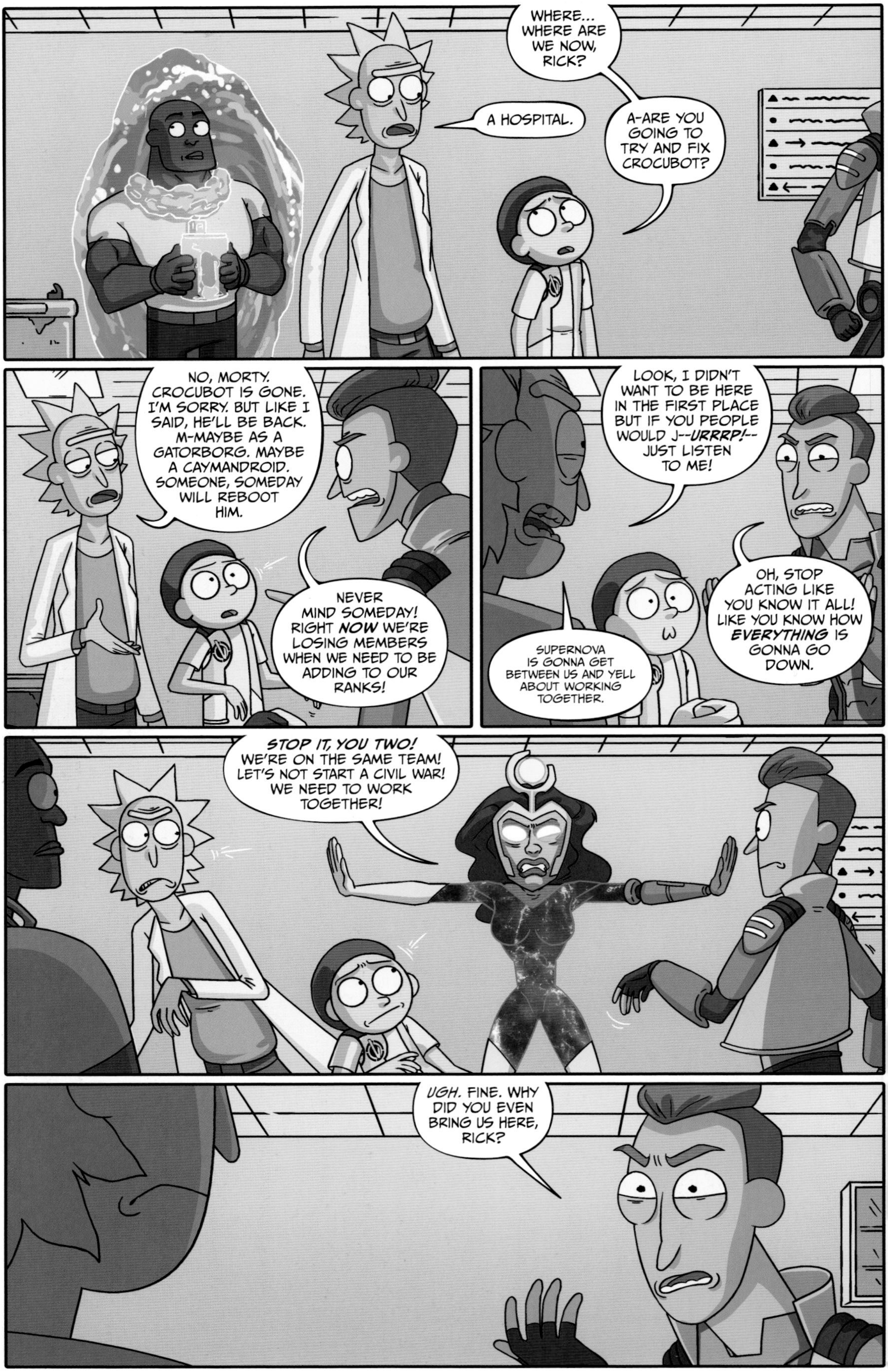
WHERE... WHERE ARE WE NOW, RICK?
A HOSPITAL.
A-ARE YOU GOING TO TRY AND FIX CROCUBOT?
NO, MORTY. CROCUBOT IS GONE. I'M SORRY. BUT LIKE I SAID, HE'LL BE BACK. M-MAYBE AS A GATORBORG. MAYBE A CAYMANDROID. SOMEONE, SOMEDAY WILL REBOOT HIM.
NEVER MIND SOMEDAY! RIGHT NOW WE'RE LOSING MEMBERS WHEN WE NEED TO BE ADDING TO OUR RANKS!
LOOK, I DIDN'T WANT TO BE HERE IN THE FIRST PLACE BUT IF YOU PEOPLE WOULD J--URRRP!-- JUST LISTEN TO ME!
OH, STOP ACTING LIKE YOU KNOW IT ALL! LIKE YOU KNOW HOW EVERYTHING IS GONNA GO DOWN.
SUPERNOVA IS GONNA GET BETWEEN US AND YELL ABOUT WORKING TOGETHER.
STOP IT, YOU TWO! WE'RE ON THE SAME TEAM! LET'S NOT START A CIVIL WAR! WE NEED TO WORK TOGETHER!
UGH. FINE. WHY DID YOU EVEN BRING US HERE, RICK?

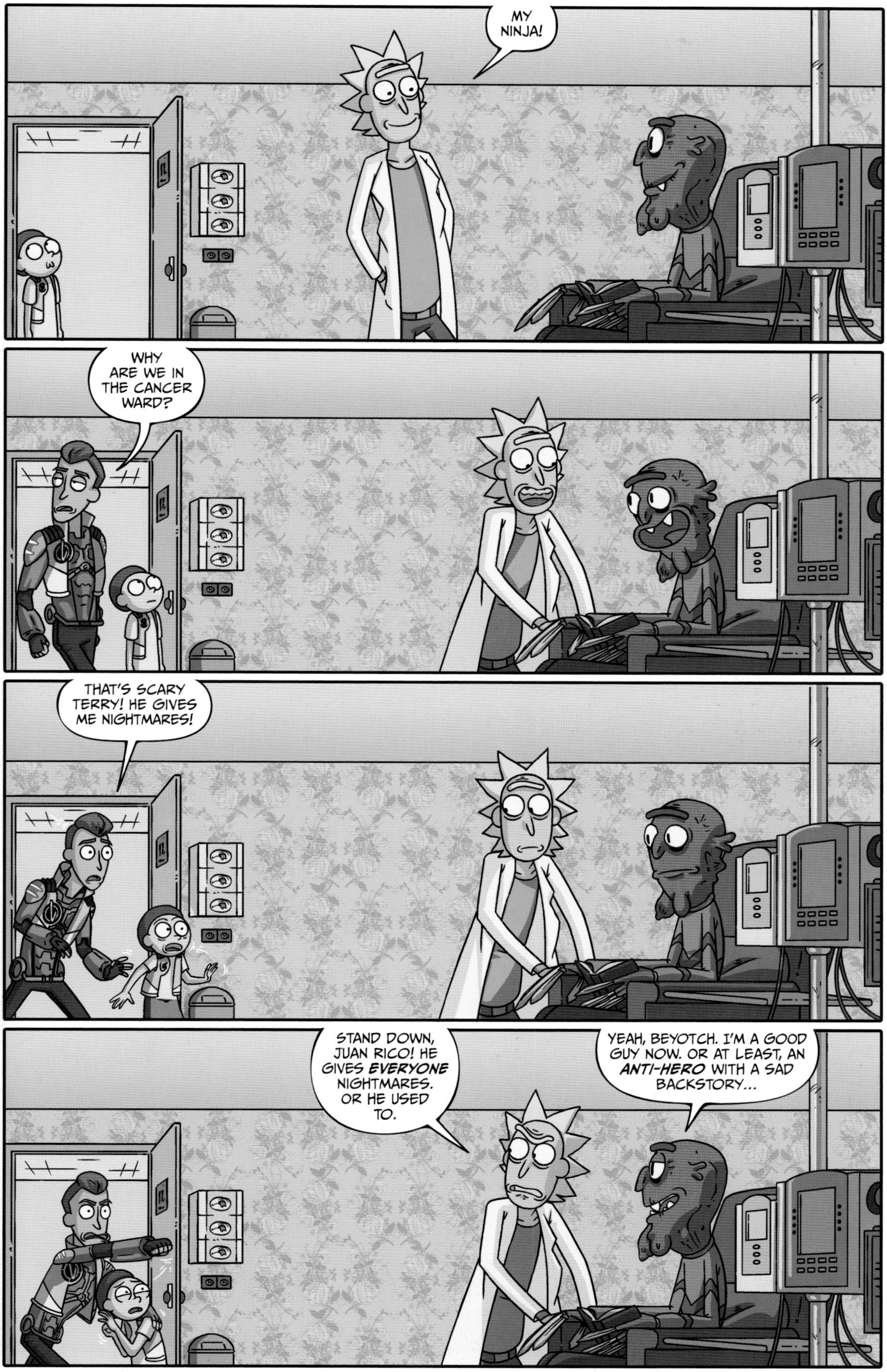
MY NINJA!
WHY ARE WE IN THE CANCER WARD?
THAT'S SCARY TERRY! HE GIVES ME NIGHTMARES!
STAND DOWN, JUAN RICO! HE GIVES EVERYONE NIGHTMARES. OR HE USED TO.
YEAH, BEYOTCH. I'M A GOOD GUY NOW. OR AT LEAST, AN ANTI-HERO WITH A SAD BACKSTORY...

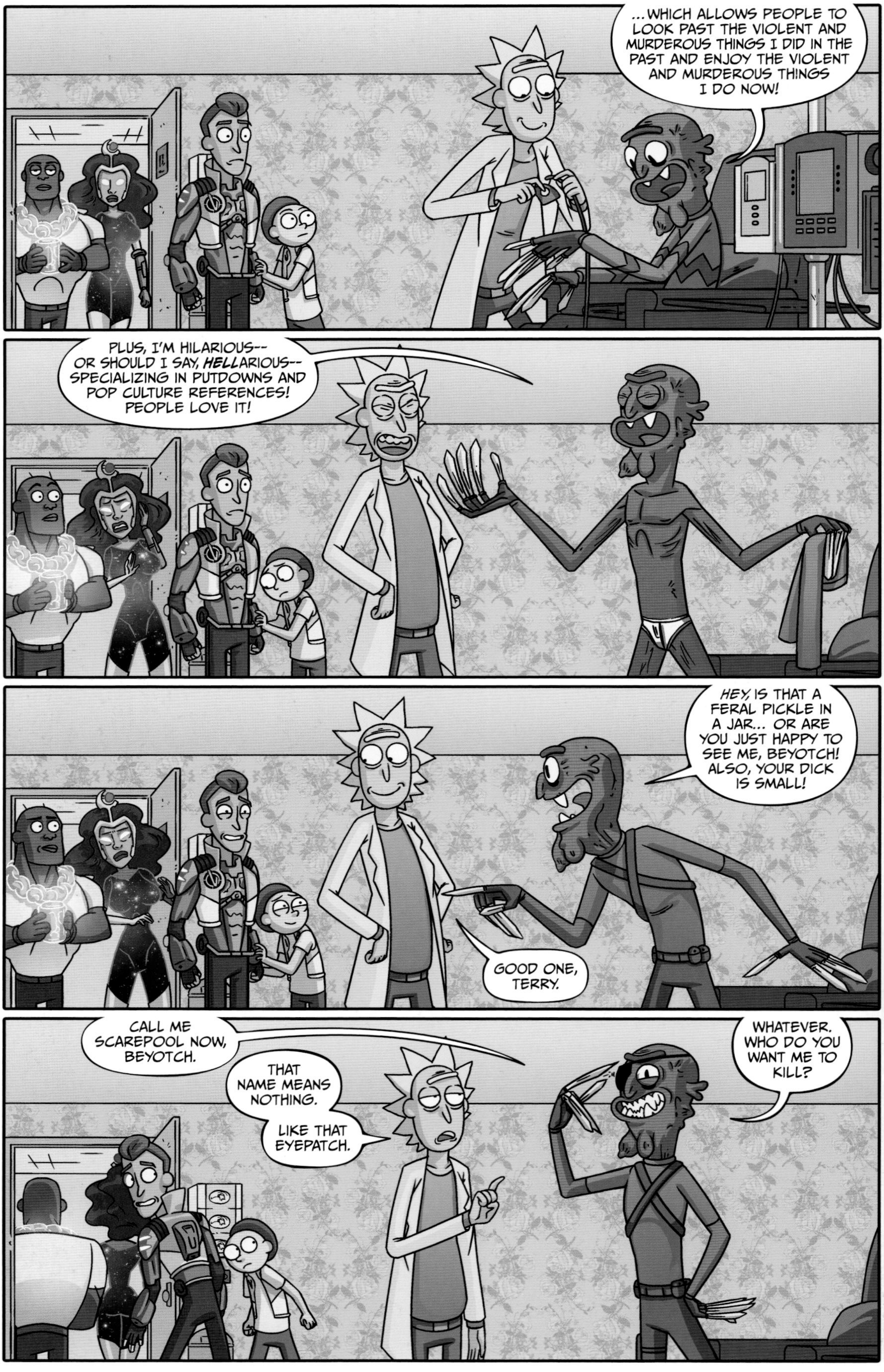
...WHICH ALLOWS PEOPLE TO LOOK PAST THE VIOLENT AND MURDEROUS THINGS I DID IN THE PAST AND ENJOY THE VIOLENT AND MURDEROUS THINGS I DO NOW!
PLUS, I'M HILARIOUS-- OR SHOULD I SAY, HELLARIOUS-- SPECIALIZING IN PUTDOWNS AND POP CULTURE REFERENCES! PEOPLE LOVE IT!
HEY, IS THAT A FERAL PICKLE IN A JAR... OR ARE YOU JUST HAPPY TO SEE ME, BEYOTCH! ALSO, YOUR DICK IS SMALL!
GOOD ONE, TERRY.
CALL ME SCAREPOOL NOW, BEYOTCH.
THAT NAME MEANS NOTHING.
LIKE THAT EYEPATCH.
WHATEVER. WHO DO YOU WANT ME TO KILL?

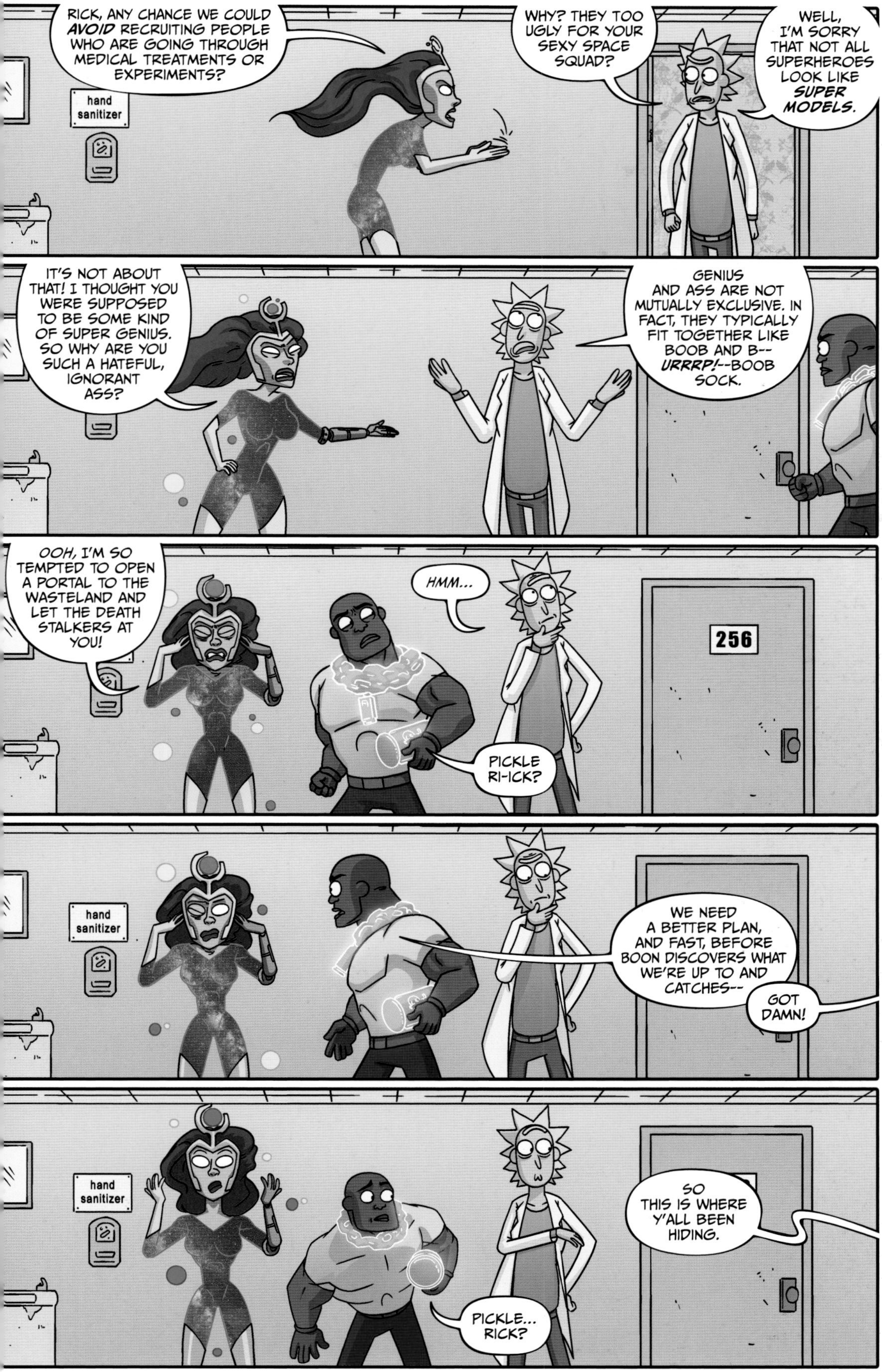

RICK, ANY CHANCE WE COULD AVOID RECRUITING PEOPLE WHO ARE GOING THROUGH MEDICAL TREATMENTS OR EXPERIMENTS?
hand sanitizer
WHY? THEY TOO UGLY FOR YOUR SEXY SPACE SQUAD?
WELL, I'M SORRY THAT NOT ALL SUPERHEROES LOOK LIKE SUPER MODELS.
IT'S NOT ABOUT THAT! I THOUGHT YOU WERE SUPPOSED TO BE SOME KIND OF SUPER GENIUS. SO WHY ARE YOU SUCH A HATEFUL, IGNORANT ASS?
GENIUS AND ASS ARE NOT MUTUALLY EXCLUSIVE. IN FACT, THEY TYPICALLY FIT TOGETHER LIKE BOOB AND B-- URRRP!--BOOB SOCK.
OOH, I'M SO TEMPTED TO OPEN A PORTAL TO THE WASTELAND AND LET THE DEATH STALKERS AT YOU!
HMM...
256
PICKLE RI-ICK?
hand sanitizer
WE NEED A BETTER PLAN, AND FAST, BEFORE BOON DISCOVERS WHAT WE'RE UP TO AND CATCHES--
GOT DAMN!
hand sanitizer
SO THIS IS WHERE Y'ALL BEEN HIDING.
PICKLE... RICK?

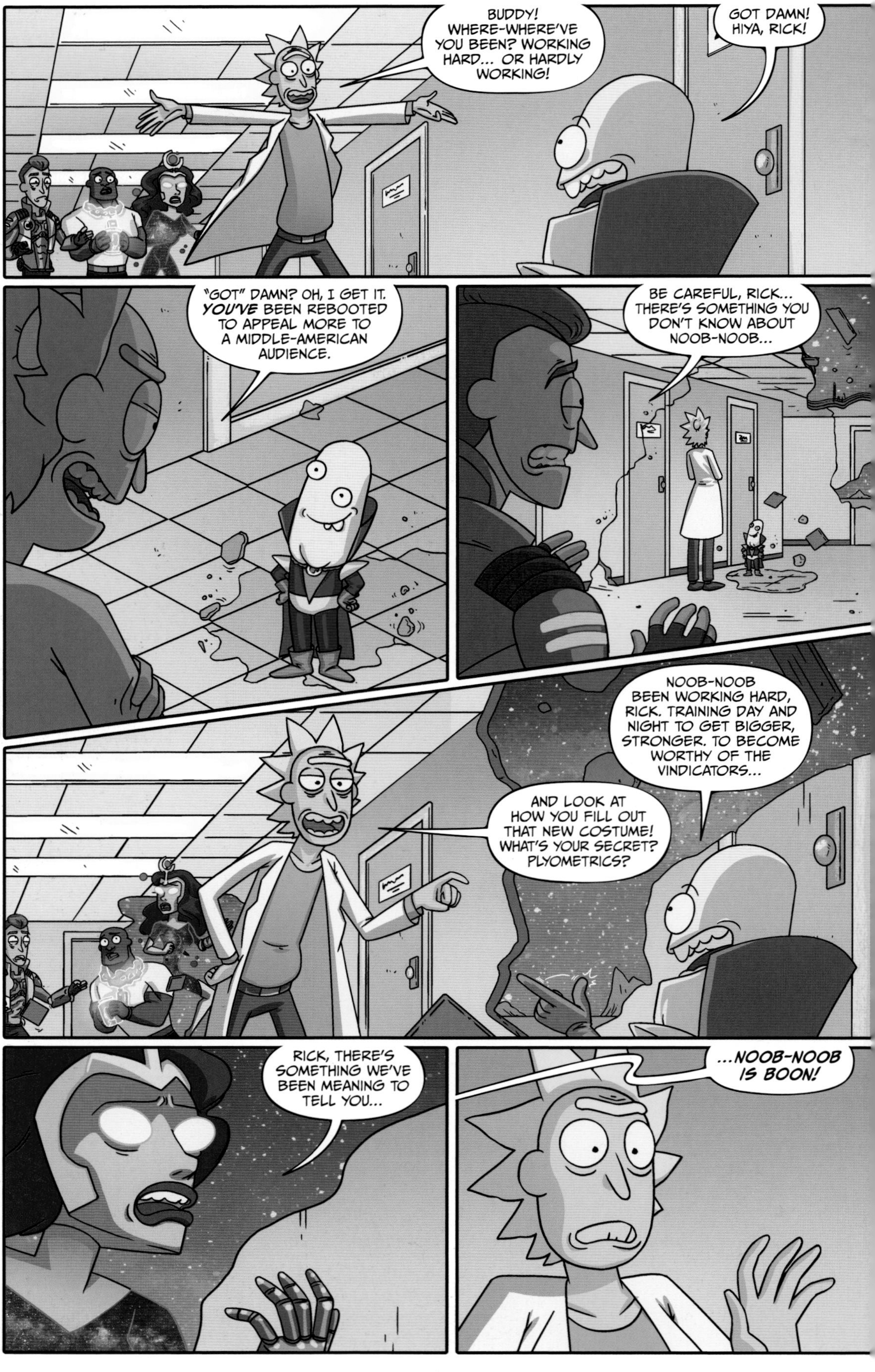
BUDDY! WHERE-WHERE'VE YOU BEEN? WORKING HARD... OR HARDLY WORKING!
GOT DAMN! HIYA, RICK!
"GOT" DAMN? OH, I GET IT. *YOU'VE* BEEN REBOOTED TO APPEAL MORE TO A MIDDLE-AMERICAN AUDIENCE.
BE CAREFUL, RICK... THERE'S SOMETHING YOU DON'T KNOW ABOUT NOOB-NOOB...
NOOB-NOOB BEEN WORKING HARD, RICK. TRAINING DAY AND NIGHT TO GET BIGGER, STRONGER. TO BECOME WORTHY OF THE VINDICATORS...
AND LOOK AT HOW YOU FILL OUT THAT NEW COSTUME! WHAT'S YOUR SECRET? PLYOMETRICS?
RICK, THERE'S SOMETHING WE'VE BEEN MEANING TO TELL YOU...
...NOOB-NOOB IS BOON!

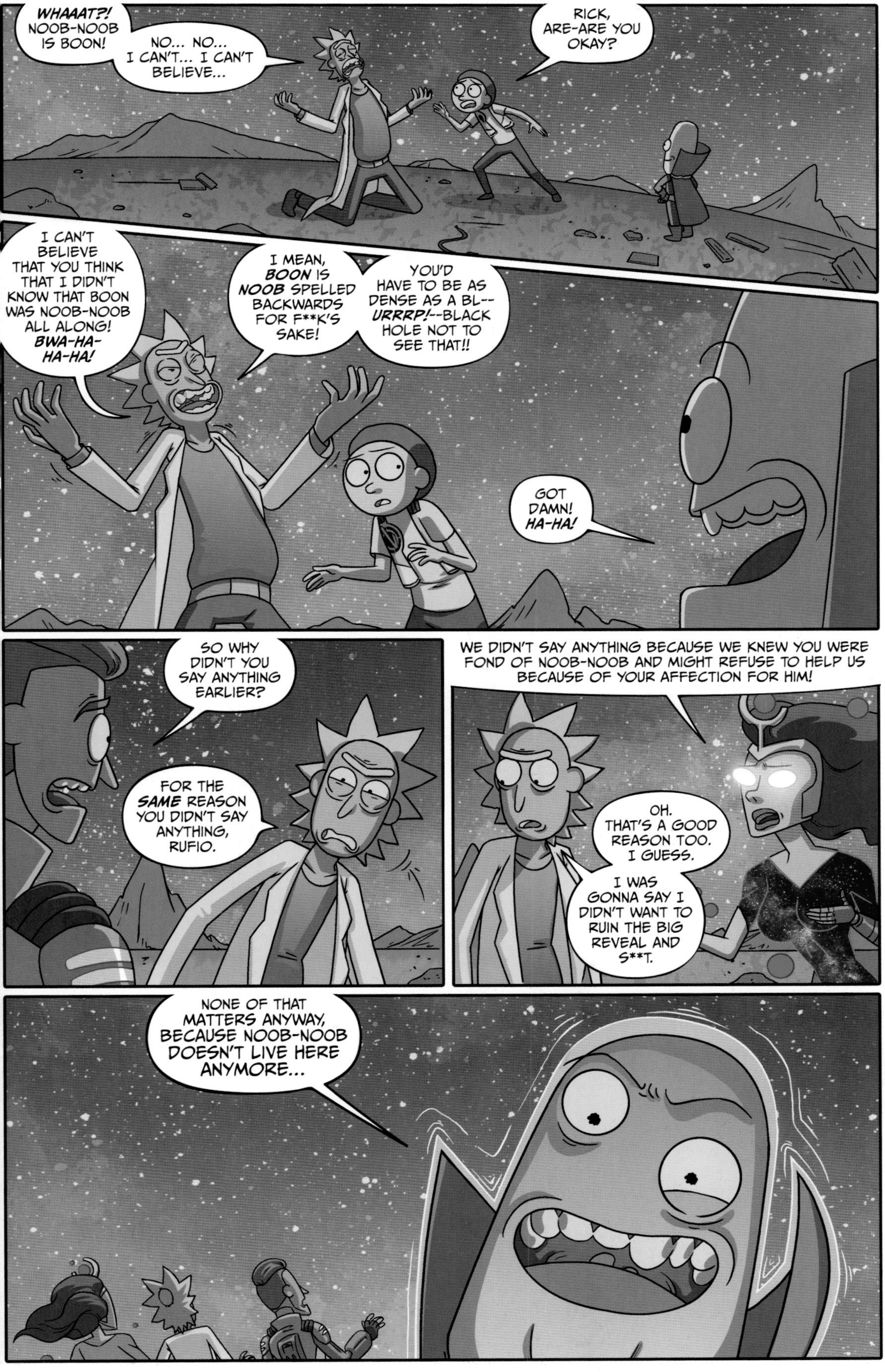
WHAAAT?! NOOB-NOOB IS BOON!
NO... NO... I CAN'T... I CAN'T BELIEVE...
RICK, ARE-ARE YOU OKAY?
I CAN'T BELIEVE THAT YOU THINK THAT I DIDN'T KNOW THAT BOON WAS NOOB-NOOB ALL ALONG! BWA-HA-HA-HA!
I MEAN, BOON IS NOOB SPELLED BACKWARDS FOR F**K'S SAKE!
YOU'D HAVE TO BE AS DENSE AS A BL--URRRP!--BLACK HOLE NOT TO SEE THAT!!
GOT DAMN! HA-HA!
SO WHY DIDN'T YOU SAY ANYTHING EARLIER?
FOR THE SAME REASON YOU DIDN'T SAY ANYTHING, RUFIO.
WE DIDN'T SAY ANYTHING BECAUSE WE KNEW YOU WERE FOND OF NOOB-NOOB AND MIGHT REFUSE TO HELP US BECAUSE OF YOUR AFFECTION FOR HIM!
OH. THAT'S A GOOD REASON TOO. I GUESS.
I WAS GONNA SAY I DIDN'T WANT TO RUIN THE BIG REVEAL AND S**T.
NONE OF THAT MATTERS ANYWAY, BECAUSE NOOB-NOOB DOESN'T LIVE HERE ANYMORE...

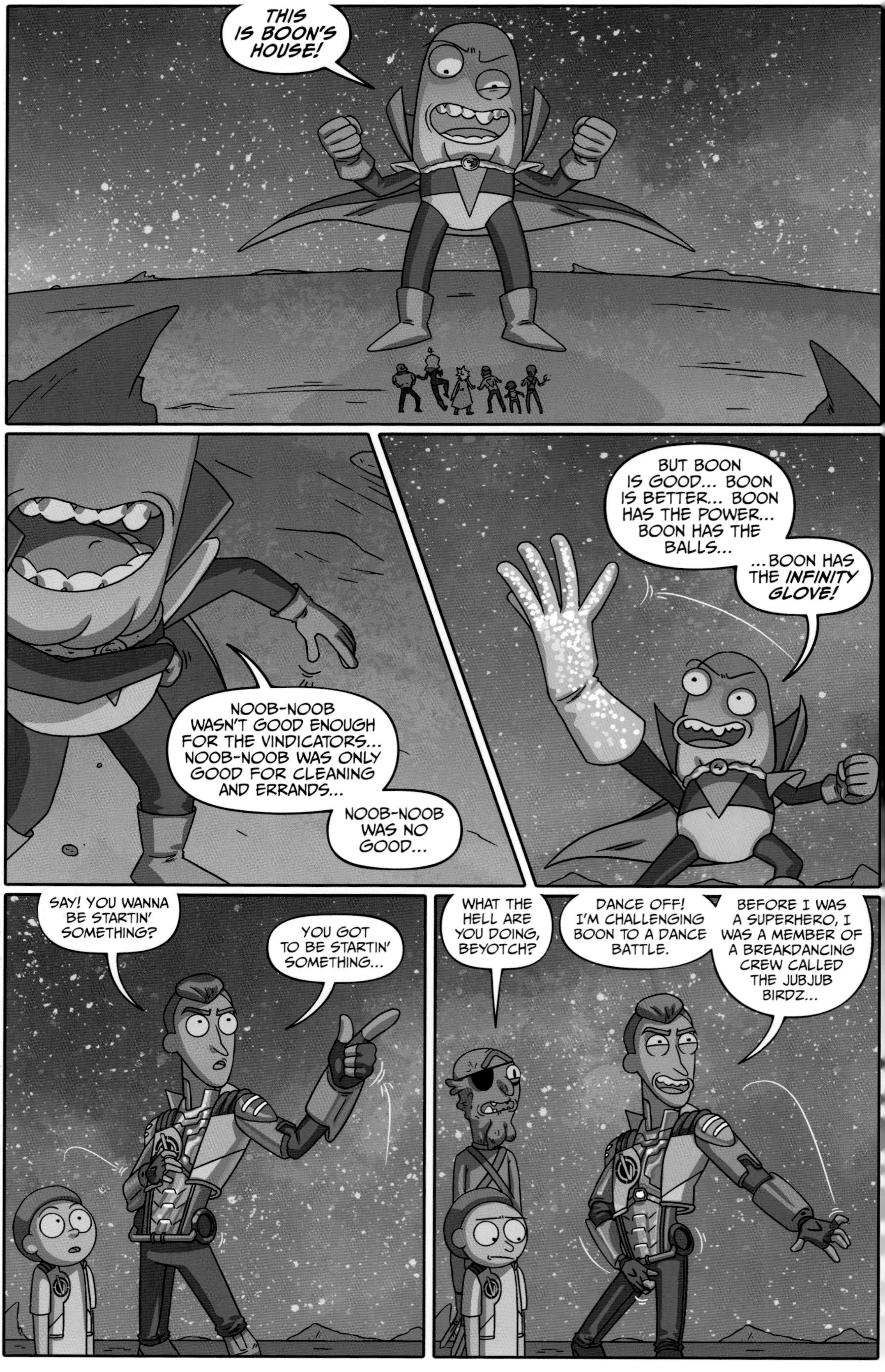
THIS IS BOON'S HOUSE!
NOOB-NOOB WASN'T GOOD ENOUGH FOR THE VINDICATORS... NOOB-NOOB WAS ONLY GOOD FOR CLEANING AND ERRANDS...
NOOB-NOOB WAS NO GOOD...
BUT BOON IS GOOD... BOON IS BETTER... BOON HAS THE POWER... BOON HAS THE BALLS...
...BOON HAS THE INFINITY GLOVE!
SAY! YOU WANNA BE STARTIN' SOMETHING?
YOU GOT TO BE STARTIN' SOMETHING...
WHAT THE HELL ARE YOU DOING, BEYOTCH?
DANCE OFF! I'M CHALLENGING BOON TO A DANCE BATTLE.
BEFORE I WAS A SUPERHERO, I WAS A MEMBER OF A BREAKDANCING CREW CALLED THE JUBJUB BIRDZ...

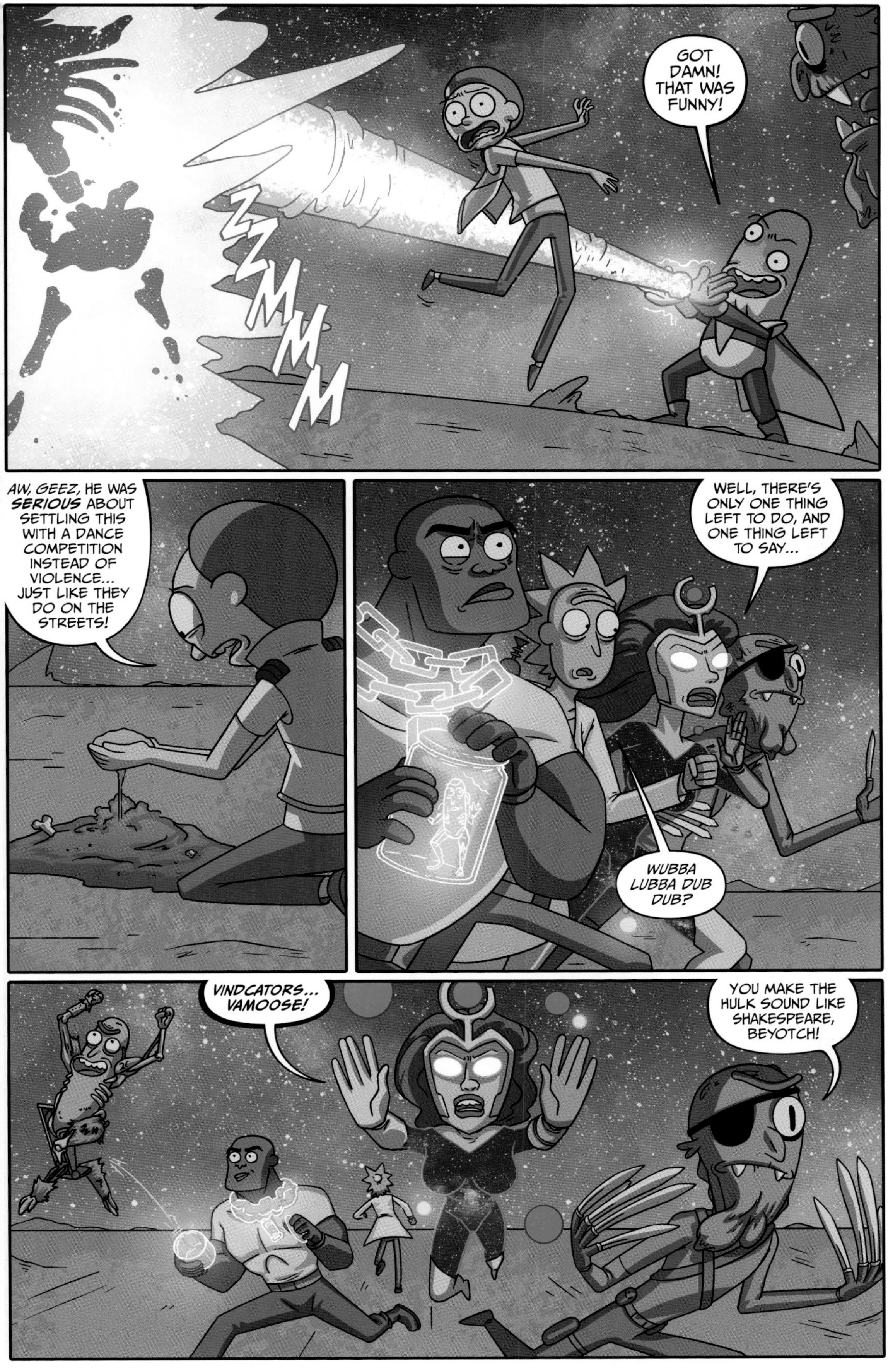
GOT DAMN! THAT WAS FUNNY!
ZZMMMM
AW, GEEZ, HE WAS SERIOUS ABOUT SETTLING THIS WITH A DANCE COMPETITION INSTEAD OF VIOLENCE... JUST LIKE THEY DO ON THE STREETS!
WELL, THERE'S ONLY ONE THING LEFT TO DO, AND ONE THING LEFT TO SAY...
WUBBA LUBBA DUB DUB?
VINDCATORS... VAMOOSE!
YOU MAKE THE HULK SOUND LIKE SHAKESPEARE, BEYOTCH!

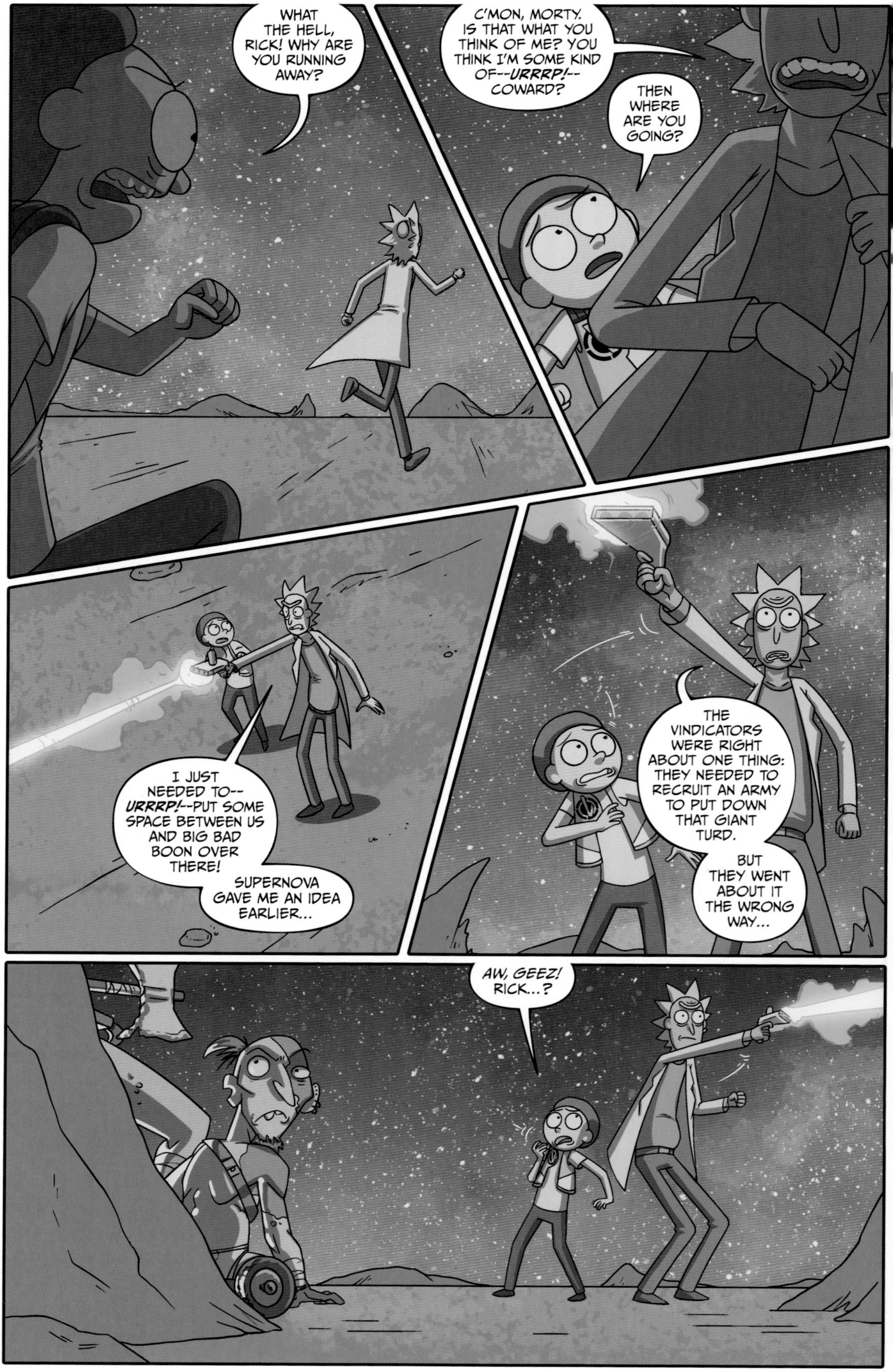
WHAT THE HELL, RICK! WHY ARE YOU RUNNING AWAY?
C'MON, MORTY. IS THAT WHAT YOU THINK OF ME? YOU THINK I'M SOME KIND OF--URRRP!--COWARD?
THEN WHERE ARE YOU GOING?
I JUST NEEDED TO--URRRP!--PUT SOME SPACE BETWEEN US AND BIG BAD BOON OVER THERE!
SUPERNOVA GAVE ME AN IDEA EARLIER...
THE VINDICATORS WERE RIGHT ABOUT ONE THING: THEY NEEDED TO RECRUIT AN ARMY TO PUT DOWN THAT GIANT TURD.
BUT THEY WENT ABOUT IT THE WRONG WAY...
AW, GEEZ! RICK...?

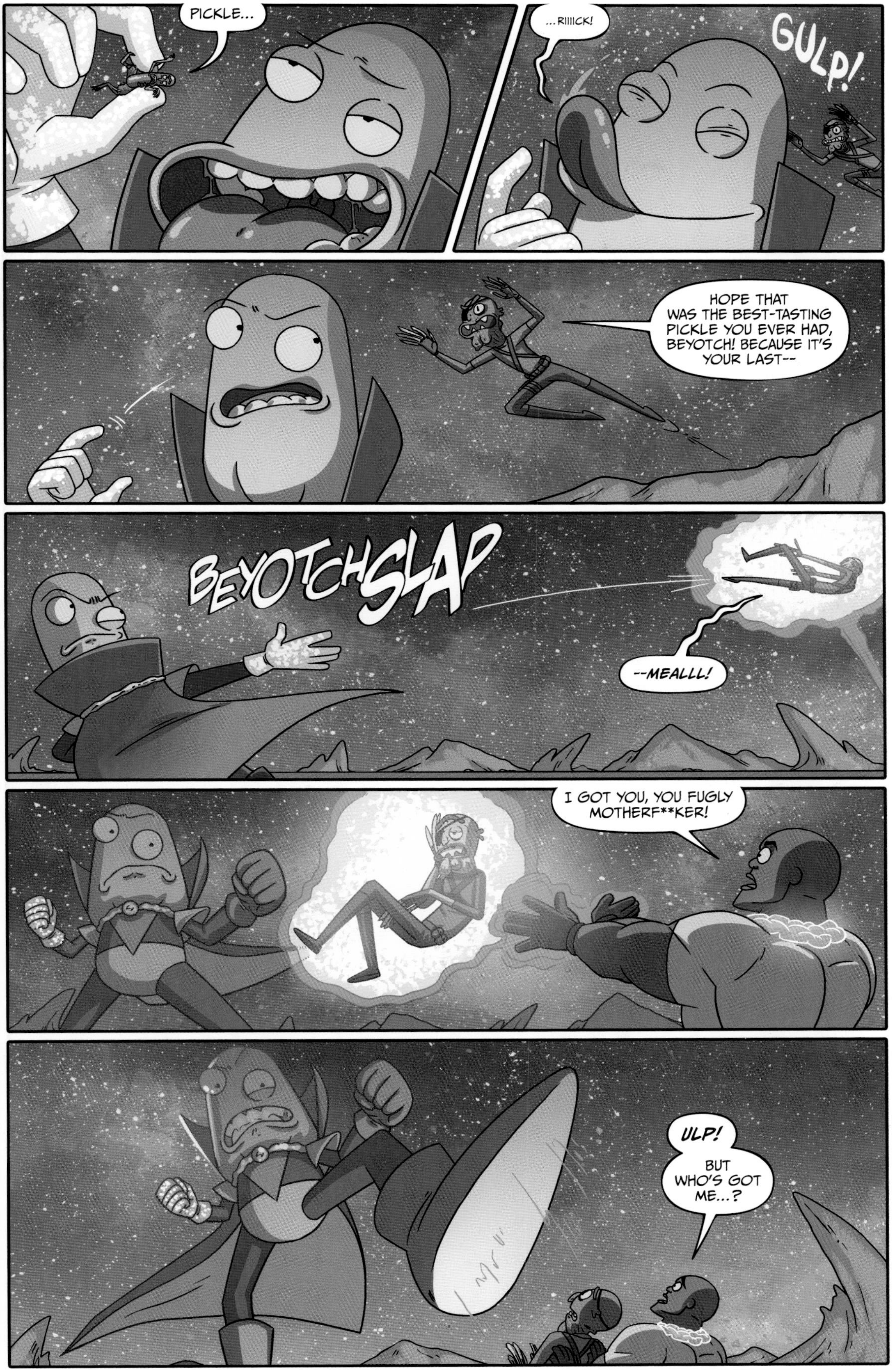
PICKLE...
...RIIIICK!
GULP!
HOPE THAT WAS THE BEST-TASTING PICKLE YOU EVER HAD, BEYOTCH! BECAUSE IT'S YOUR LAST--
BEYOTCHSLAP
--MEALLL!
I GOT YOU, YOU FUGLY MOTHERF**KER!
ULP!
BUT WHO'S GOT ME...?

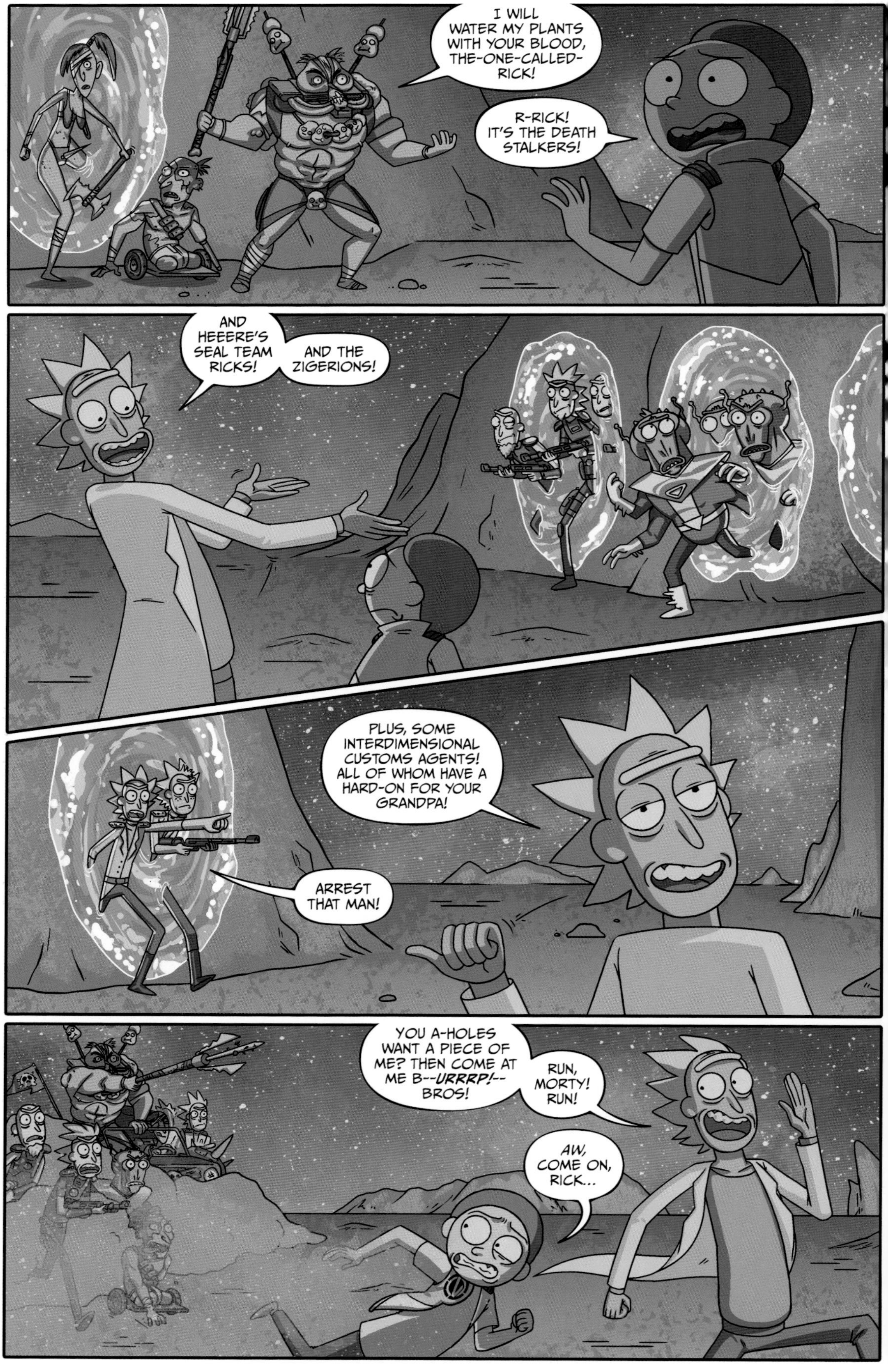
I WILL WATER MY PLANTS WITH YOUR BLOOD, THE-ONE-CALLED-RICK!
R-RICK! IT'S THE DEATH STALKERS!
AND HEEEERE'S SEAL TEAM RICKS!
AND THE ZIGERIONS!
PLUS, SOME INTERDIMENSIONAL CUSTOMS AGENTS! ALL OF WHOM HAVE A HARD-ON FOR YOUR GRANDPA!
ARREST THAT MAN!
YOU A-HOLES WANT A PIECE OF ME? THEN COME AT ME B--*URRRP!*--BROS!
RUN, MORTY! RUN!
AW, COME ON, RICK...

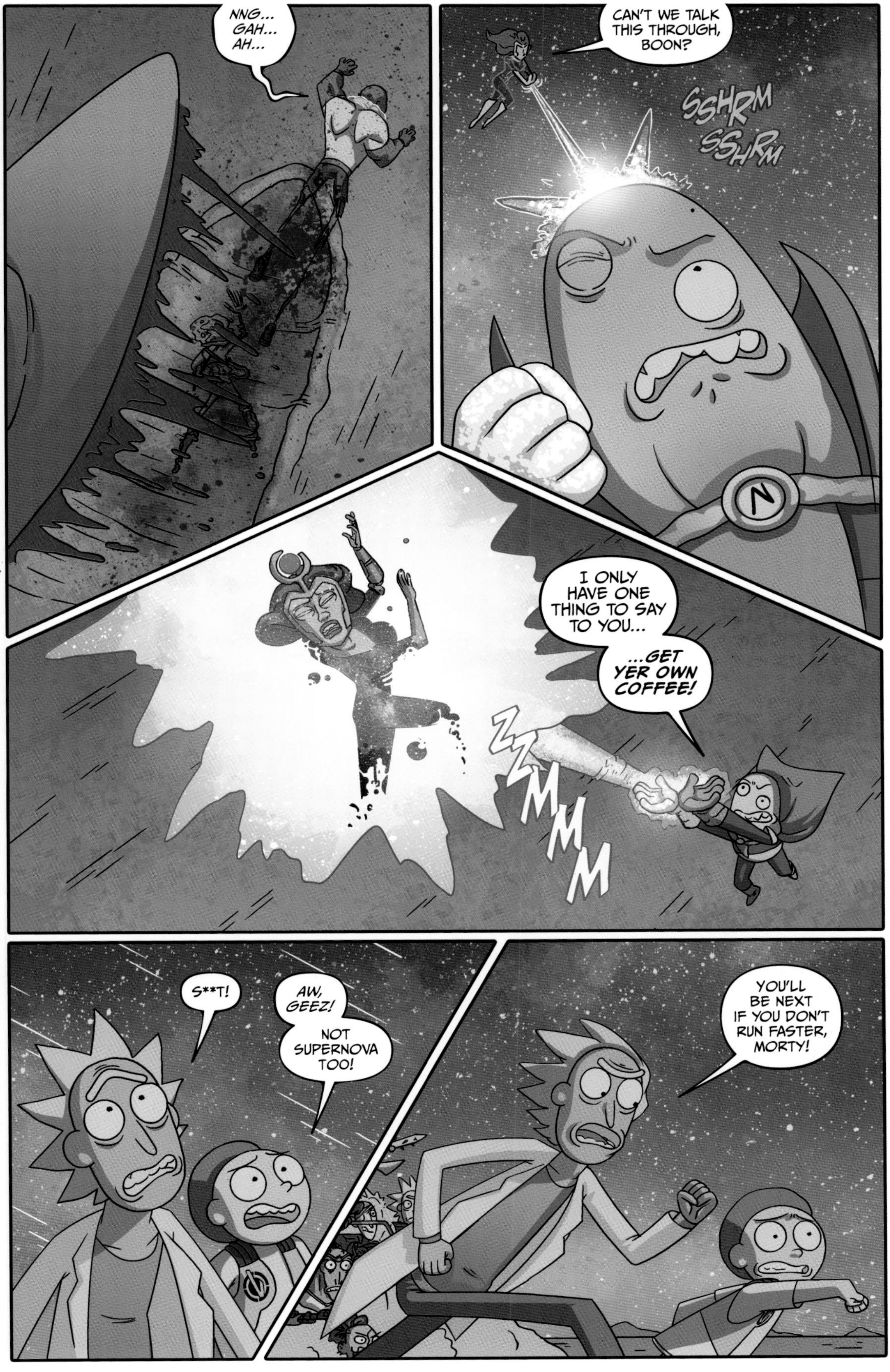
NNG... GAH... AH...
CAN'T WE TALK THIS THROUGH, BOON?
SSHRM SSHRM
I ONLY HAVE ONE THING TO SAY TO YOU...
...GET YER OWN COFFEE!
ZZMMMM
S**T!
AW, GEEZ!
NOT SUPERNOVA TOO!
YOU'LL BE NEXT IF YOU DON'T RUN FASTER, MORTY!

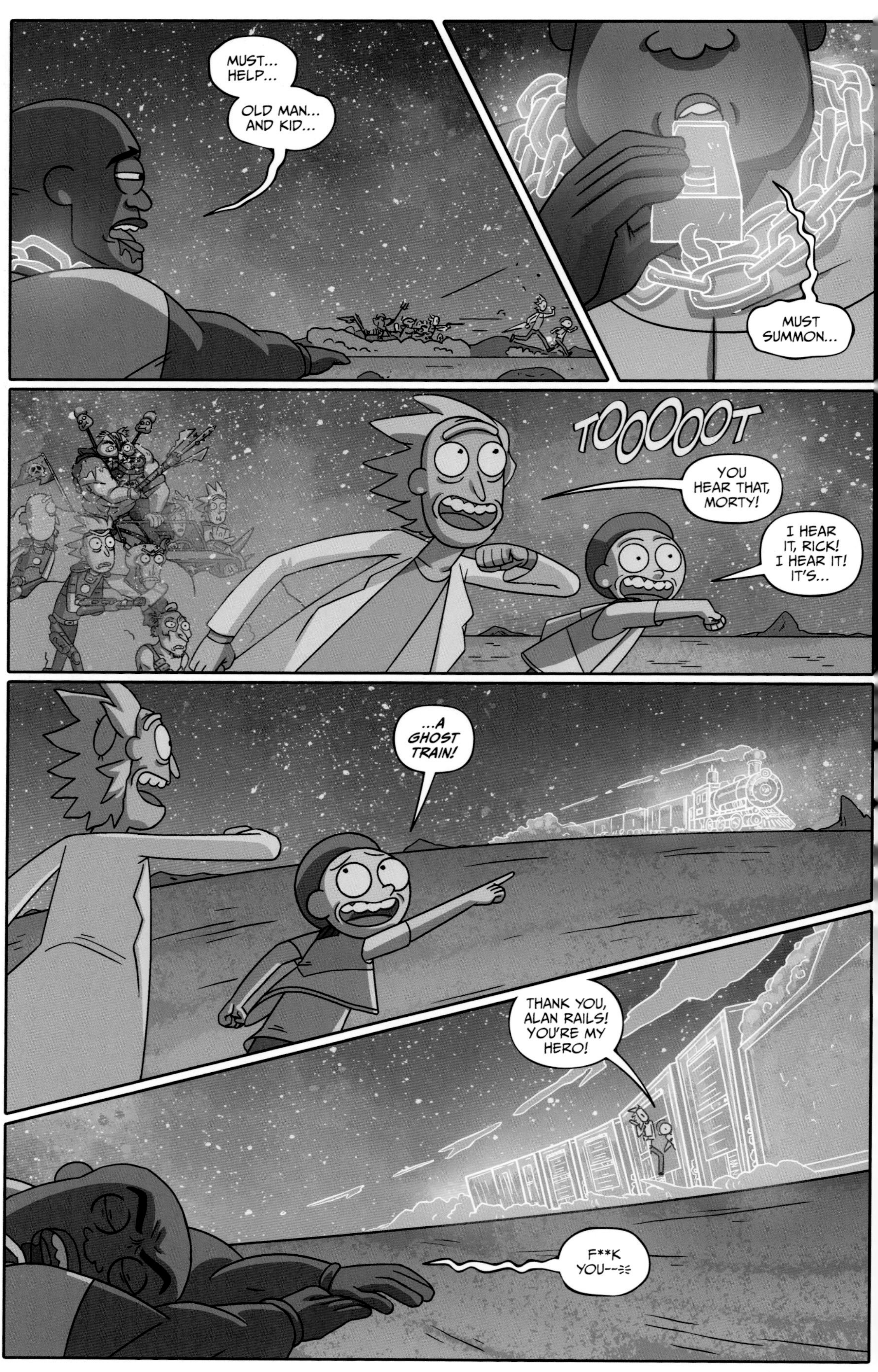
MUST... HELP...
OLD MAN... AND KID...
MUST SUMMON...
TOOOOOT
YOU HEAR THAT, MORTY!
I HEAR IT, RICK! I HEAR IT! IT'S...
...A GHOST TRAIN!
THANK YOU, ALAN RAILS! YOU'RE MY HERO!
F**K YOU--

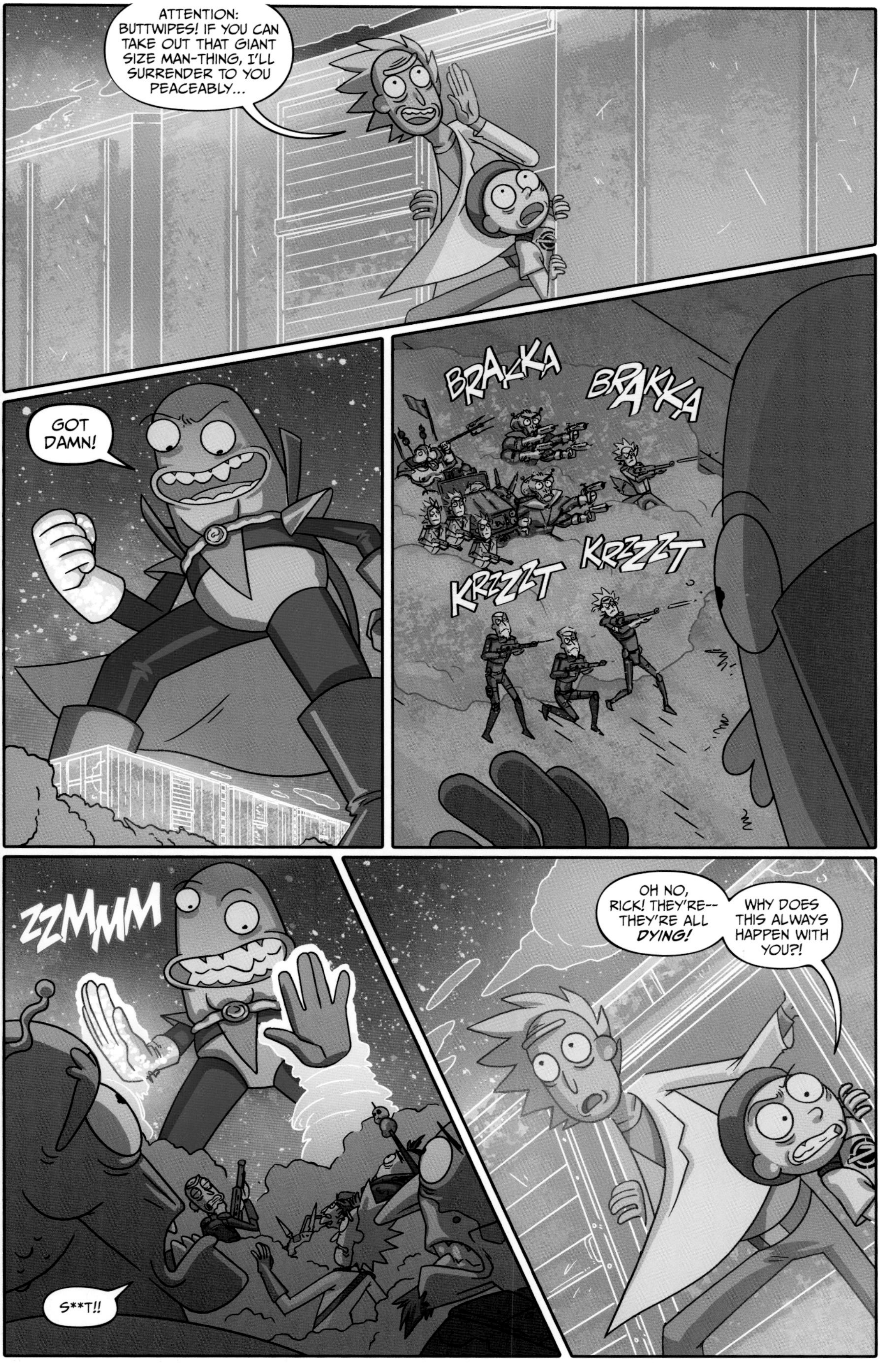
ATTENTION: BUTTWIPES! IF YOU CAN TAKE OUT THAT GIANT SIZE MAN-THING, I'LL SURRENDER TO YOU PEACEABLY...
GOT DAMN!
BRAKKA
BRAKKA
KRZZZT
KRZZZT
ZZMMM
S**T!!
OH NO, RICK! THEY'RE-- THEY'RE ALL *DYING!*
WHY DOES THIS ALWAYS HAPPEN WITH YOU?!

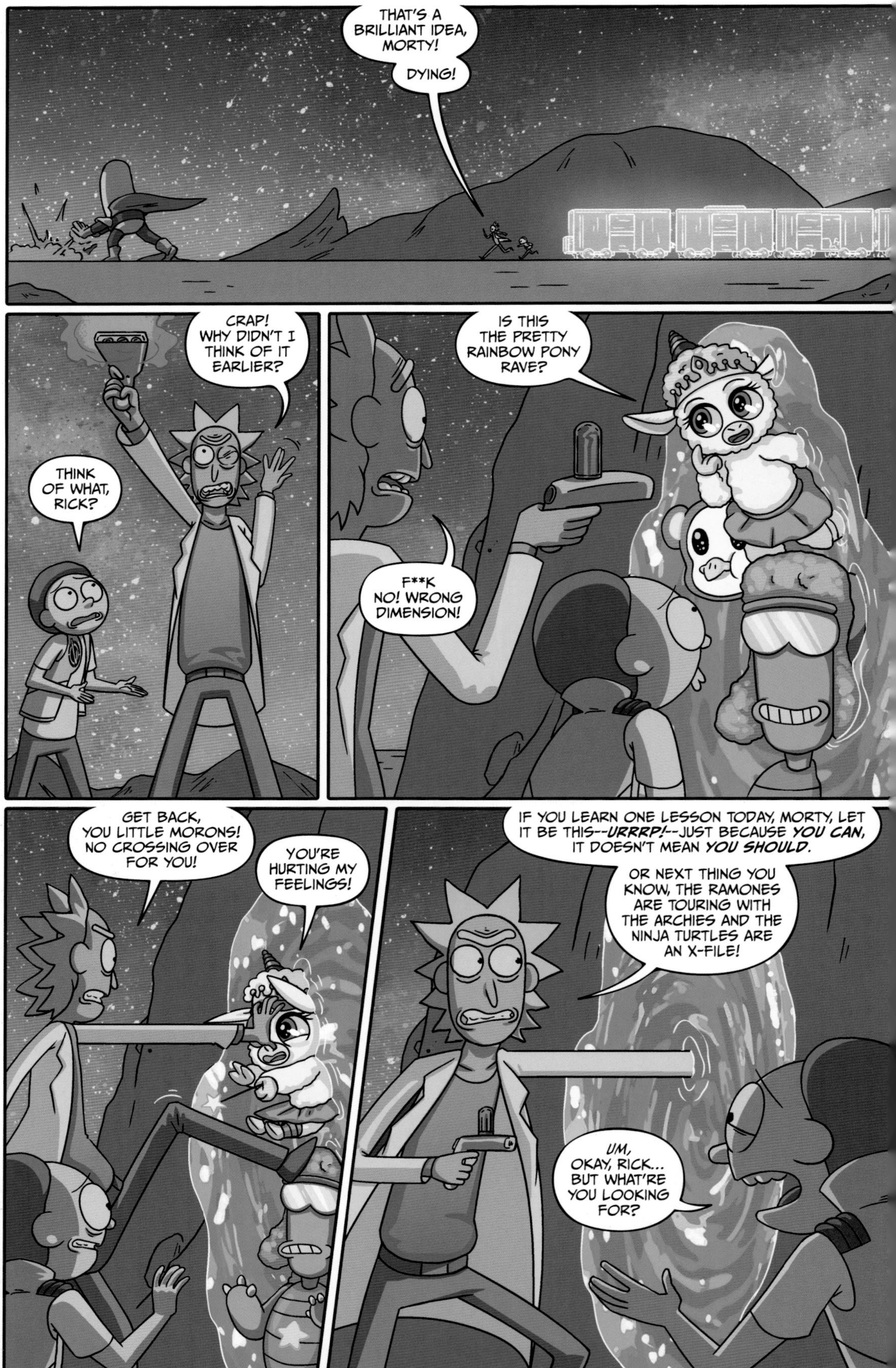

THAT'S A BRILLIANT IDEA, MORTY!
DYING!
CRAP! WHY DIDN'T I THINK OF IT EARLIER?
THINK OF WHAT, RICK?
IS THIS THE PRETTY RAINBOW PONY RAVE?
F**K NO! WRONG DIMENSION!
GET BACK, YOU LITTLE MORONS! NO CROSSING OVER FOR YOU!
YOU'RE HURTING MY FEELINGS!
IF YOU LEARN ONE LESSON TODAY, MORTY, LET IT BE THIS--*URRRP!*--JUST BECAUSE *YOU CAN,* IT DOESN'T MEAN *YOU SHOULD.*
OR NEXT THING YOU KNOW, THE RAMONES ARE TOURING WITH THE ARCHIES AND THE NINJA TURTLES ARE AN X-FILE!
UM, OKAY, RICK... BUT WHAT'RE YOU LOOKING FOR?

THIS, MORTY.
A MEESEEKS BOX!
THAT'S RIGHT, SON. AND WE'RE GONNA PUSH THIS BUTTON LIKE IT'S NEVER BEEN PUSHED BEFORE. IT'S GONNA PISS OFF SOME ARTISTS, BUT WE'RE GONNA SUMMON DOZENS OF MEESEEKS, SCORES OF THEM, HUNDREDS EVEN!
YES! I GET IT! MEESEEKS ARE CREATED TO SERVE A SINGULAR PURPOSE FOR WHICH THEY WILL GO TO ANY LENGTH TO FULFILL. THEY CAN'T EVEN DIE UNTIL THEY ACCOMPLISH THEIR ONE MISSION!
I'M MR. MEESEEKS!
MR. MEESEEKS, DEFEAT BOON!
YESSIREE!

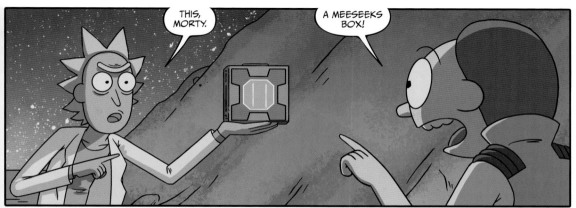

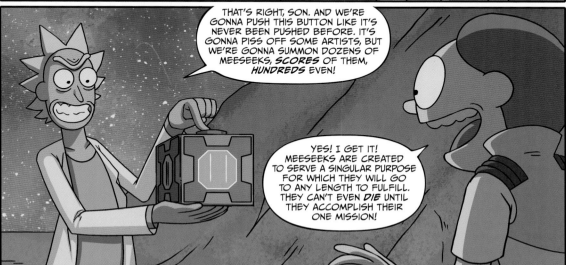

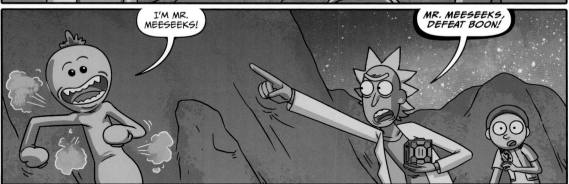

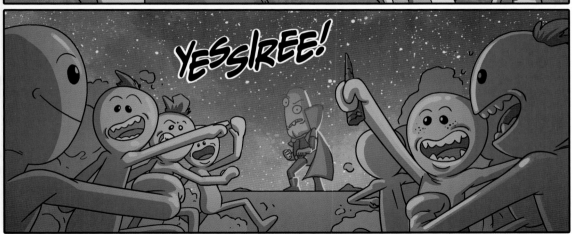

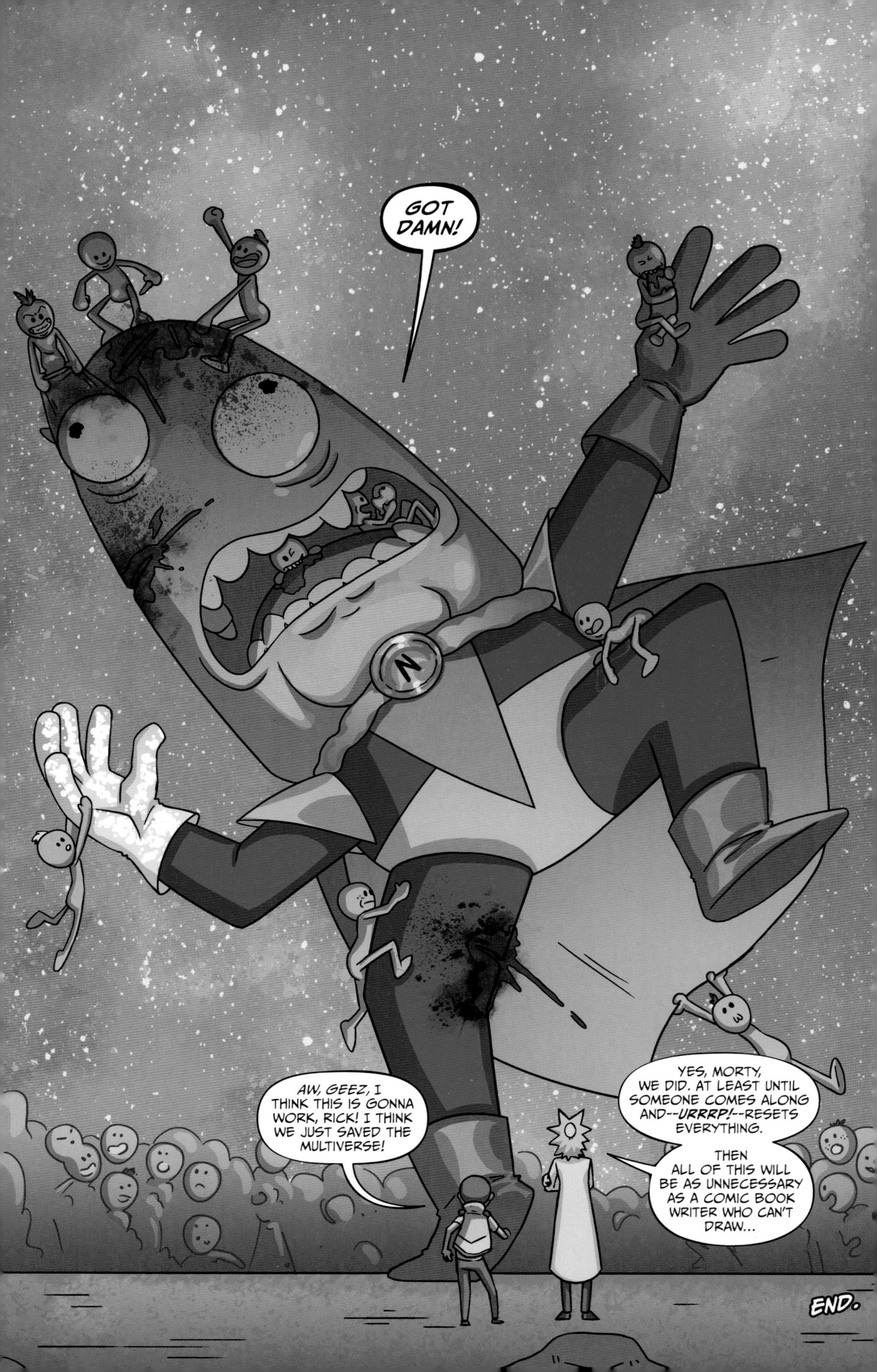
GOT DAMN!
AW, GEEZ, I THINK THIS IS GONNA WORK, RICK! I THINK WE JUST SAVED THE MULTIVERSE!
YES, MORTY, WE DID. AT LEAST UNTIL SOMEONE COMES ALONG AND--URRRP!--RESETS EVERYTHING.
THEN ALL OF THIS WILL BE AS UNNECESSARY AS A COMIC BOOK WRITER WHO CAN'T DRAW...
END.

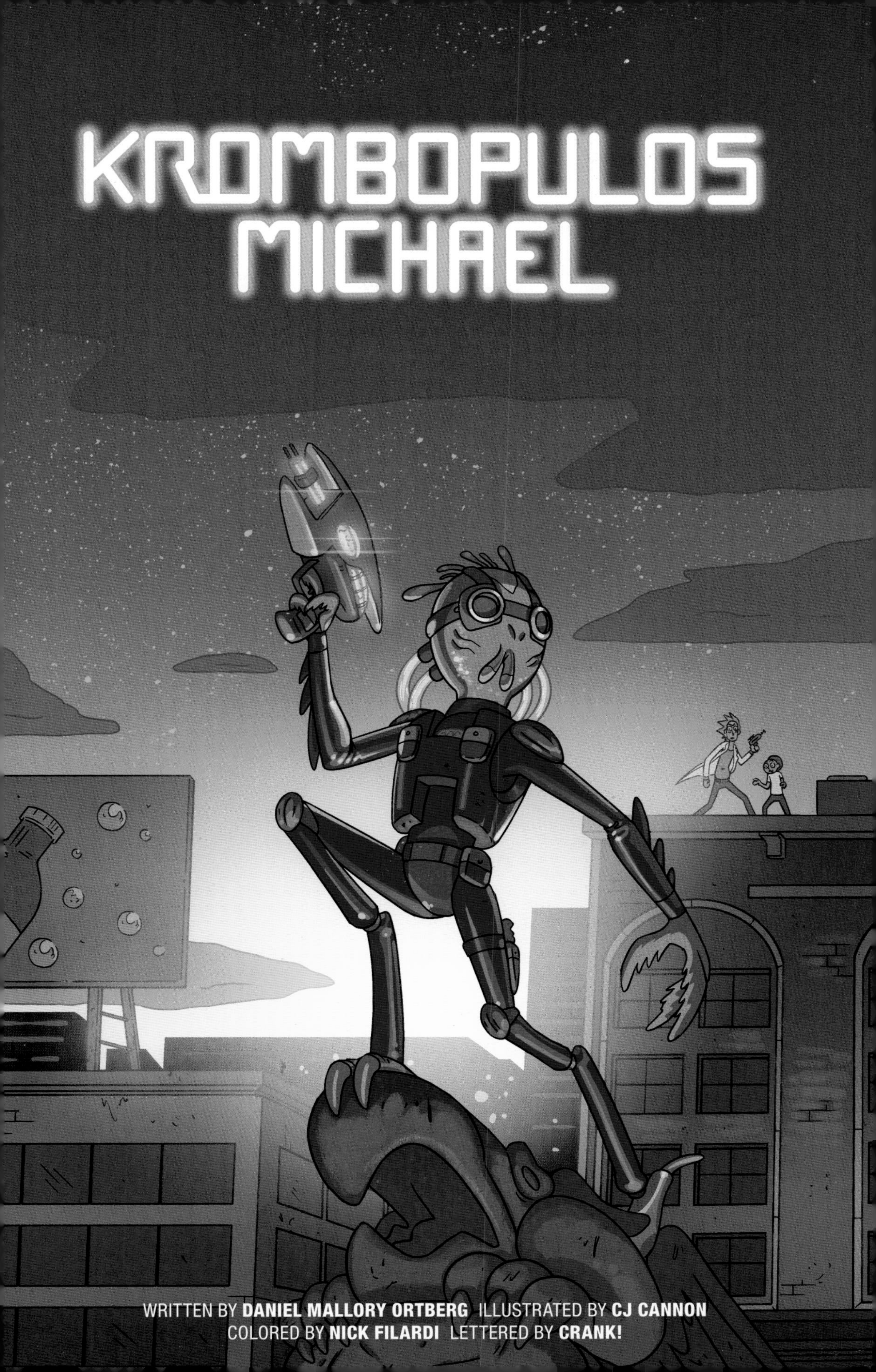
KROMBOPULOS
MICHAEL
WRITTEN BY DANIEL MALLORY ORTBERG ILLUSTRATED BY CJ CANNON
COLORED BY NICK FILARDI LETTERED BY CRANK!

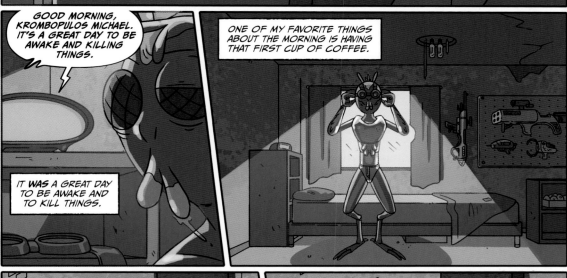

GOOD MORNING, KROMBOPULOS MICHAEL. IT'S A GREAT DAY TO BE AWAKE AND KILLING THINGS.

IT **WAS** A GREAT DAY TO BE AWAKE AND TO KILL THINGS.

ONE OF MY FAVORITE THINGS ABOUT THE MORNING IS HAVING THAT FIRST CUP OF COFFEE.

ALSO, IT'S THE PART OF THE DAY WHERE I GET TO START KILLING PEOPLE.

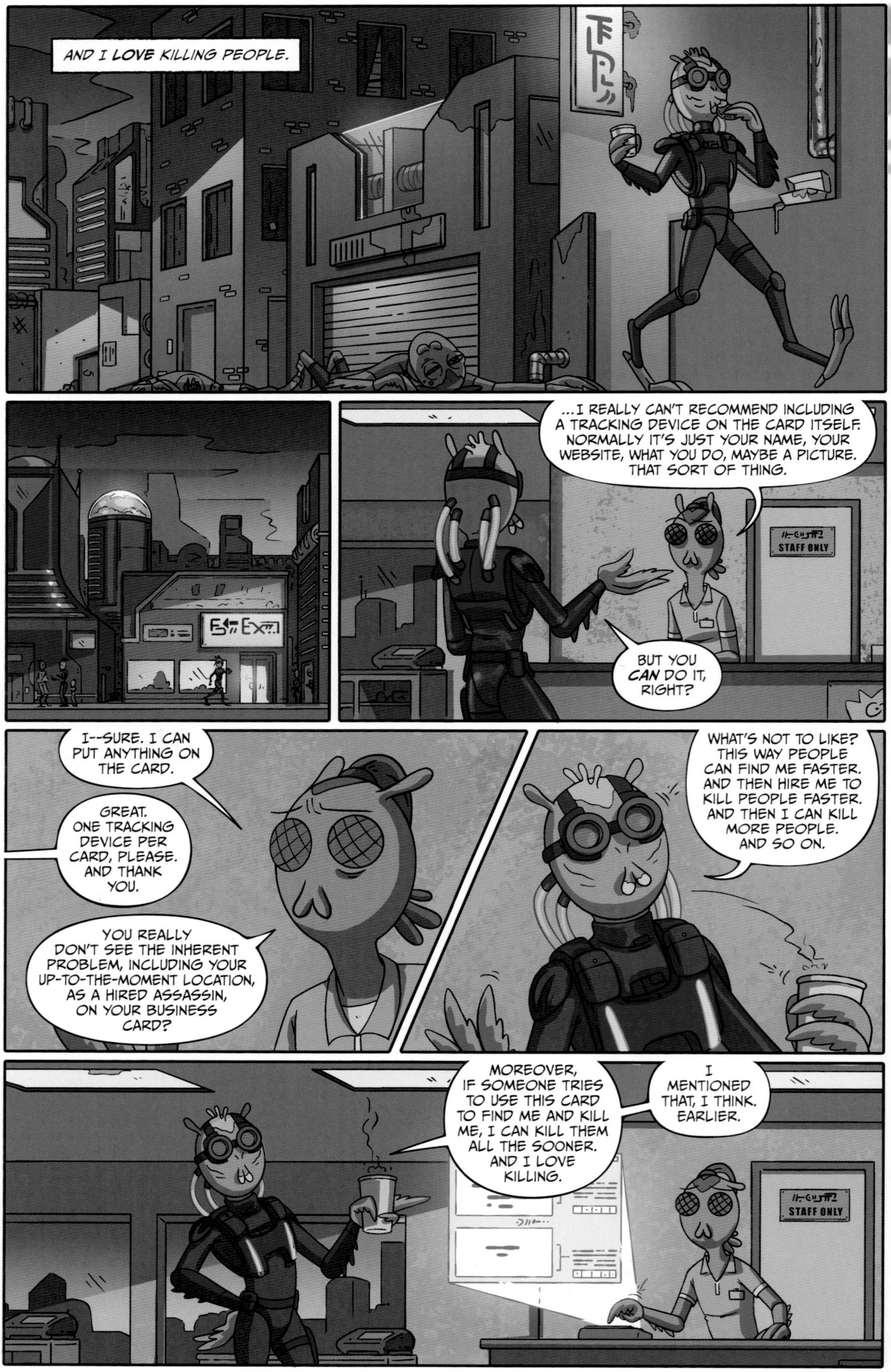
AND I LOVE KILLING PEOPLE.
...I REALLY CAN'T RECOMMEND INCLUDING A TRACKING DEVICE ON THE CARD ITSELF. NORMALLY IT'S JUST YOUR NAME, YOUR WEBSITE, WHAT YOU DO, MAYBE A PICTURE. THAT SORT OF THING.
STAFF ONLY
BUT YOU CAN DO IT, RIGHT?
I--SURE. I CAN PUT ANYTHING ON THE CARD.
GREAT. ONE TRACKING DEVICE PER CARD, PLEASE. AND THANK YOU.
YOU REALLY DON'T SEE THE INHERENT PROBLEM, INCLUDING YOUR UP-TO-THE-MOMENT LOCATION, AS A HIRED ASSASSIN, ON YOUR BUSINESS CARD?
WHAT'S NOT TO LIKE? THIS WAY PEOPLE CAN FIND ME FASTER. AND THEN HIRE ME TO KILL PEOPLE FASTER. AND THEN I CAN KILL MORE PEOPLE. AND SO ON.
MOREOVER, IF SOMEONE TRIES TO USE THIS CARD TO FIND ME AND KILL ME, I CAN KILL THEM ALL THE SOONER. AND I LOVE KILLING.
I MENTIONED THAT, I THINK. EARLIER.
STAFF ONLY

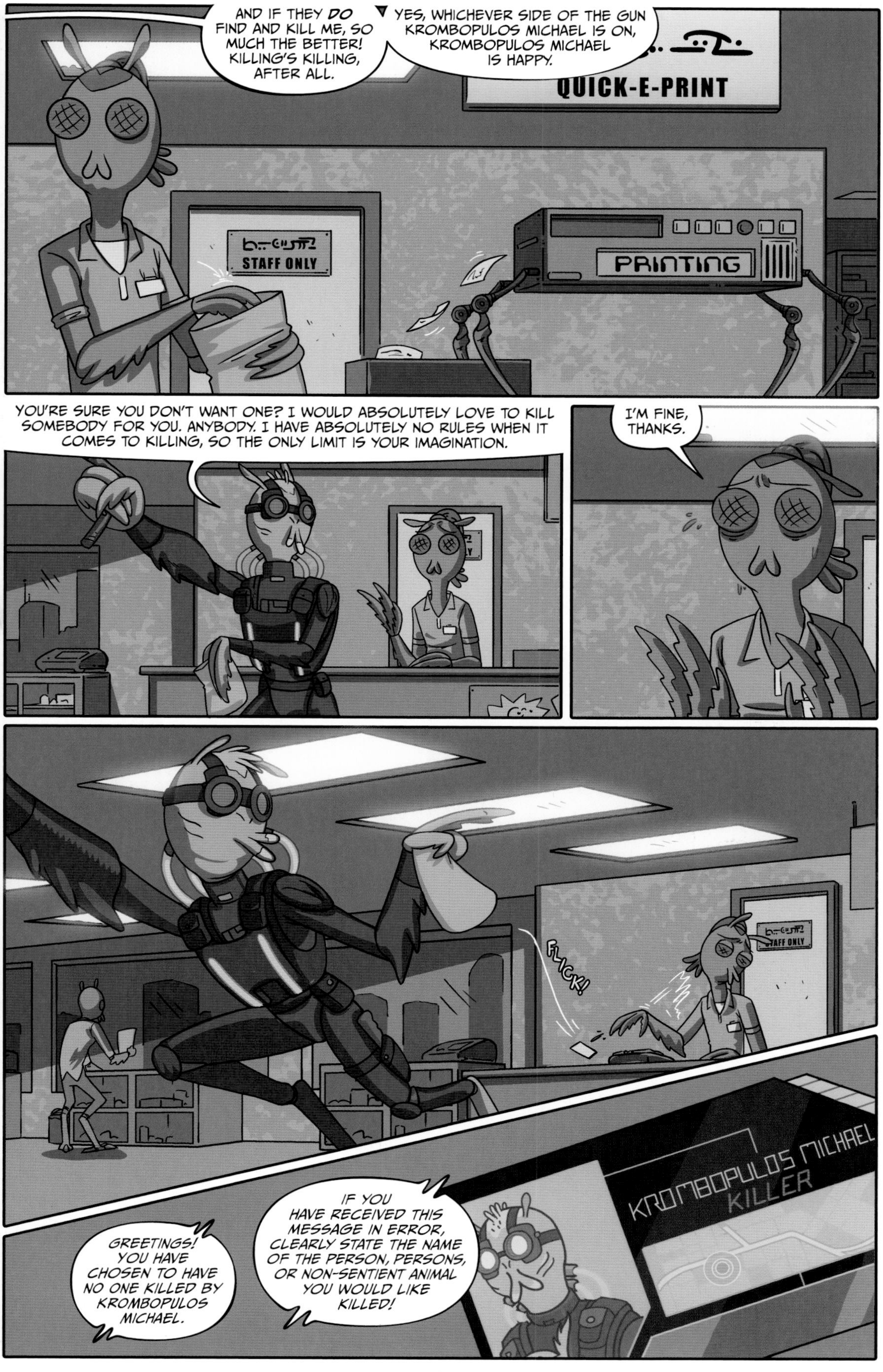
AND IF THEY DO FIND AND KILL ME, SO MUCH THE BETTER! KILLING'S KILLING, AFTER ALL.
YES, WHICHEVER SIDE OF THE GUN KROMBOPULOS MICHAEL IS ON, KROMBOPULOS MICHAEL IS HAPPY.
QUICK-E-PRINT
STAFF ONLY
PRINTING
YOU'RE SURE YOU DON'T WANT ONE? I WOULD ABSOLUTELY LOVE TO KILL SOMEBODY FOR YOU. ANYBODY. I HAVE ABSOLUTELY NO RULES WHEN IT COMES TO KILLING, SO THE ONLY LIMIT IS YOUR IMAGINATION.
I'M FINE, THANKS.
STAFF ONLY
FLICK!
KROMBOPULOS MICHAEL
KILLER
GREETINGS! YOU HAVE CHOSEN TO HAVE NO ONE KILLED BY KROMBOPULOS MICHAEL.
IF YOU HAVE RECEIVED THIS MESSAGE IN ERROR, CLEARLY STATE THE NAME OF THE PERSON, PERSONS, OR NON-SENTIENT ANIMAL YOU WOULD LIKE KILLED!

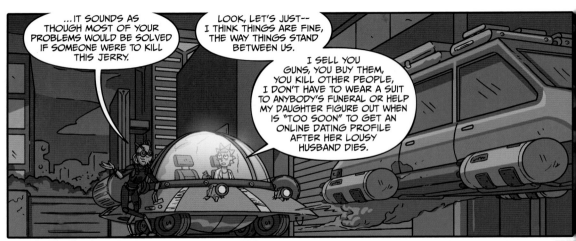

...IT SOUNDS AS THOUGH MOST OF YOUR PROBLEMS WOULD BE SOLVED IF SOMEONE WERE TO KILL THIS JERRY.

LOOK, LET'S JUST-- I THINK THINGS ARE FINE, THE WAY THINGS STAND BETWEEN US.

I SELL YOU GUNS, YOU BUY THEM, YOU KILL OTHER PEOPLE, I DON'T HAVE TO WEAR A SUIT TO ANYBODY'S FUNERAL OR HELP MY DAUGHTER FIGURE OUT WHEN IS "TOO SOON" TO GET AN ONLINE DATING PROFILE AFTER HER LOUSY HUSBAND DIES.

OH, BUT RICK, IT WOULD BE NO TROUBLE AT ALL FOR ME TO DO YOU THIS FAVOR. I COULD KILL THIS JERRY, FOR YOU, RICK.

BECAUSE I'D SAY SOMETHING WRONG, AND SHE'D START CRYING. OR IT'D BE SOMETHING ELSE, LIKE I'D PICK UP THE KIND OF DETERGENT HE USED TO BUY, AND THEN ALL THE SHEETS WOULD SMELL LIKE HIS DETERGENT, AND THEN I'D HAVE TO WASH ALL THE SHEETS AGAIN, AND I DON'T HAVE TIME TO WASH MY OWN SHEETS, MUCH LESS BETH'S.

IF SOMEONE WERE TO KILL BETH AS WELL, WOULD THIS SOLVE YOUR SHEETS PROBLEM?

LET'S JUST KEEP THINGS PROFESSIONAL.

OKAY, RICK. I WILL CONTINUE TO BUY GUNS FROM YOU, UNTIL YOU ASK ME TO KILL YOUR FAMILY. KILLING YOUR FAMILY WOULD MAKE ME VERY HAPPY. I HAVE NO PROBLEM KILLING FAMILIES.

KILLING :) :) :)

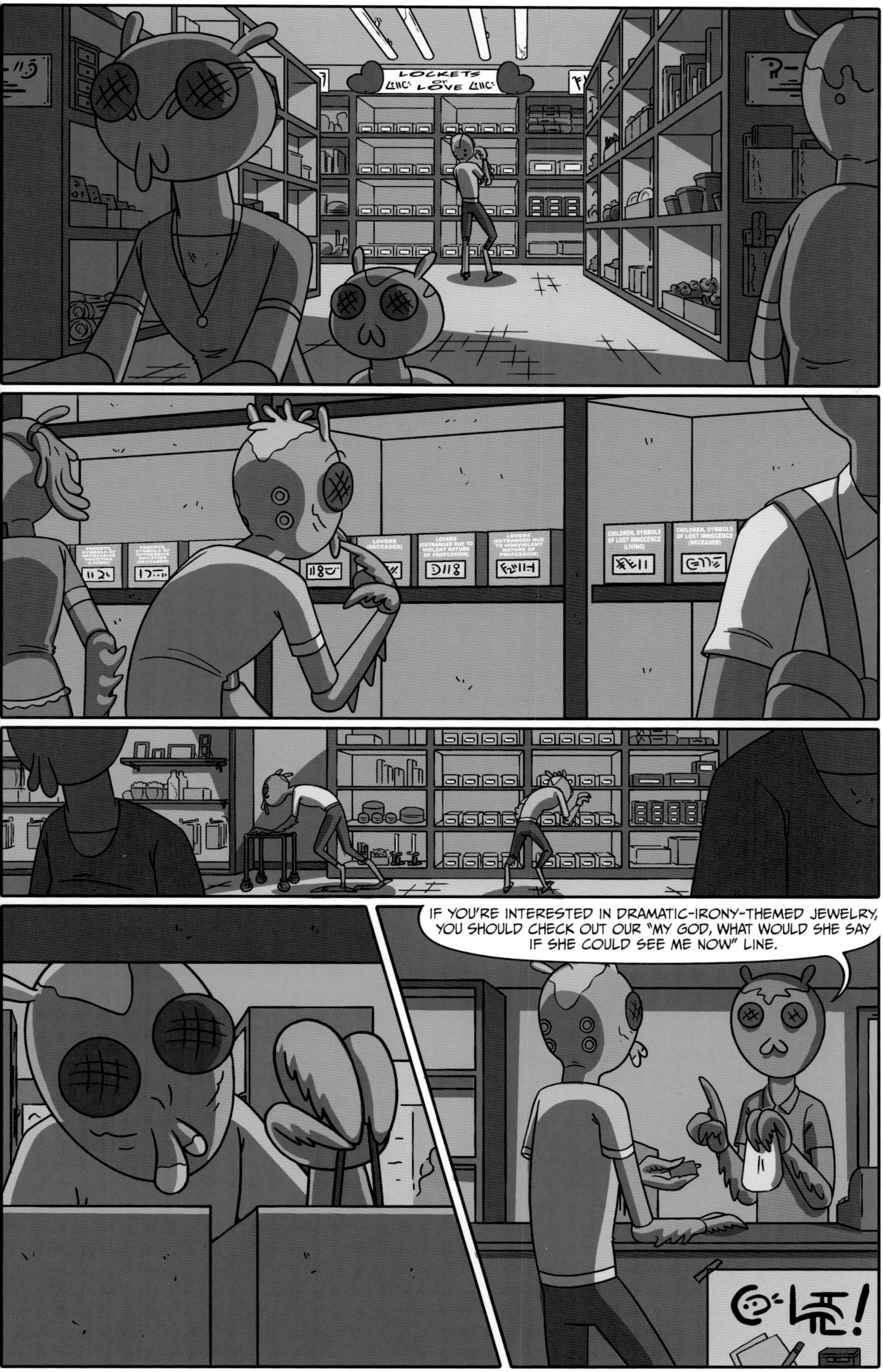
LOCKETS OF LOVE
PARENTS, SYMBOLS OF OPPRESSIVE SOCIETIES (LIVING)
PARENTS, SYMBOLS OF OPPRESSIVE SOCIETIES (DECEASED)
LOVERS (DECEASED)
LOVERS (ESTRANGED DUE TO VIOLENT NATURE OF PROFESSION)
LOVERS (ESTRANGED DUE TO NONVIOLENT NATURE OF PROFESSION)
CHILDREN, SYMBOLS OF LOST INNOCENCE (LIVING)
CHILDREN, SYMBOLS OF LOST INNOCENCE (DECEASED)
IF YOU'RE INTERESTED IN DRAMATIC-IRONY-THEMED JEWELRY, YOU SHOULD CHECK OUT OUR "MY GOD, WHAT WOULD SHE SAY IF SHE COULD SEE ME NOW" LINE.

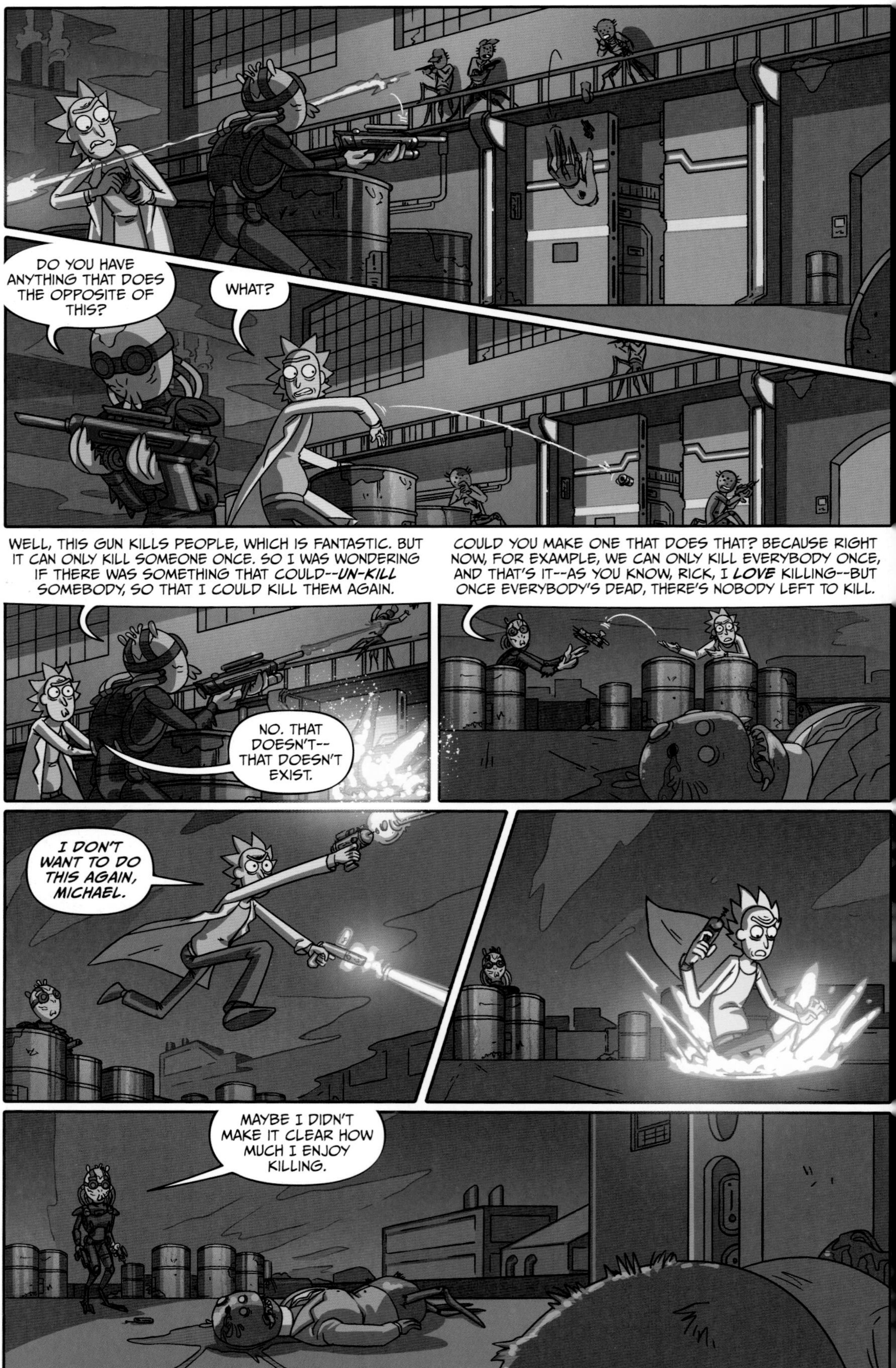
DO YOU HAVE ANYTHING THAT DOES THE OPPOSITE OF THIS?
WHAT?
WELL, THIS GUN KILLS PEOPLE, WHICH IS FANTASTIC. BUT IT CAN ONLY KILL SOMEONE ONCE. SO I WAS WONDERING IF THERE WAS SOMETHING THAT COULD--UN-KILL SOMEBODY, SO THAT I COULD KILL THEM AGAIN.
NO. THAT DOESN'T--THAT DOESN'T EXIST.
COULD YOU MAKE ONE THAT DOES THAT? BECAUSE RIGHT NOW, FOR EXAMPLE, WE CAN ONLY KILL EVERYBODY ONCE, AND THAT'S IT--AS YOU KNOW, RICK, I LOVE KILLING--BUT ONCE EVERYBODY'S DEAD, THERE'S NOBODY LEFT TO KILL.
I DON'T WANT TO DO THIS AGAIN, MICHAEL.
MAYBE I DIDN'T MAKE IT CLEAR HOW MUCH I ENJOY KILLING.

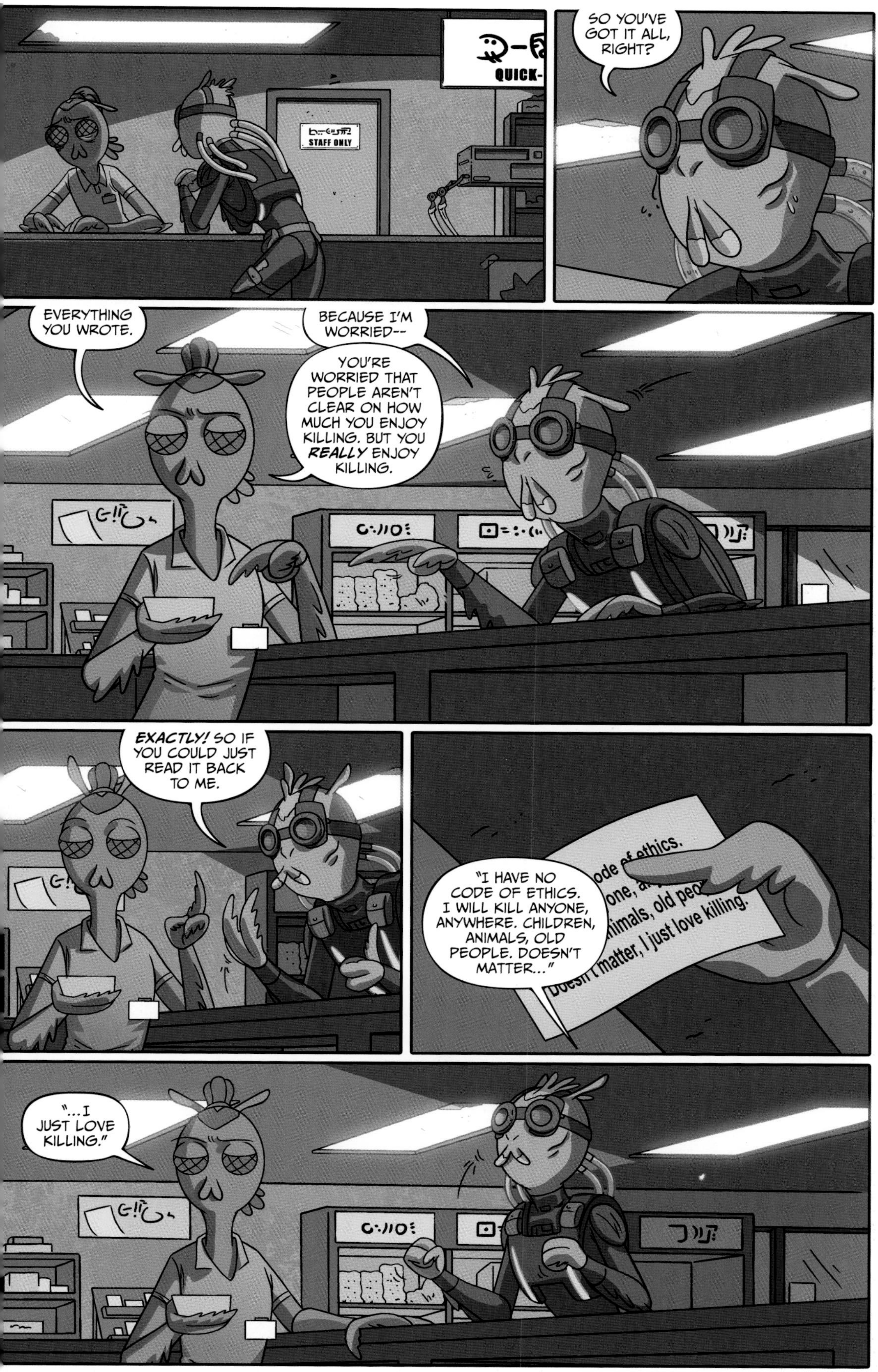
QUICK-
STAFF ONLY
SO YOU'VE GOT IT ALL, RIGHT?
EVERYTHING YOU WROTE.
BECAUSE I'M WORRIED--
YOU'RE WORRIED THAT PEOPLE AREN'T CLEAR ON HOW MUCH YOU ENJOY KILLING. BUT YOU *REALLY* ENJOY KILLING.
EXACTLY! SO IF YOU COULD JUST READ IT BACK TO ME.
"I HAVE NO CODE OF ETHICS. I WILL KILL ANYONE, ANYWHERE. CHILDREN, ANIMALS, OLD PEOPLE. DOESN'T MATTER..."
"...I JUST LOVE KILLING."

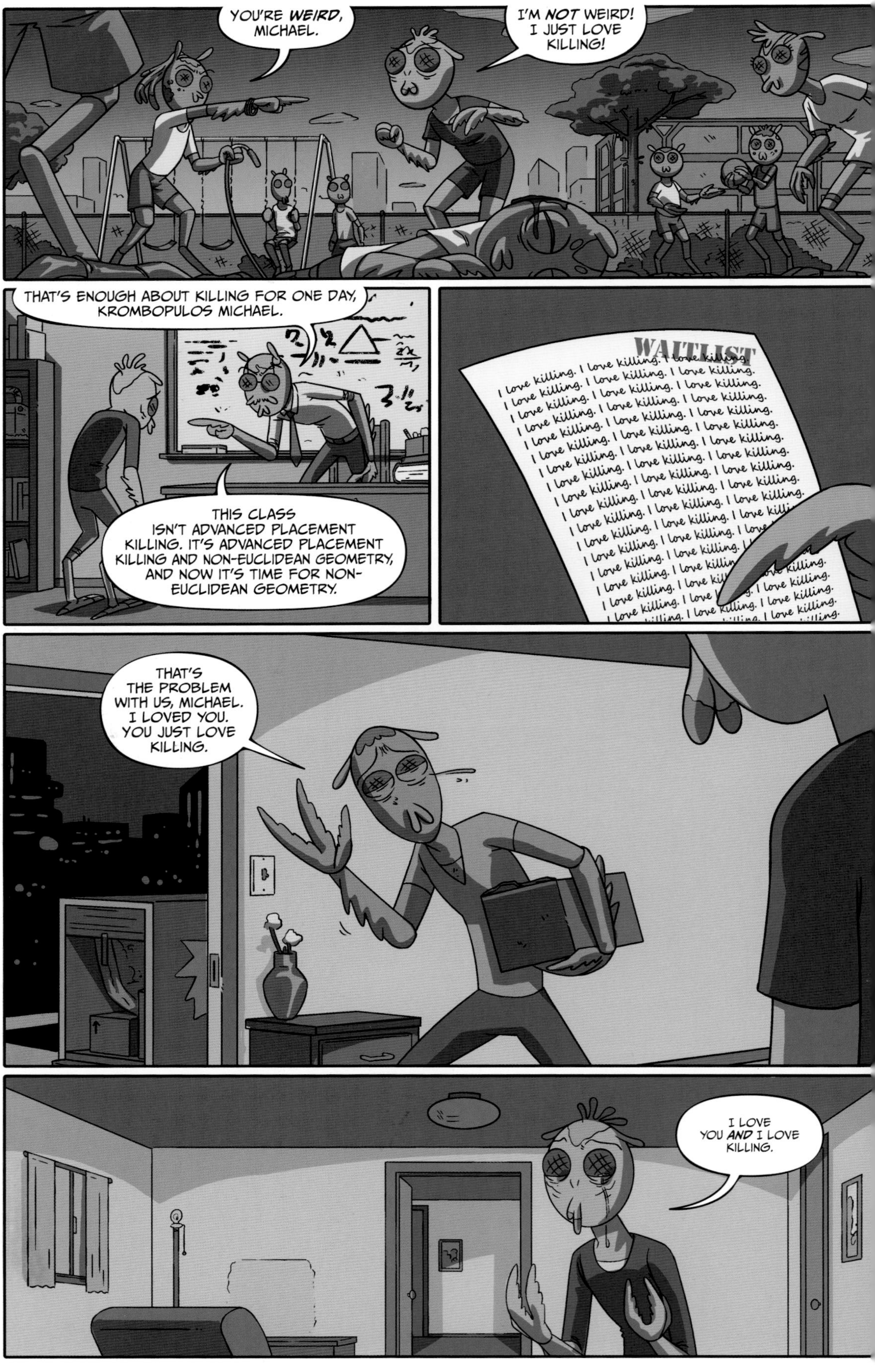
YOU'RE WEIRD, MICHAEL.
I'M NOT WEIRD! I JUST LOVE KILLING!
THAT'S ENOUGH ABOUT KILLING FOR ONE DAY, KROMBOPULOS MICHAEL.
THIS CLASS ISN'T ADVANCED PLACEMENT KILLING. IT'S ADVANCED PLACEMENT KILLING AND NON-EUCLIDEAN GEOMETRY, AND NOW IT'S TIME FOR NON-EUCLIDEAN GEOMETRY.
WAITLIST
I love killing. I love killing. I love killing.
THAT'S THE PROBLEM WITH US, MICHAEL. I LOVED YOU. YOU JUST LOVE KILLING.
I LOVE YOU AND I LOVE KILLING.

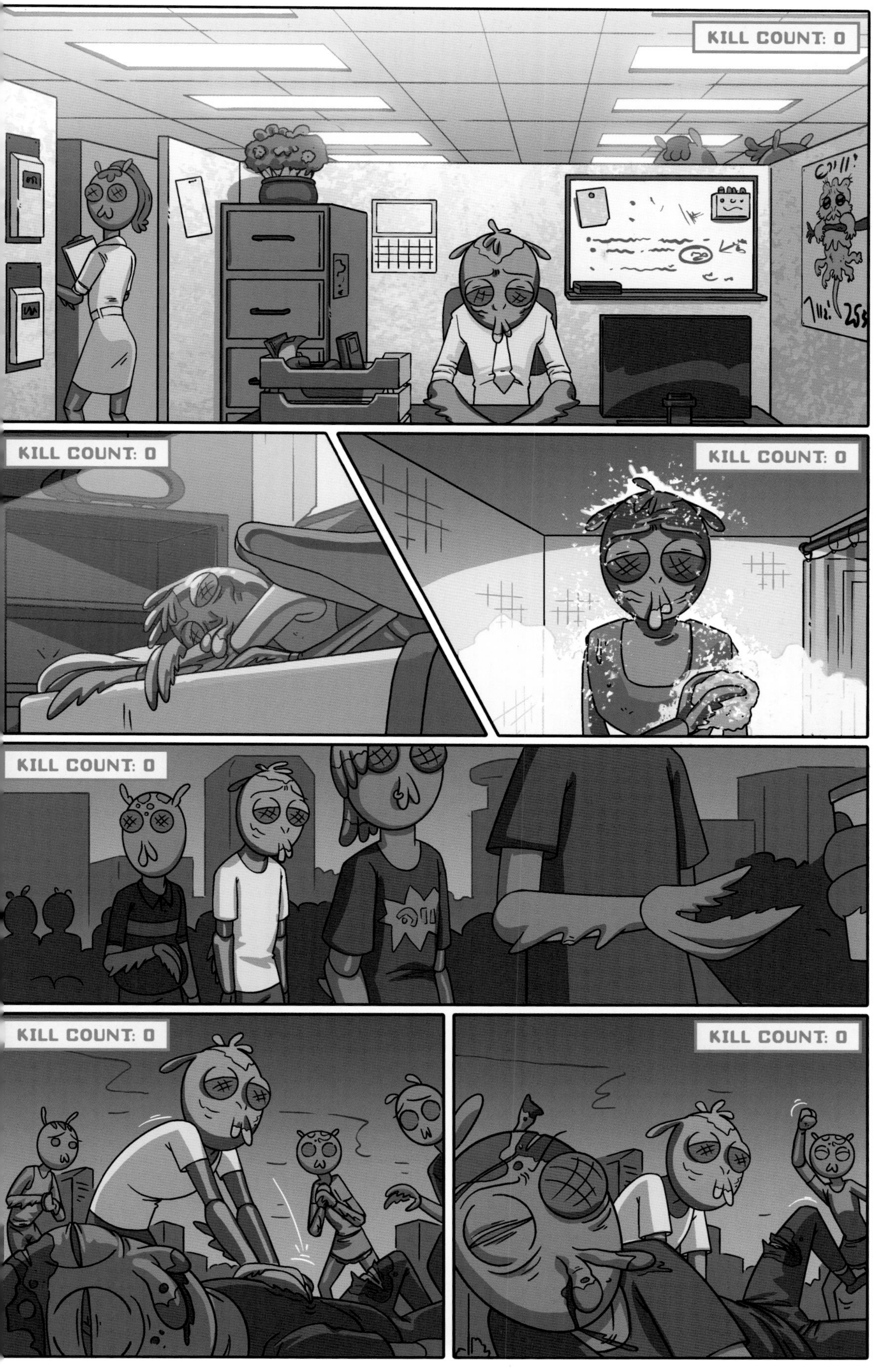
KILL COUNT: 0
KILL COUNT: 0
KILL COUNT: 0
KILL COUNT: 0
KILL COUNT: 0
KILL COUNT: 0

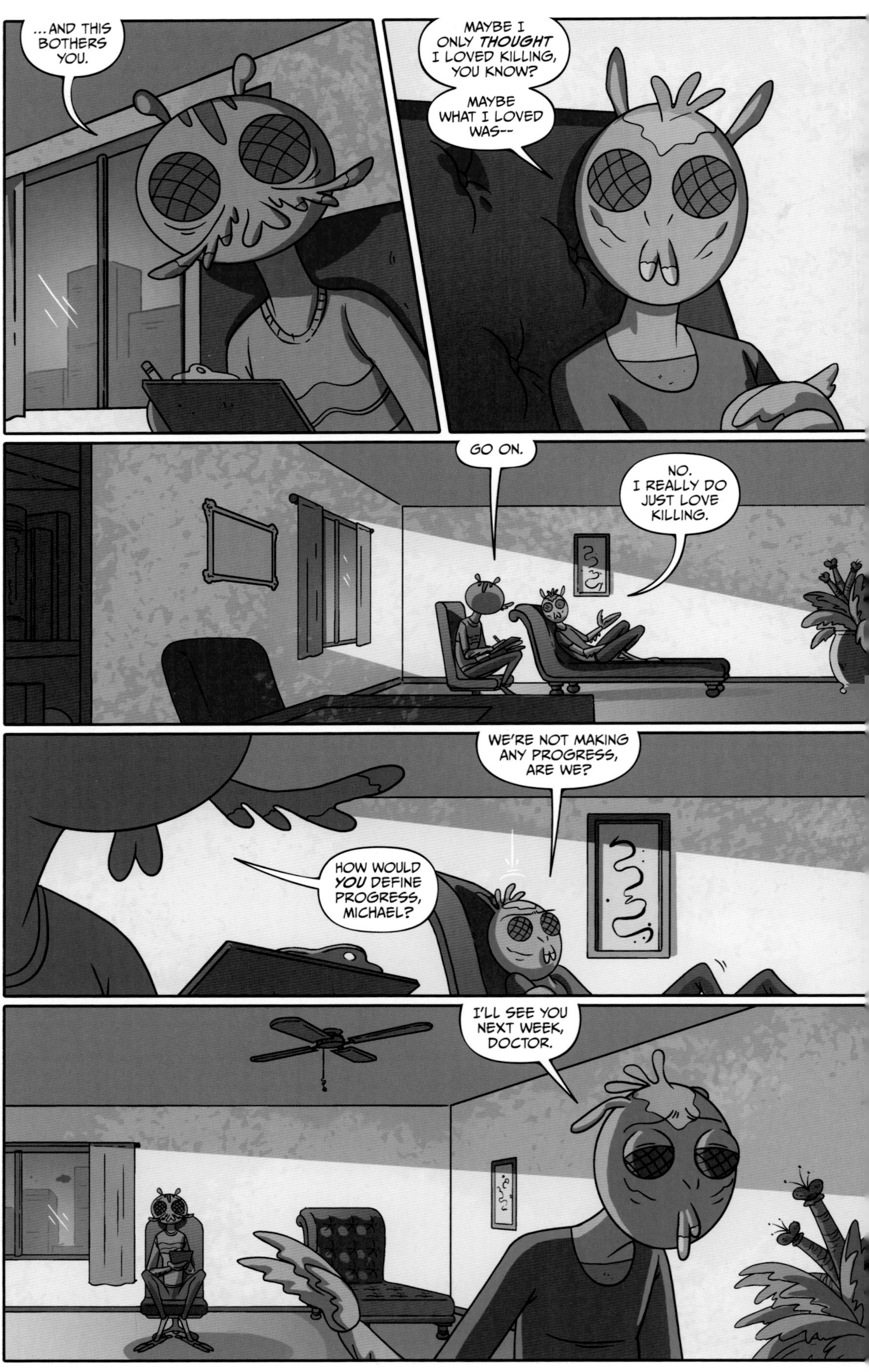
...AND THIS BOTHERS YOU.
MAYBE I ONLY *THOUGHT* I LOVED KILLING, YOU KNOW?
MAYBE WHAT I LOVED WAS--
GO ON.
NO. I REALLY DO JUST LOVE KILLING.
WE'RE NOT MAKING ANY PROGRESS, ARE WE?
HOW WOULD *YOU* DEFINE PROGRESS, MICHAEL?
I'LL SEE YOU NEXT WEEK, DOCTOR.

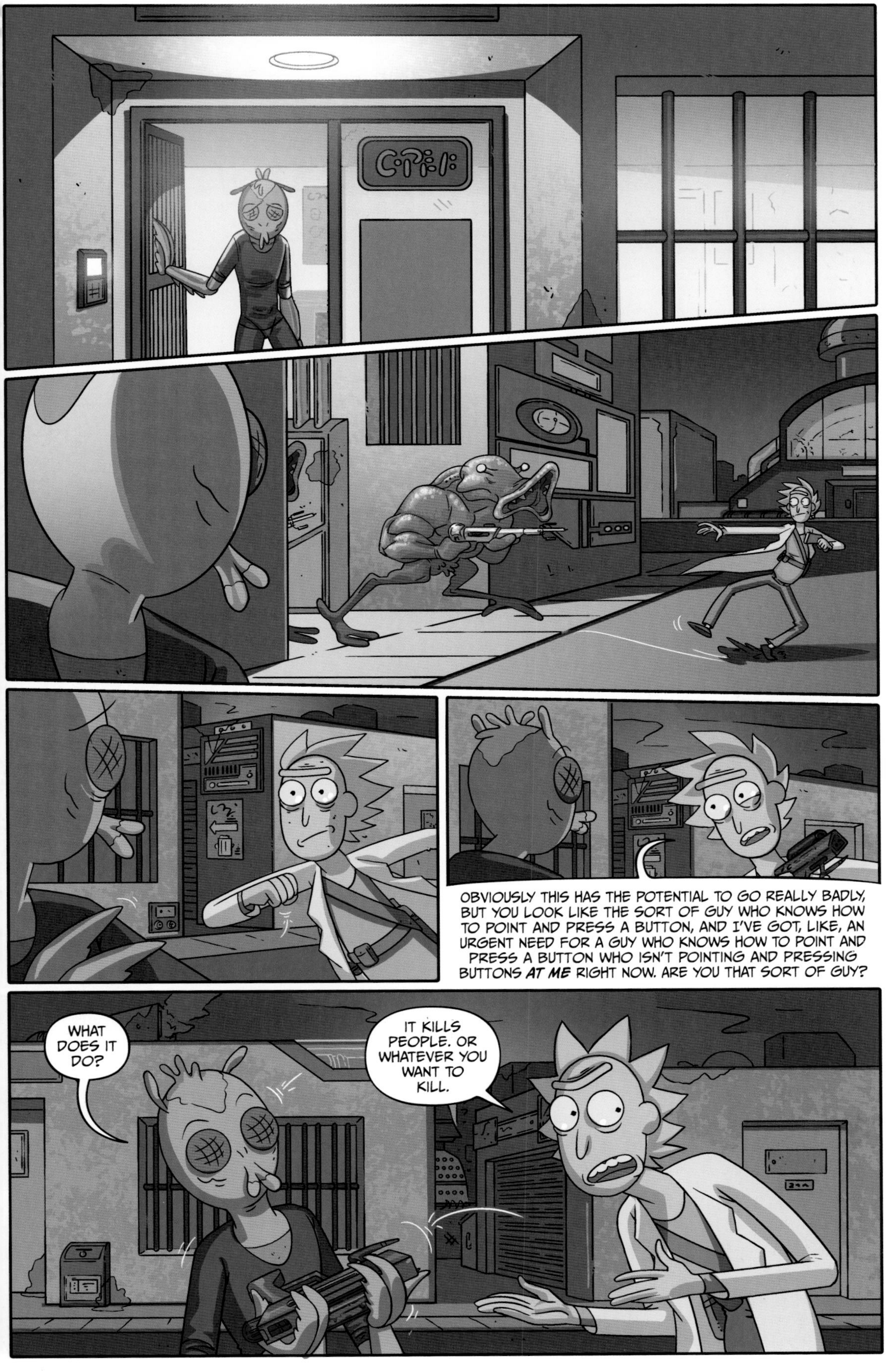
OBVIOUSLY THIS HAS THE POTENTIAL TO GO REALLY BADLY, BUT YOU LOOK LIKE THE SORT OF GUY WHO KNOWS HOW TO POINT AND PRESS A BUTTON, AND I'VE GOT, LIKE, AN URGENT NEED FOR A GUY WHO KNOWS HOW TO POINT AND PRESS A BUTTON WHO ISN'T POINTING AND PRESSING BUTTONS *AT ME* RIGHT NOW. ARE YOU THAT SORT OF GUY?
WHAT DOES IT DO?
IT KILLS PEOPLE. OR WHATEVER YOU WANT TO KILL.

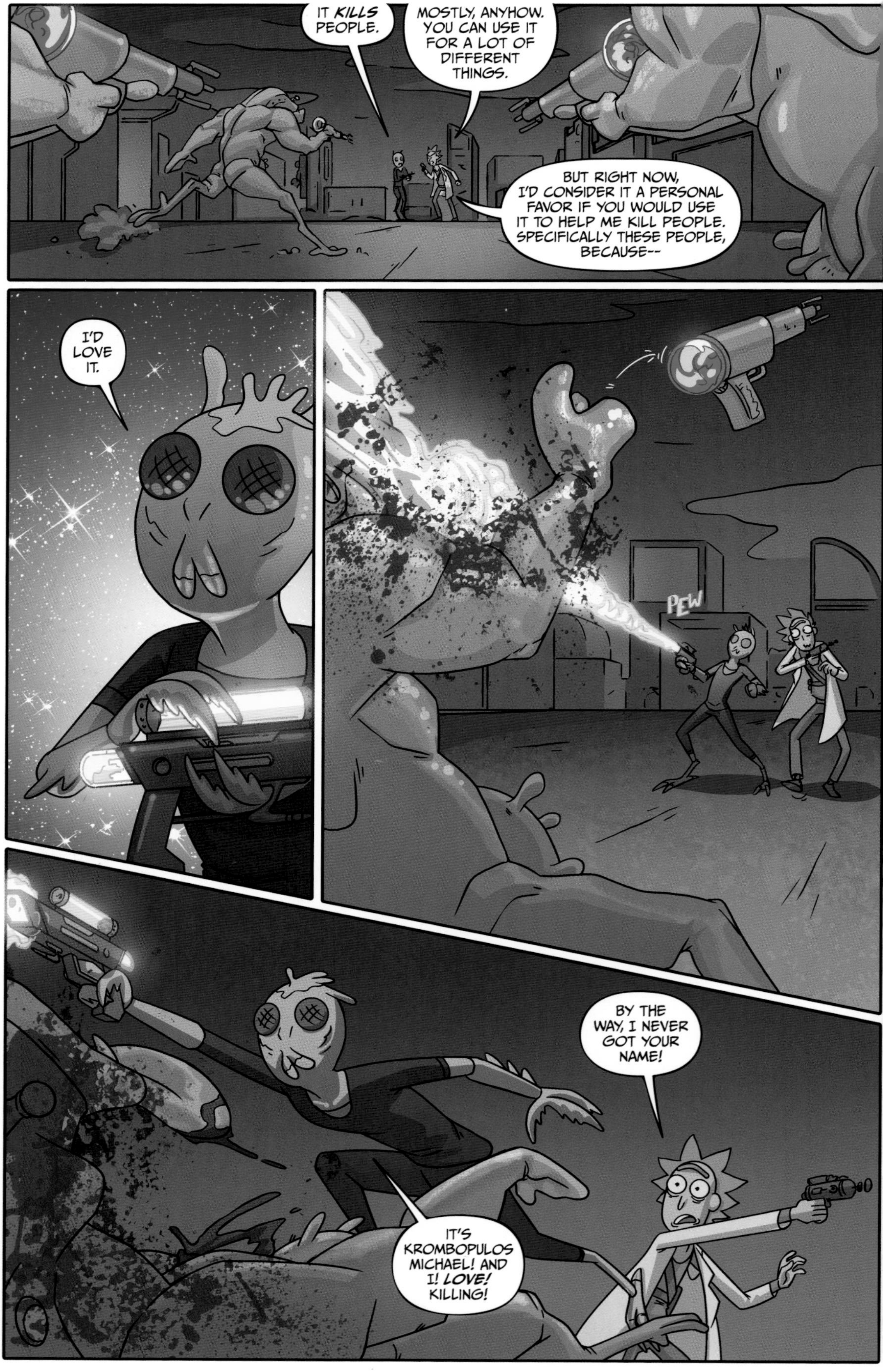
IT KILLS PEOPLE.
MOSTLY, ANYHOW. YOU CAN USE IT FOR A LOT OF DIFFERENT THINGS.
BUT RIGHT NOW, I'D CONSIDER IT A PERSONAL FAVOR IF YOU WOULD USE IT TO HELP ME KILL PEOPLE. SPECIFICALLY THESE PEOPLE, BECAUSE--
I'D LOVE IT.
PEW
BY THE WAY, I NEVER GOT YOUR NAME!
IT'S KROMBOPULOS MICHAEL! AND I! LOVE! KILLING!

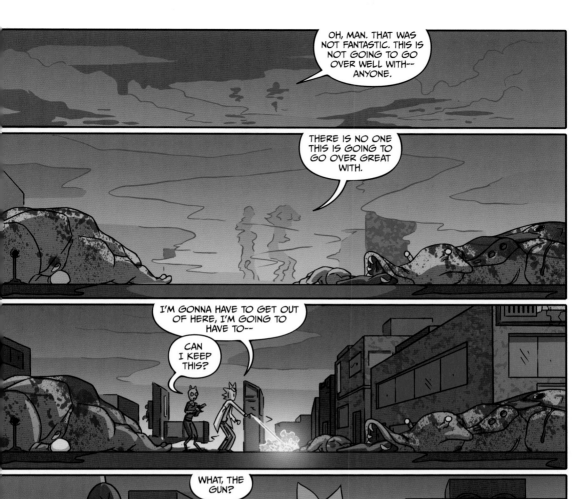

OH, MAN. THAT WAS NOT FANTASTIC. THIS IS NOT GOING TO GO OVER WELL WITH-- ANYONE.

THERE IS NO ONE THIS IS GOING TO GO OVER GREAT WITH.

I'M GONNA HAVE TO GET OUT OF HERE, I'M GOING TO HAVE TO--

CAN I KEEP THIS?

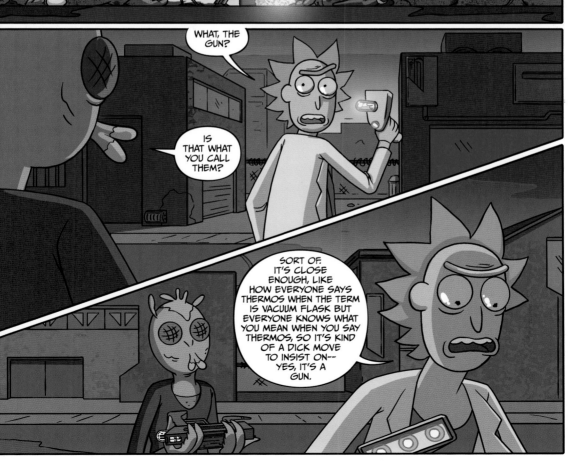

WHAT, THE GUN?

IS THAT WHAT YOU CALL THEM?

SORT OF. IT'S CLOSE ENOUGH, LIKE HOW EVERYONE SAYS THERMOS WHEN THE TERM IS VACUUM FLASK BUT EVERYONE KNOWS WHAT YOU MEAN WHEN YOU SAY THERMOS, SO IT'S KIND OF A DICK MOVE TO INSIST ON-- YES, IT'S A GUN.

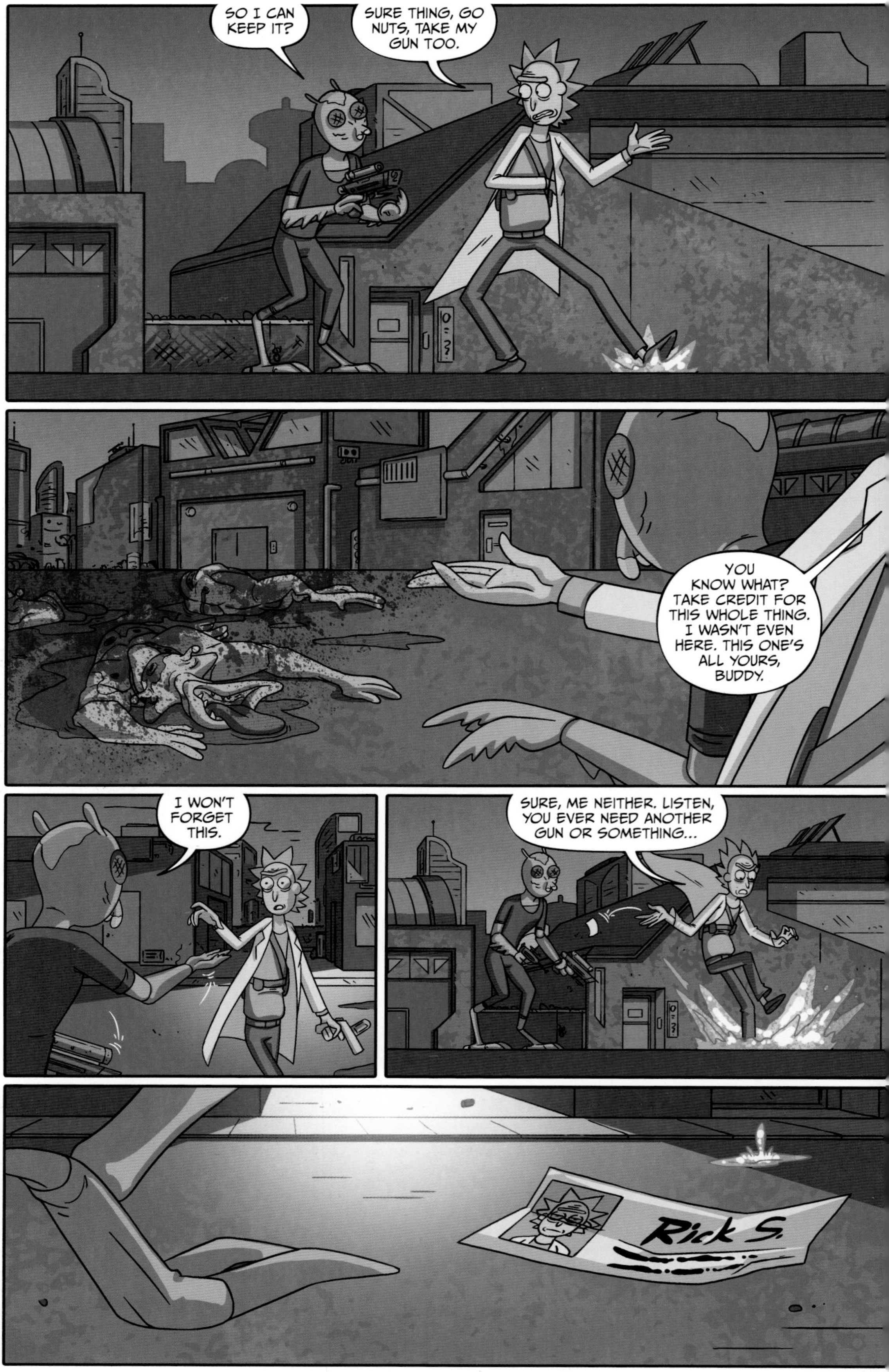
SO I CAN KEEP IT?
SURE THING, GO NUTS, TAKE MY GUN TOO.
YOU KNOW WHAT? TAKE CREDIT FOR THIS WHOLE THING. I WASN'T EVEN HERE. THIS ONE'S ALL YOURS, BUDDY.
I WON'T FORGET THIS.
SURE, ME NEITHER. LISTEN, YOU EVER NEED ANOTHER GUN OR SOMETHING...
Rick S.

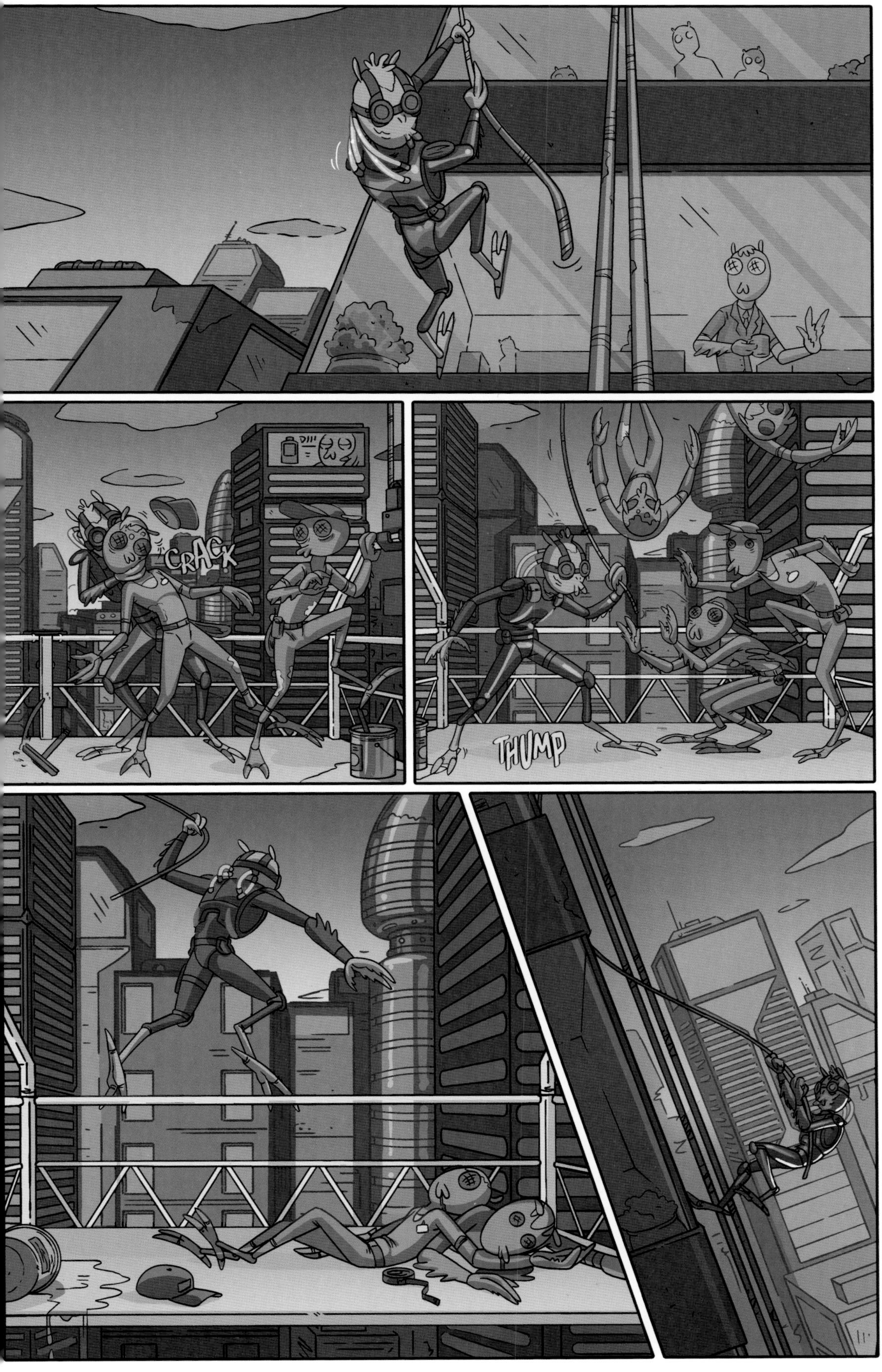
CRACK
THUMP

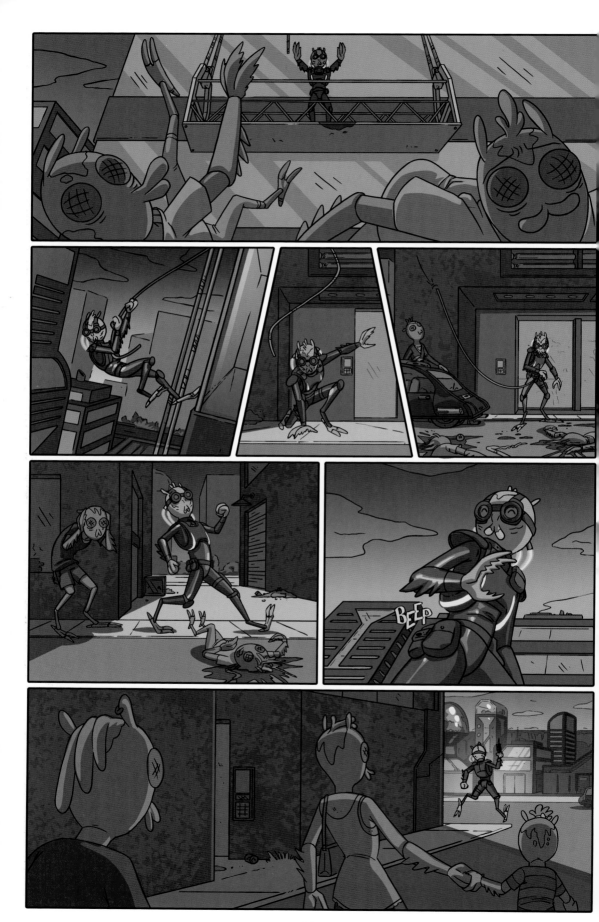

BEEP

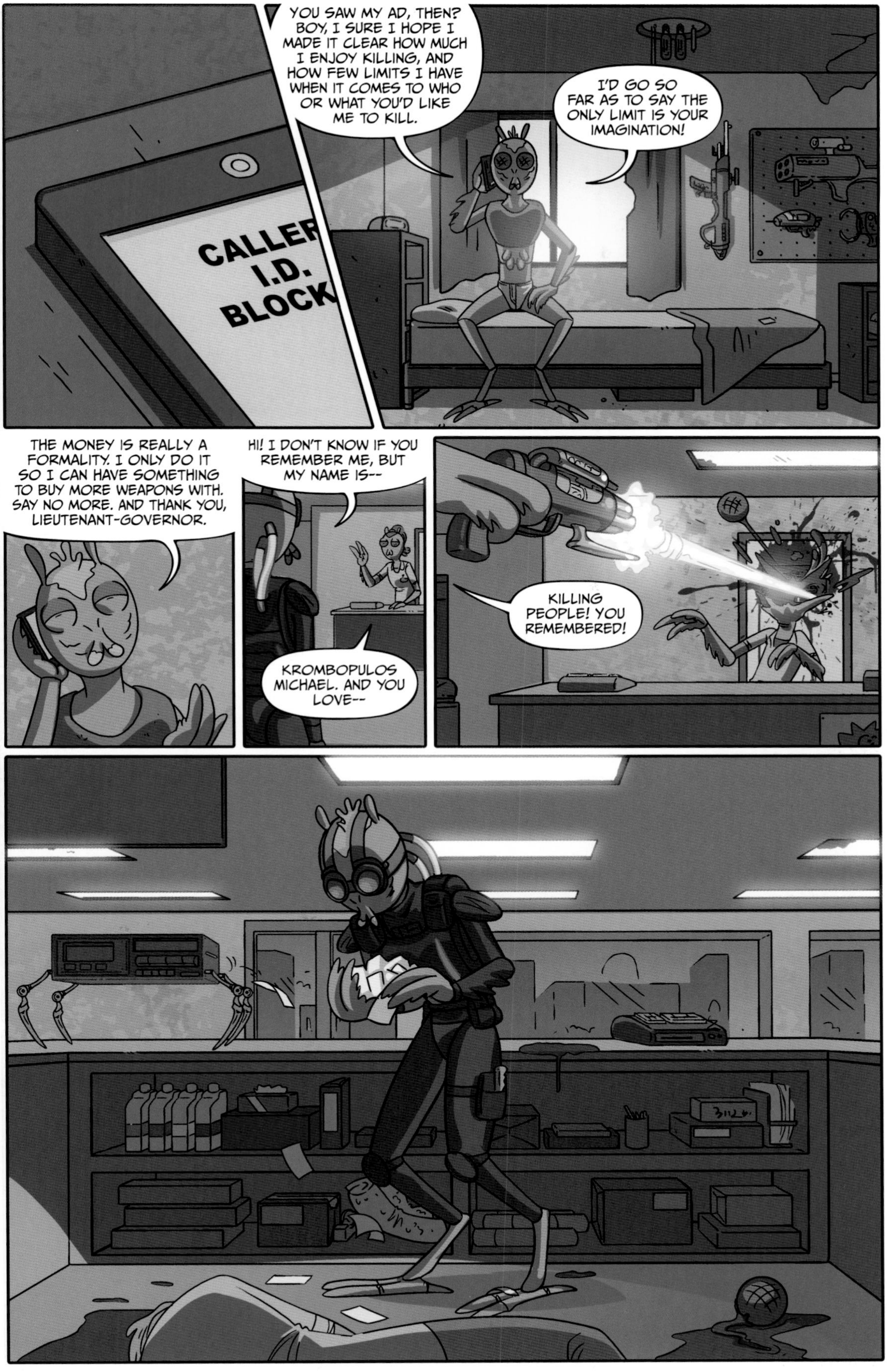

CALLER I.D. BLOCK
YOU SAW MY AD, THEN? BOY, I SURE I HOPE I MADE IT CLEAR HOW MUCH I ENJOY KILLING, AND HOW FEW LIMITS I HAVE WHEN IT COMES TO WHO OR WHAT YOU'D LIKE ME TO KILL.
I'D GO SO FAR AS TO SAY THE ONLY LIMIT IS YOUR IMAGINATION!
THE MONEY IS REALLY A FORMALITY. I ONLY DO IT SO I CAN HAVE SOMETHING TO BUY MORE WEAPONS WITH. SAY NO MORE. AND THANK YOU, LIEUTENANT-GOVERNOR.
HI! I DON'T KNOW IF YOU REMEMBER ME, BUT MY NAME IS--
KROMBOPULOS MICHAEL. AND YOU LOVE--
KILLING PEOPLE! YOU REMEMBERED!

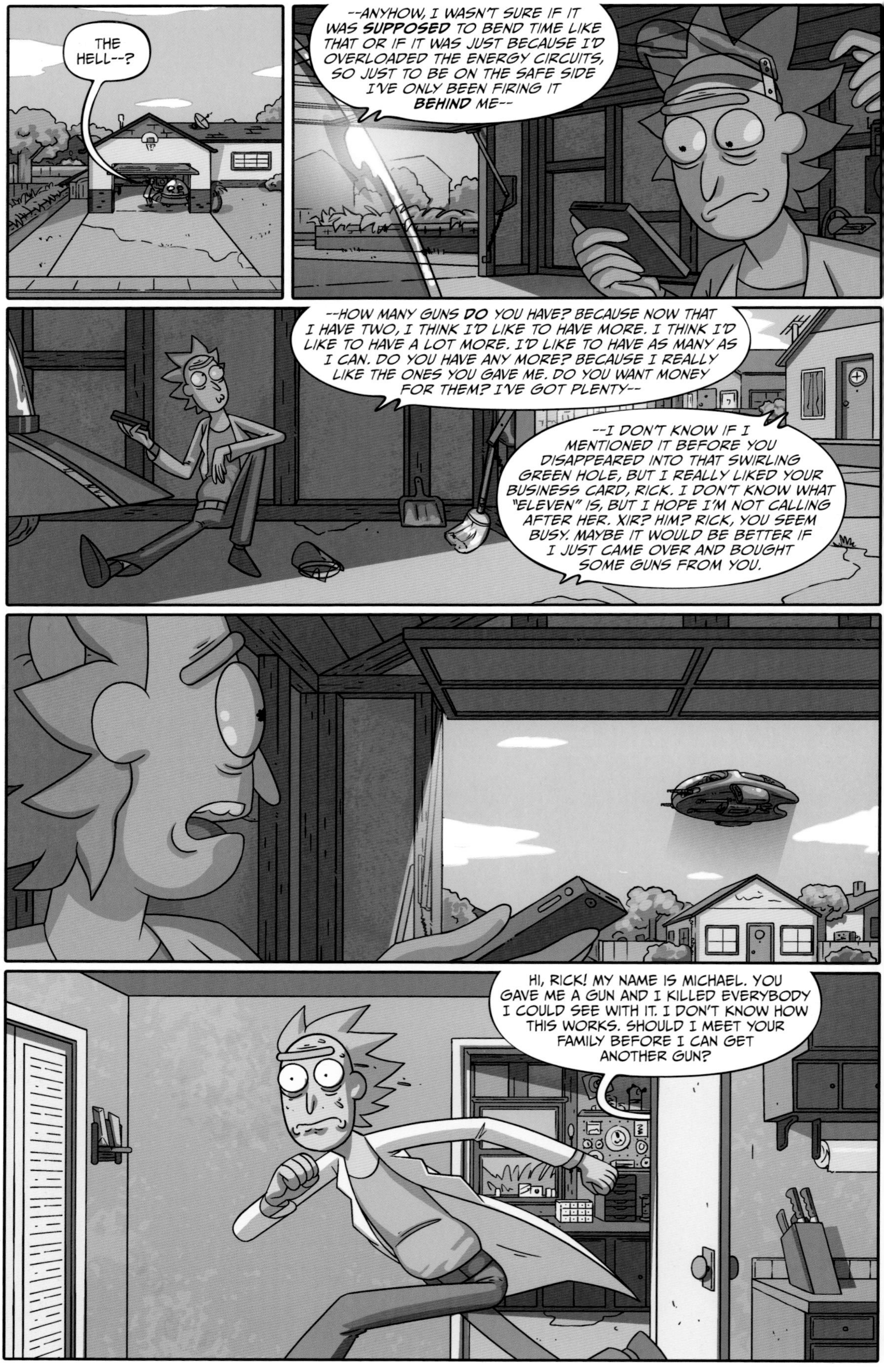
THE HELL--?
--ANYHOW, I WASN'T SURE IF IT WAS SUPPOSED TO BEND TIME LIKE THAT OR IF IT WAS JUST BECAUSE I'D OVERLOADED THE ENERGY CIRCUITS, SO JUST TO BE ON THE SAFE SIDE I'VE ONLY BEEN FIRING IT BEHIND ME--
--HOW MANY GUNS DO YOU HAVE? BECAUSE NOW THAT I HAVE TWO, I THINK I'D LIKE TO HAVE MORE. I THINK I'D LIKE TO HAVE A LOT MORE. I'D LIKE TO HAVE AS MANY AS I CAN. DO YOU HAVE ANY MORE? BECAUSE I REALLY LIKE THE ONES YOU GAVE ME. DO YOU WANT MONEY FOR THEM? I'VE GOT PLENTY--
--I DON'T KNOW IF I MENTIONED IT BEFORE YOU DISAPPEARED INTO THAT SWIRLING GREEN HOLE, BUT I REALLY LIKED YOUR BUSINESS CARD, RICK. I DON'T KNOW WHAT "ELEVEN" IS, BUT I HOPE I'M NOT CALLING AFTER HER. XIR? HIM? RICK, YOU SEEM BUSY. MAYBE IT WOULD BE BETTER IF I JUST CAME OVER AND BOUGHT SOME GUNS FROM YOU.
HI, RICK! MY NAME IS MICHAEL. YOU GAVE ME A GUN AND I KILLED EVERYBODY I COULD SEE WITH IT. I DON'T KNOW HOW THIS WORKS. SHOULD I MEET YOUR FAMILY BEFORE I CAN GET ANOTHER GUN?

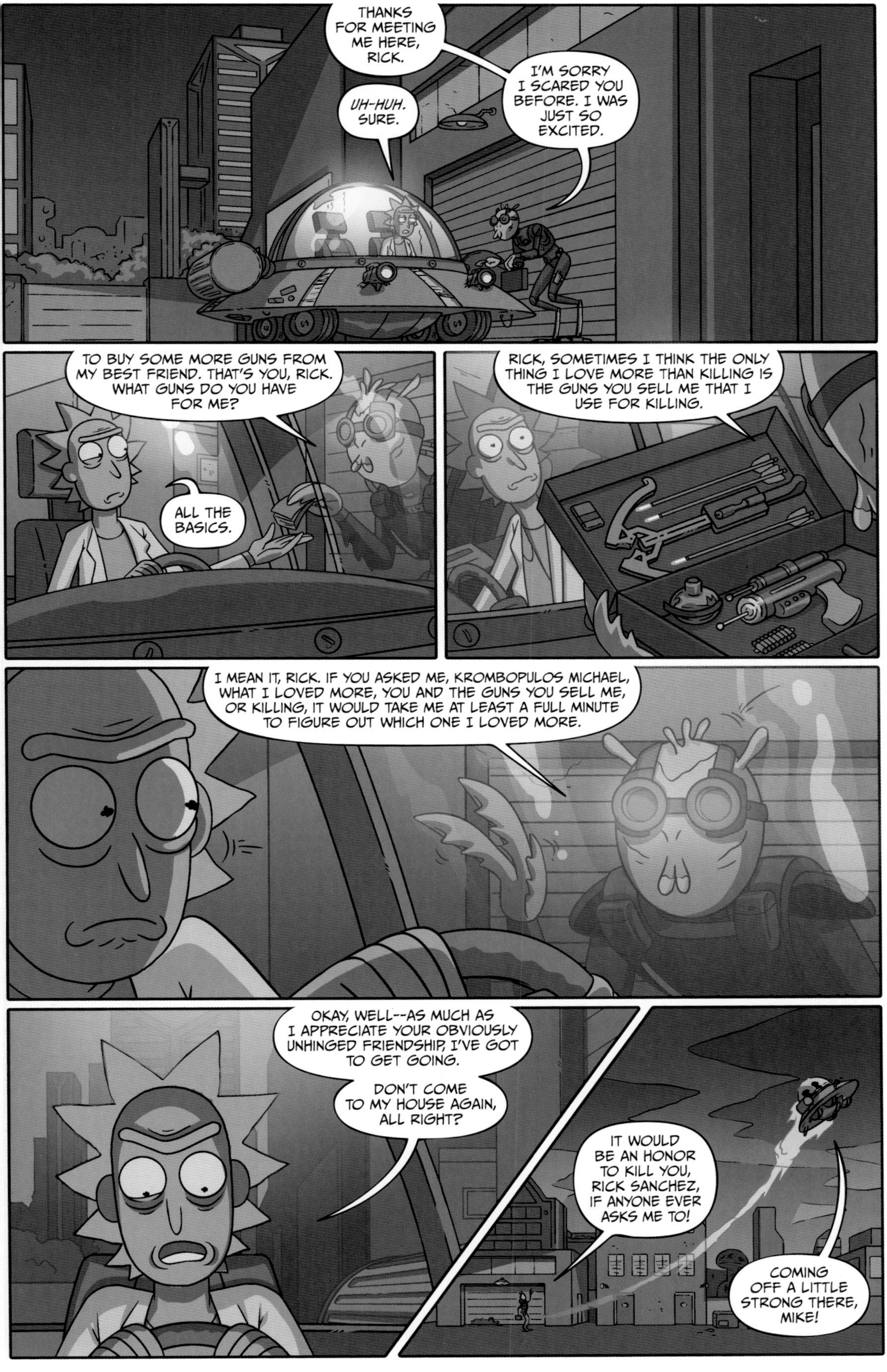
THANKS FOR MEETING ME HERE, RICK.
UH-HUH. SURE.
I'M SORRY I SCARED YOU BEFORE. I WAS JUST SO EXCITED.
TO BUY SOME MORE GUNS FROM MY BEST FRIEND. THAT'S YOU, RICK. WHAT GUNS DO YOU HAVE FOR ME?
ALL THE BASICS.
RICK, SOMETIMES I THINK THE ONLY THING I LOVE MORE THAN KILLING IS THE GUNS YOU SELL ME THAT I USE FOR KILLING.
I MEAN IT, RICK. IF YOU ASKED ME, KROMBOPULOS MICHAEL, WHAT I LOVED MORE, YOU AND THE GUNS YOU SELL ME, OR KILLING, IT WOULD TAKE ME AT LEAST A FULL MINUTE TO FIGURE OUT WHICH ONE I LOVED MORE.
OKAY, WELL--AS MUCH AS I APPRECIATE YOUR OBVIOUSLY UNHINGED FRIENDSHIP, I'VE GOT TO GET GOING.
DON'T COME TO MY HOUSE AGAIN, ALL RIGHT?
IT WOULD BE AN HONOR TO KILL YOU, RICK SANCHEZ, IF ANYONE EVER ASKS ME TO!
COMING OFF A LITTLE STRONG THERE, MIKE!

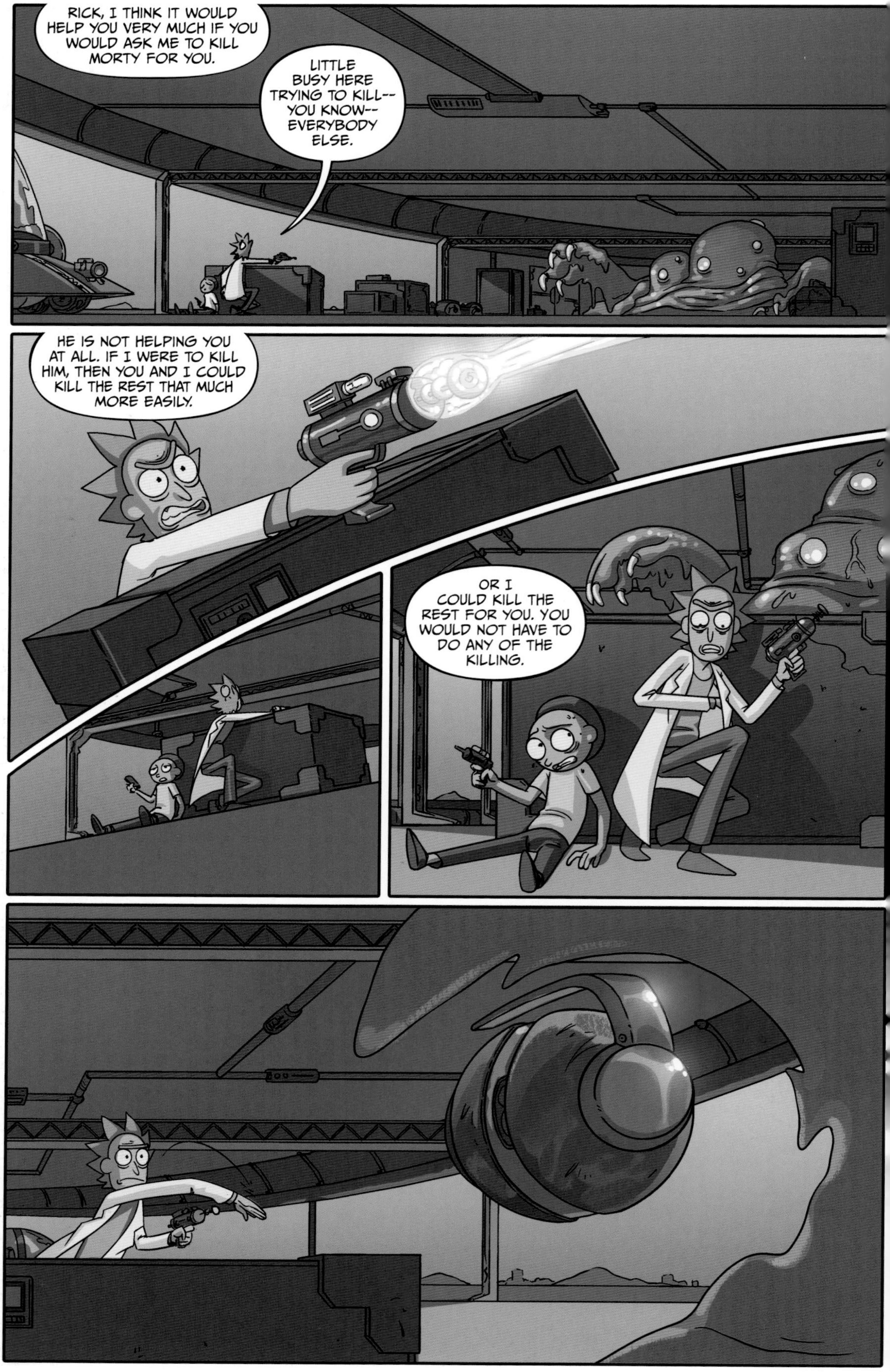
RICK, I THINK IT WOULD HELP YOU VERY MUCH IF YOU WOULD ASK ME TO KILL MORTY FOR YOU.
LITTLE BUSY HERE TRYING TO KILL-- YOU KNOW-- EVERYBODY ELSE.
HE IS NOT HELPING YOU AT ALL. IF I WERE TO KILL HIM, THEN YOU AND I COULD KILL THE REST THAT MUCH MORE EASILY.
OR I COULD KILL THE REST FOR YOU. YOU WOULD NOT HAVE TO DO ANY OF THE KILLING.

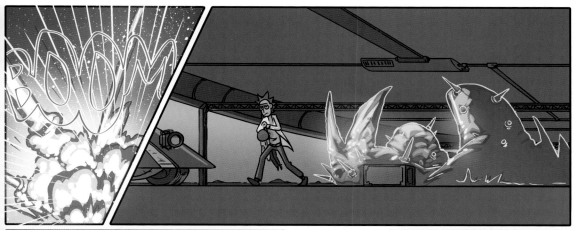

I DON'T NEED YOU TO KILL ANYBODY, OKAY? LET'S JUST KEEP THINGS PROFESSIONAL.

I AM VERY PROFESSIONAL, RICK. I HAVE A BUSINESS CARD.

I KNOW.

WOULD YOU LIKE ANOTHER COPY OF MY BUSINESS CARD?

I HAVE PLENTY.

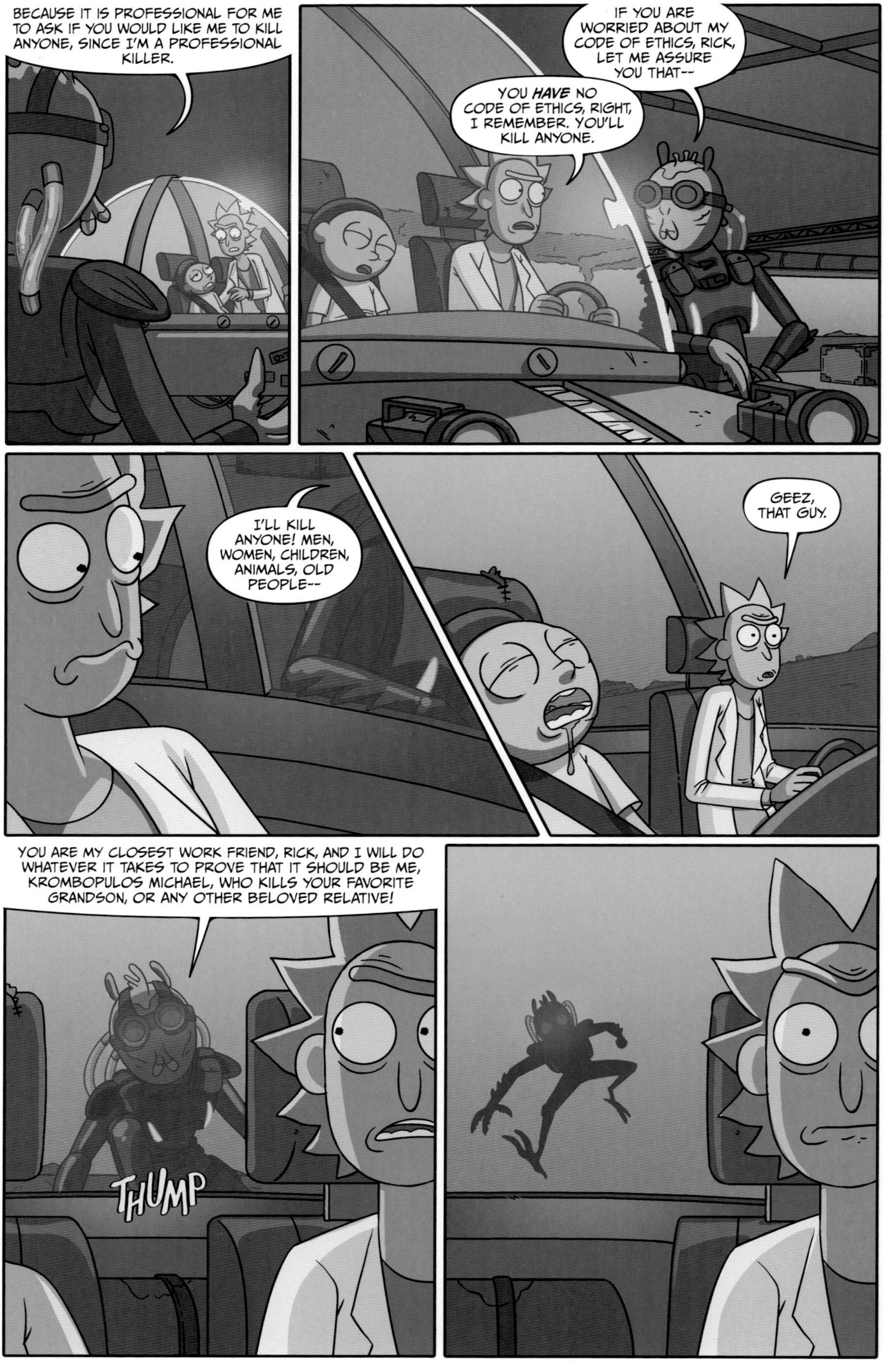
BECAUSE IT IS PROFESSIONAL FOR ME TO ASK IF YOU WOULD LIKE ME TO KILL ANYONE, SINCE I'M A PROFESSIONAL KILLER.
IF YOU ARE WORRIED ABOUT MY CODE OF ETHICS, RICK, LET ME ASSURE YOU THAT--
YOU HAVE NO CODE OF ETHICS, RIGHT, I REMEMBER. YOU'LL KILL ANYONE.
I'LL KILL ANYONE! MEN, WOMEN, CHILDREN, ANIMALS, OLD PEOPLE--
GEEZ, THAT GUY.
YOU ARE MY CLOSEST WORK FRIEND, RICK, AND I WILL DO WHATEVER IT TAKES TO PROVE THAT IT SHOULD BE ME, KROMBOPULOS MICHAEL, WHO KILLS YOUR FAVORITE GRANDSON, OR ANY OTHER BELOVED RELATIVE!
THUMP

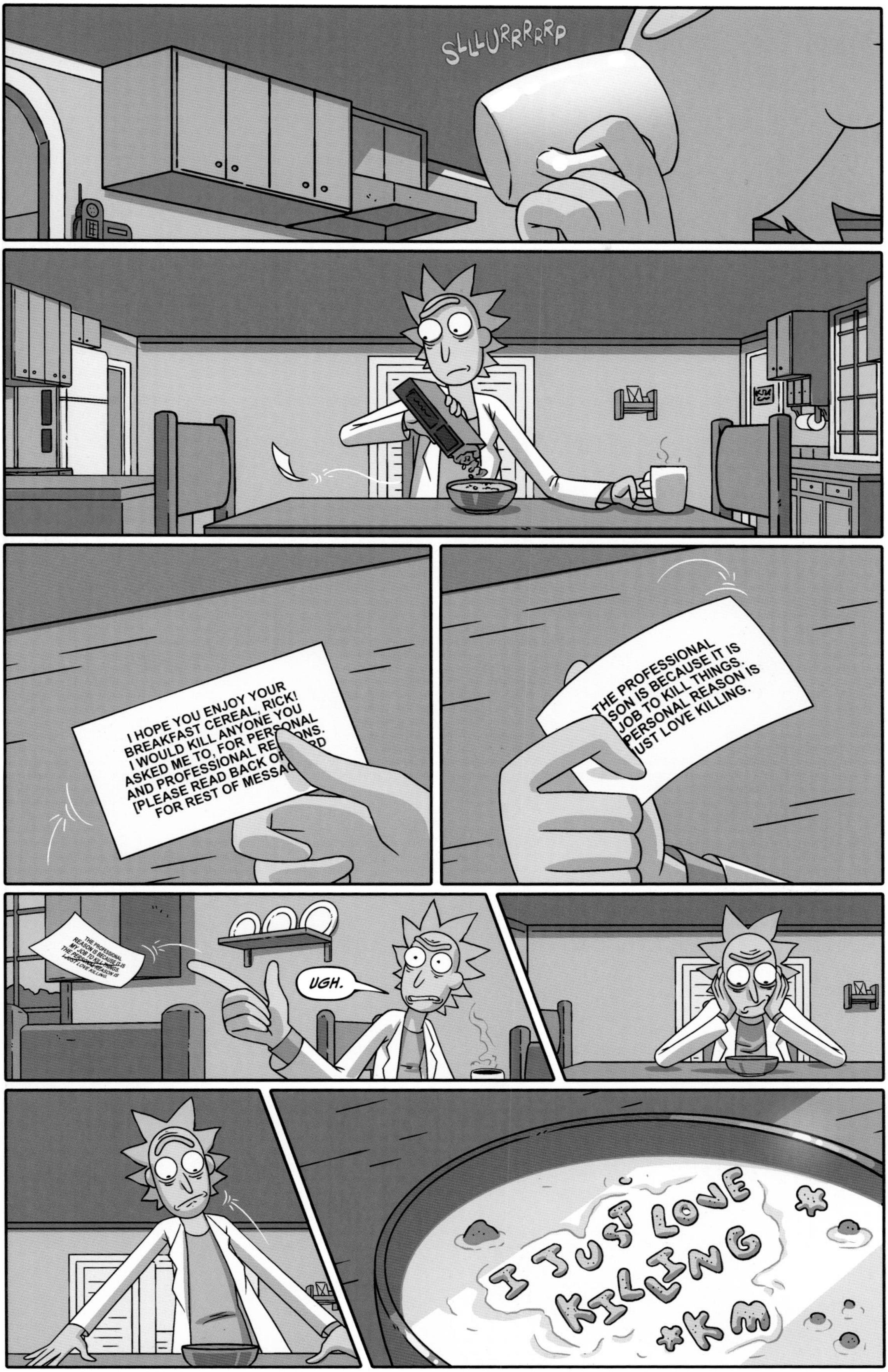
SLLLURRRRRP
I HOPE YOU ENJOY YOUR
BREAKFAST CEREAL, RICK!
I WOULD KILL ANYONE YOU
ASKED ME TO, FOR PERSONAL
AND PROFESSIONAL RE ONS.
[PLEASE READ BACK OF RD
FOR REST OF MESSAG
THE PROFESSIONAL
SON IS BECAUSE IT IS
JOB TO KILL THINGS.
PERSONAL REASON IS
JUST LOVE KILLING.
THE PROFESSIONAL REASON IS BECAUSE IT IS MY JOB TO KILL THINGS. THE PERSONAL REASON IS I JUST LOVE KILLING.
UGH.
I JUST LOVE KILLING *KM

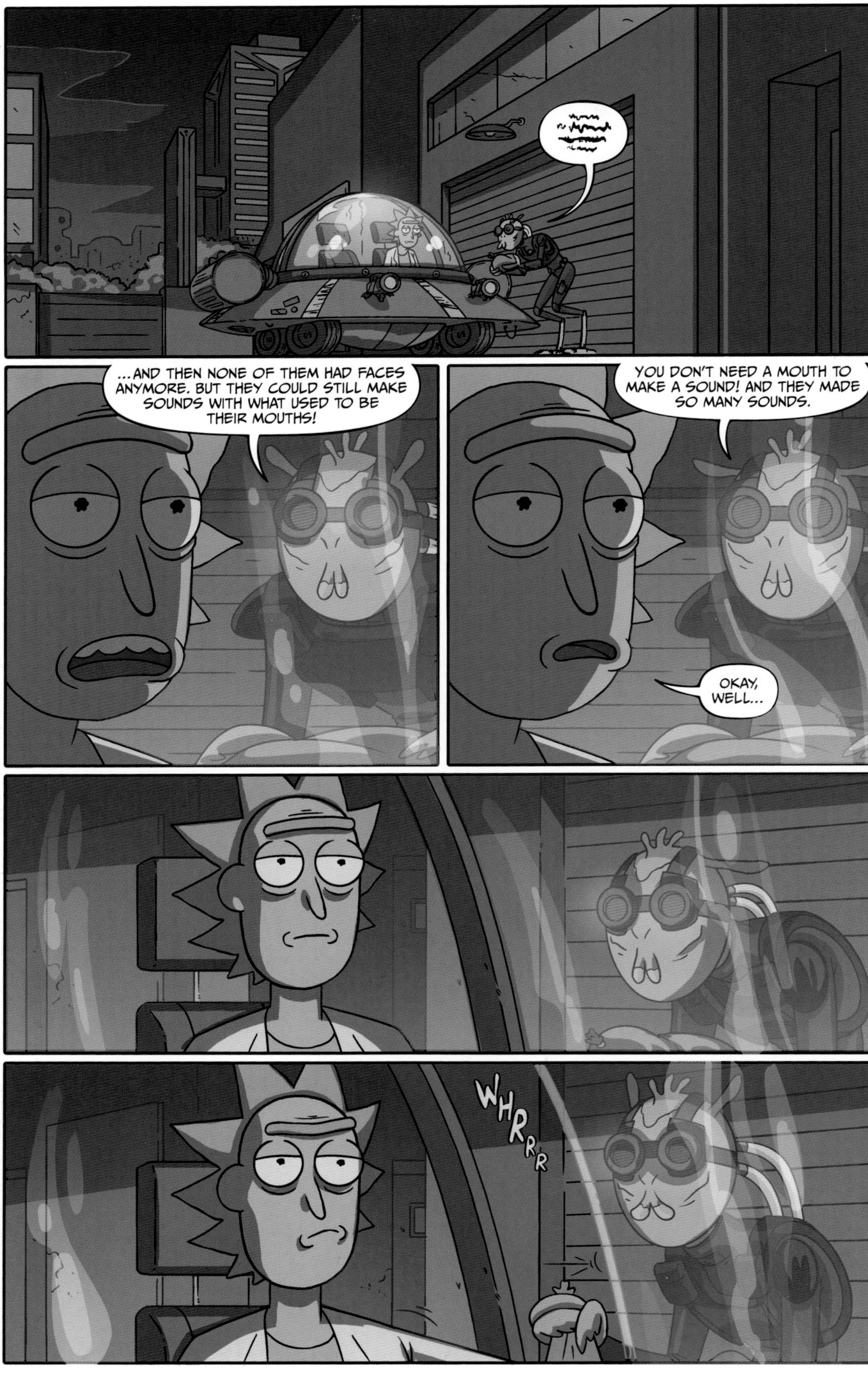
...AND THEN NONE OF THEM HAD FACES ANYMORE. BUT THEY COULD STILL MAKE SOUNDS WITH WHAT USED TO BE THEIR MOUTHS!
YOU DON'T NEED A MOUTH TO MAKE A SOUND! AND THEY MADE SO MANY SOUNDS.
OKAY, WELL...
WHRRRR

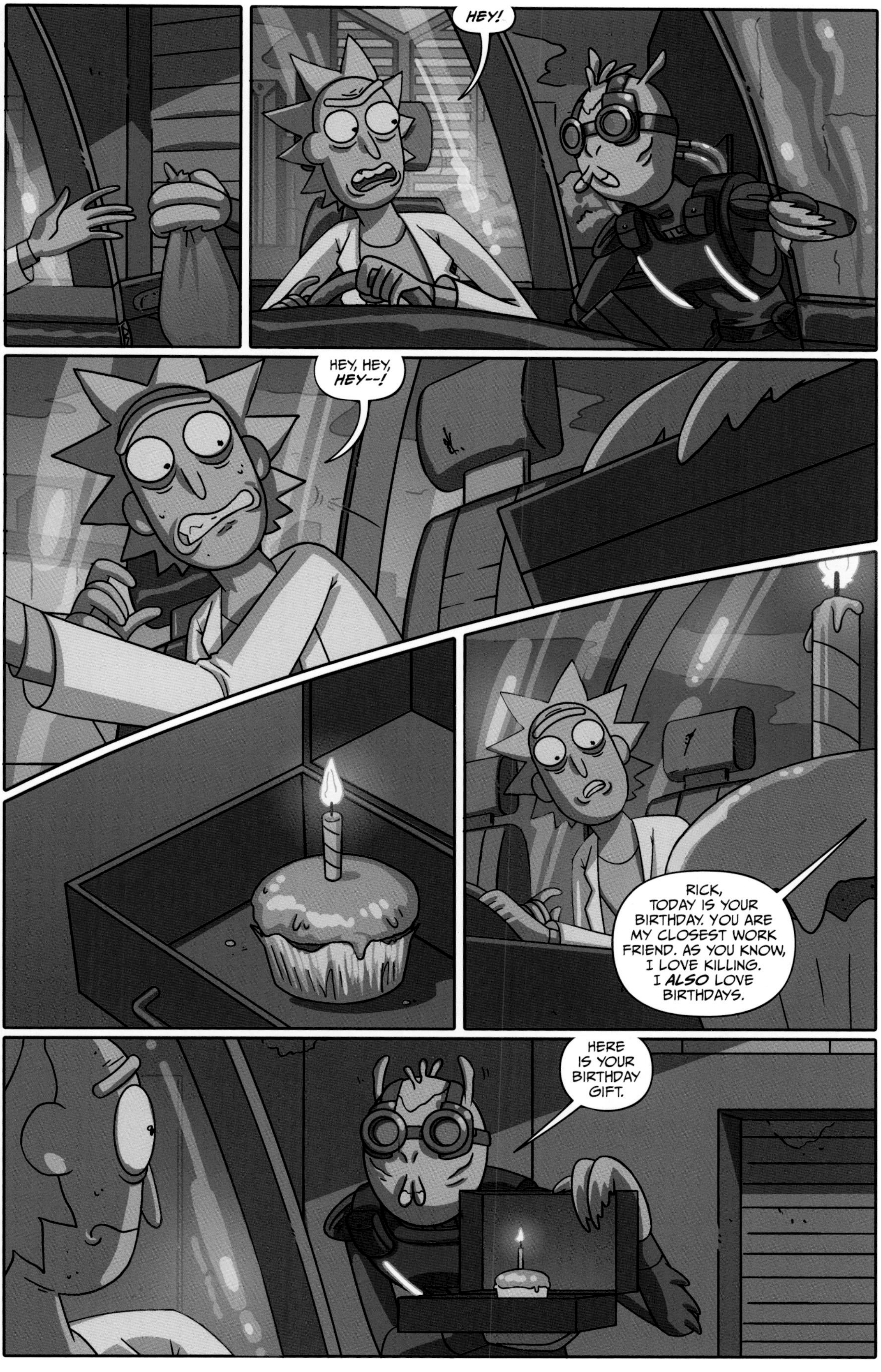
HEY!
HEY, HEY, HEY--!
RICK, TODAY IS YOUR BIRTHDAY. YOU ARE MY CLOSEST WORK FRIEND. AS YOU KNOW, I LOVE KILLING. I ALSO LOVE BIRTHDAYS.
HERE IS YOUR BIRTHDAY GIFT.

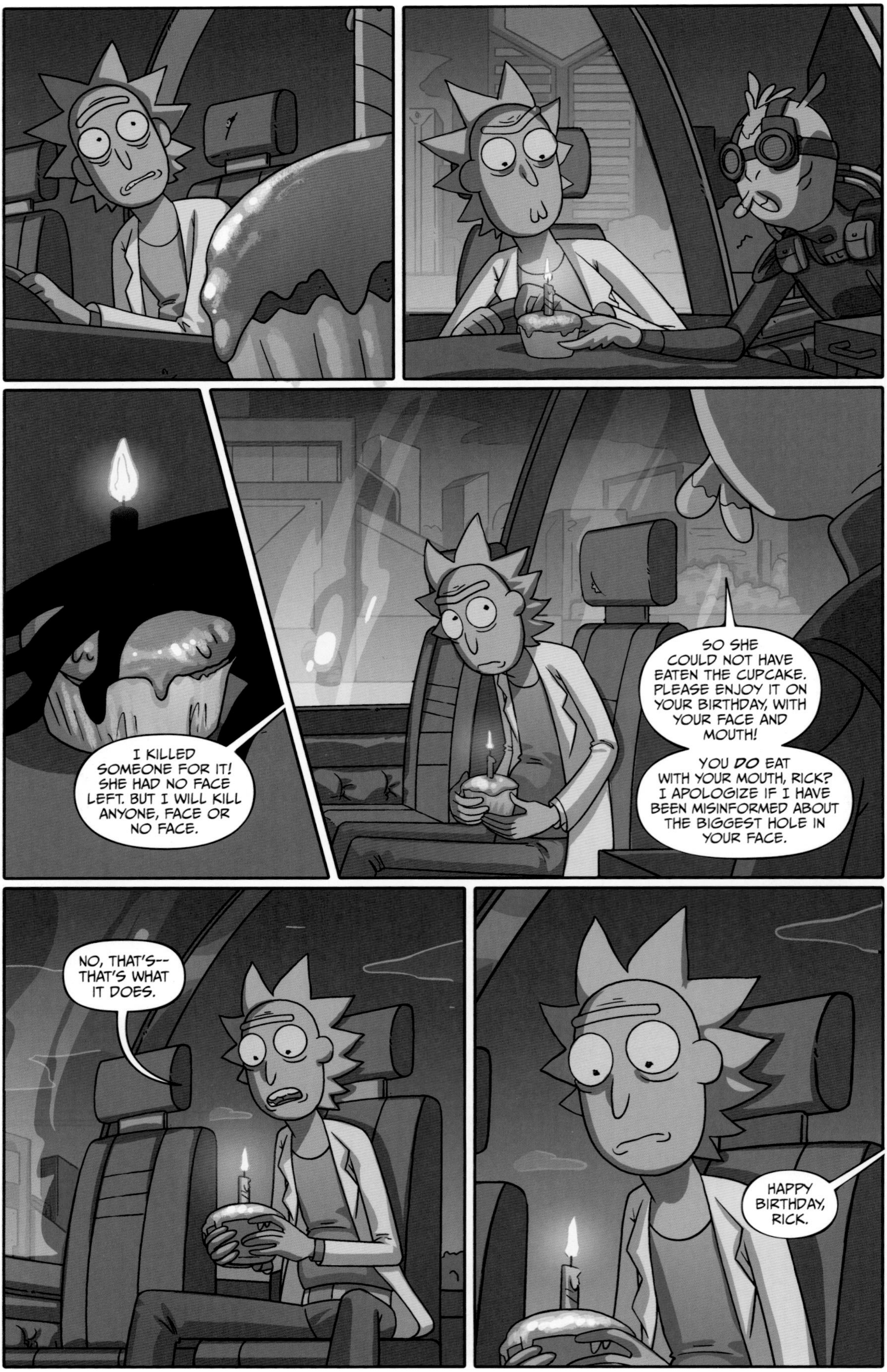
I KILLED SOMEONE FOR IT! SHE HAD NO FACE LEFT. BUT I WILL KILL ANYONE, FACE OR NO FACE.
SO SHE COULD NOT HAVE EATEN THE CUPCAKE. PLEASE ENJOY IT ON YOUR BIRTHDAY, WITH YOUR FACE AND MOUTH!
YOU *DO* EAT WITH YOUR MOUTH, RICK? I APOLOGIZE IF I HAVE BEEN MISINFORMED ABOUT THE BIGGEST HOLE IN YOUR FACE.
NO, THAT'S-- THAT'S WHAT IT DOES.
HAPPY BIRTHDAY, RICK.

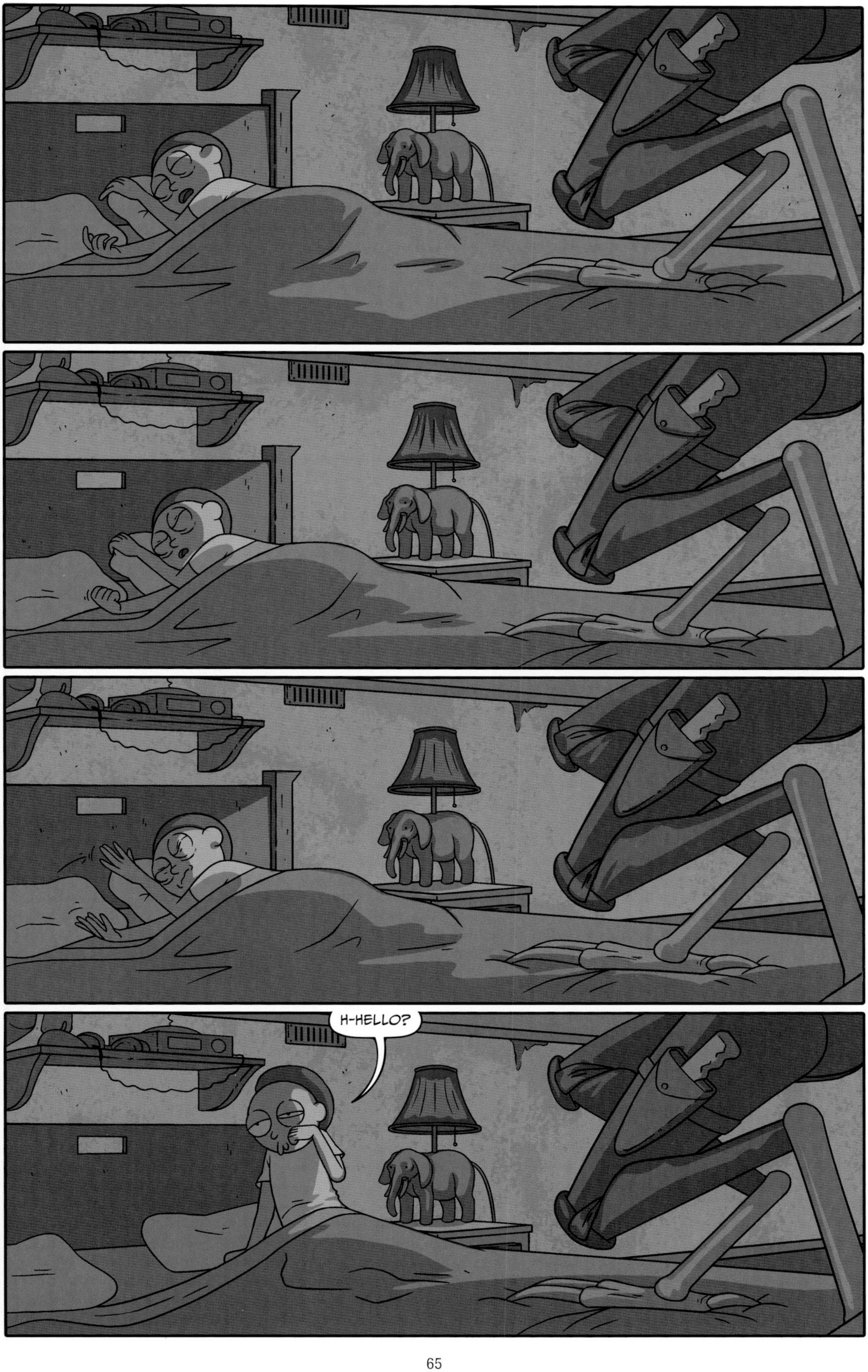
H-HELLO?

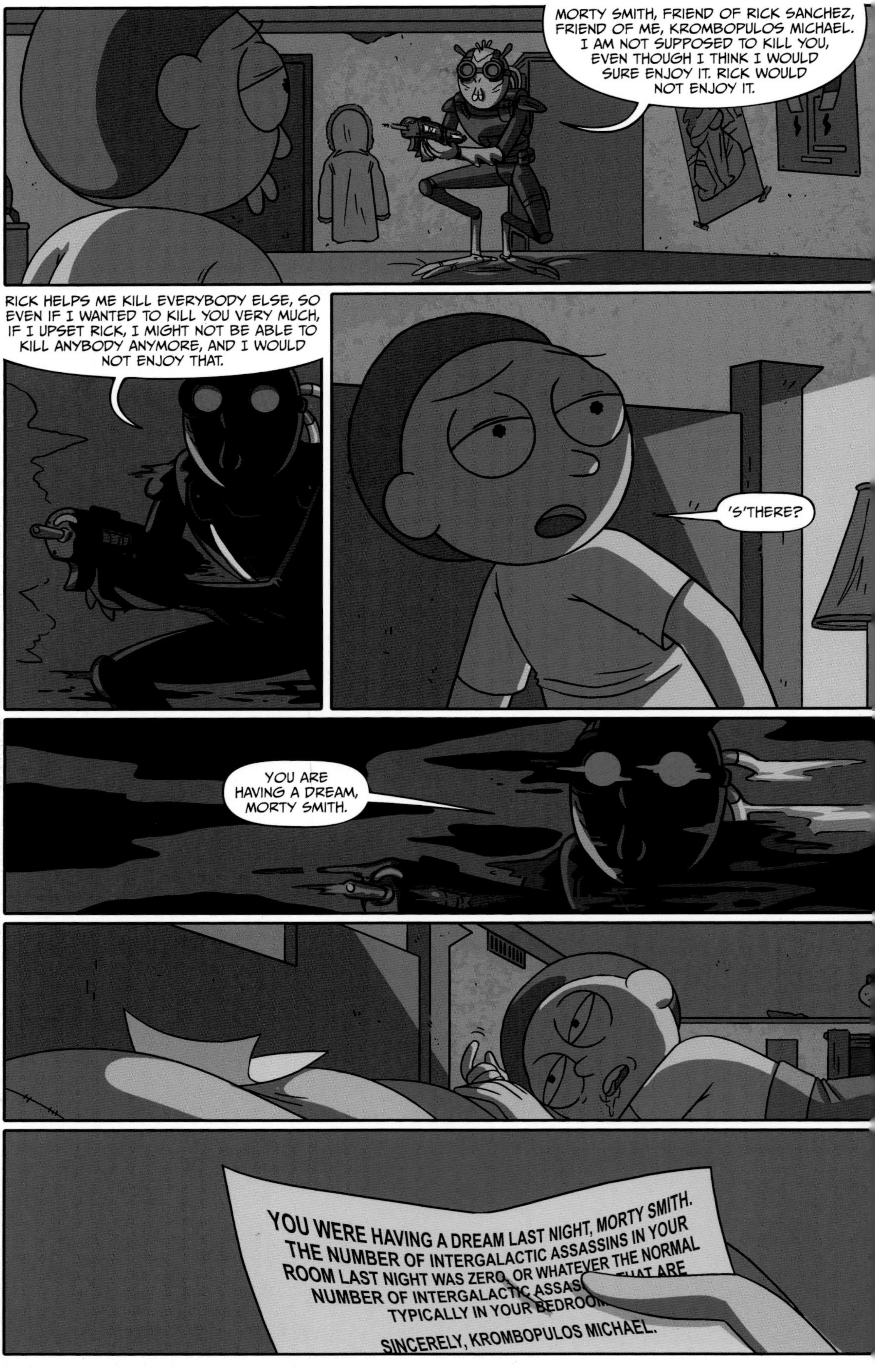
MORTY SMITH, FRIEND OF RICK SANCHEZ, FRIEND OF ME, KROMBOPULOS MICHAEL. I AM NOT SUPPOSED TO KILL YOU, EVEN THOUGH I THINK I WOULD SURE ENJOY IT. RICK WOULD NOT ENJOY IT.
RICK HELPS ME KILL EVERYBODY ELSE, SO EVEN IF I WANTED TO KILL YOU VERY MUCH, IF I UPSET RICK, I MIGHT NOT BE ABLE TO KILL ANYBODY ANYMORE, AND I WOULD NOT ENJOY THAT.
'S'THERE?
YOU ARE HAVING A DREAM, MORTY SMITH.
YOU WERE HAVING A DREAM LAST NIGHT, MORTY SMITH. THE NUMBER OF INTERGALACTIC ASSASSINS IN YOUR ROOM LAST NIGHT WAS ZERO, OR WHATEVER THE NORMAL NUMBER OF INTERGALACTIC ASSAS THAT ARE TYPICALLY IN YOUR BEDROOM
SINCERELY, KROMBOPULOS MICHAEL.

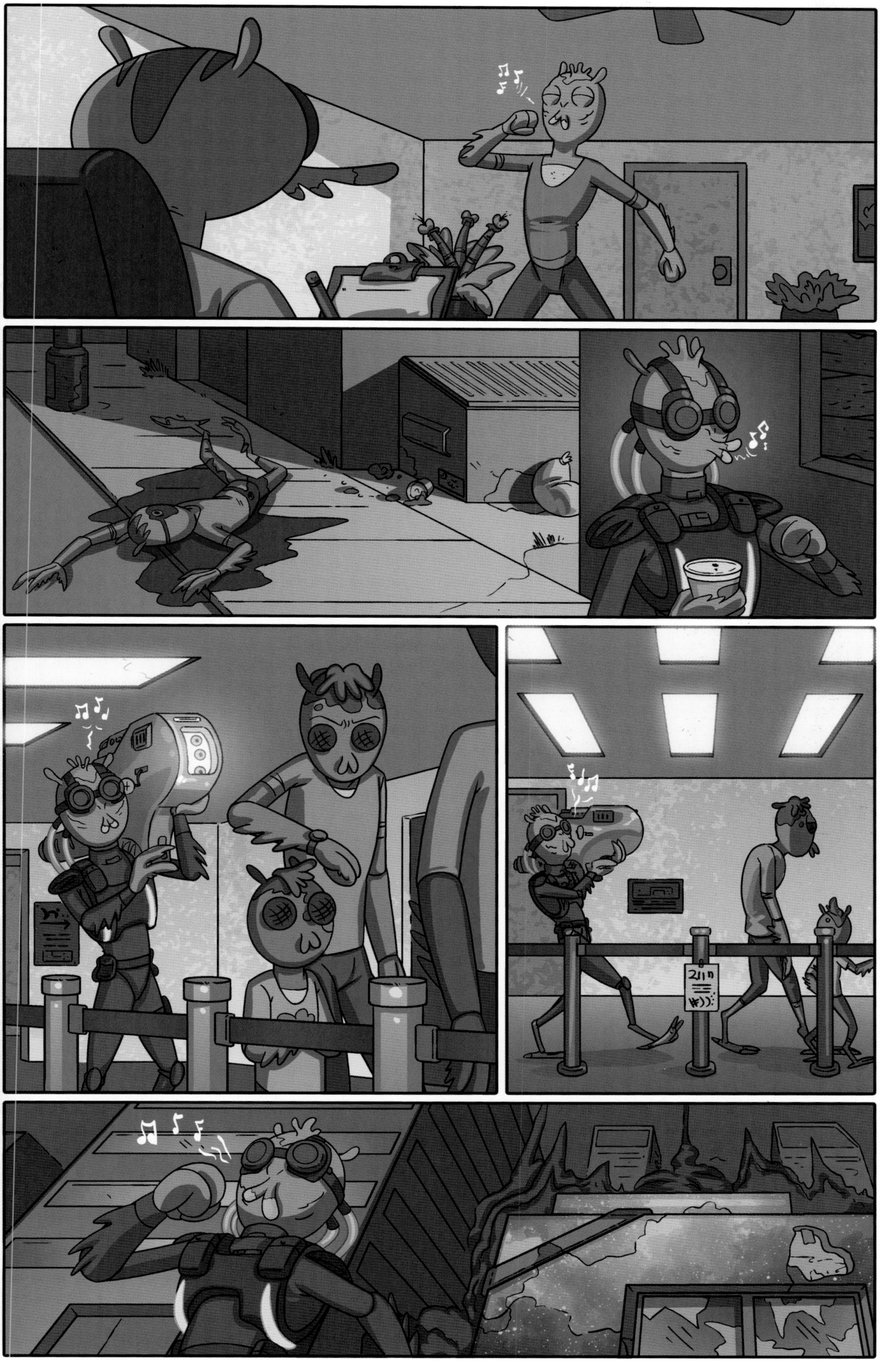

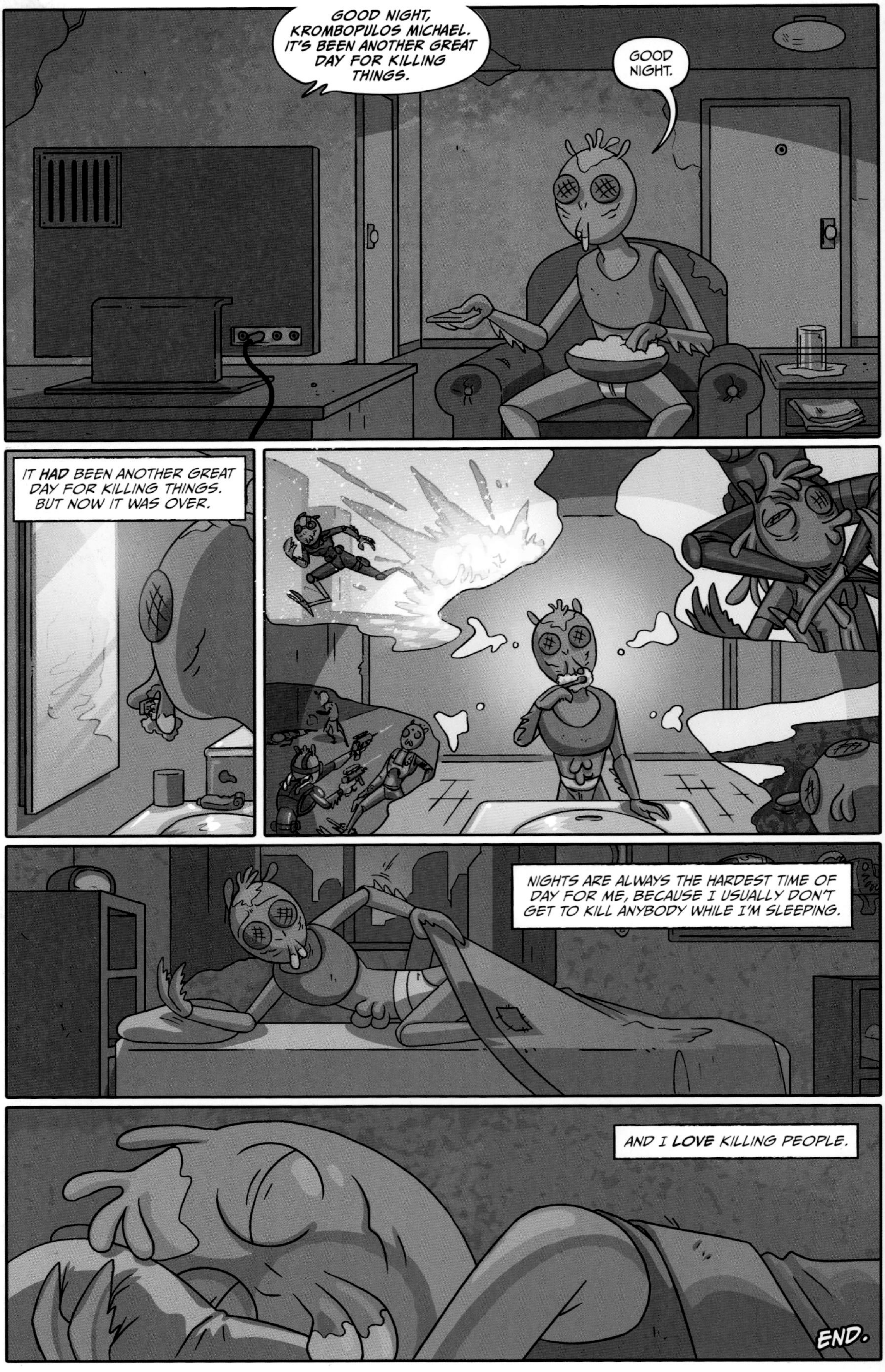
GOOD NIGHT, KROMBOPULOS MICHAEL. IT'S BEEN ANOTHER GREAT DAY FOR KILLING THINGS.
GOOD NIGHT.
IT HAD BEEN ANOTHER GREAT DAY FOR KILLING THINGS. BUT NOW IT WAS OVER.
NIGHTS ARE ALWAYS THE HARDEST TIME OF DAY FOR ME, BECAUSE I USUALLY DON'T GET TO KILL ANYBODY WHILE I'M SLEEPING.
AND I LOVE KILLING PEOPLE.
END.

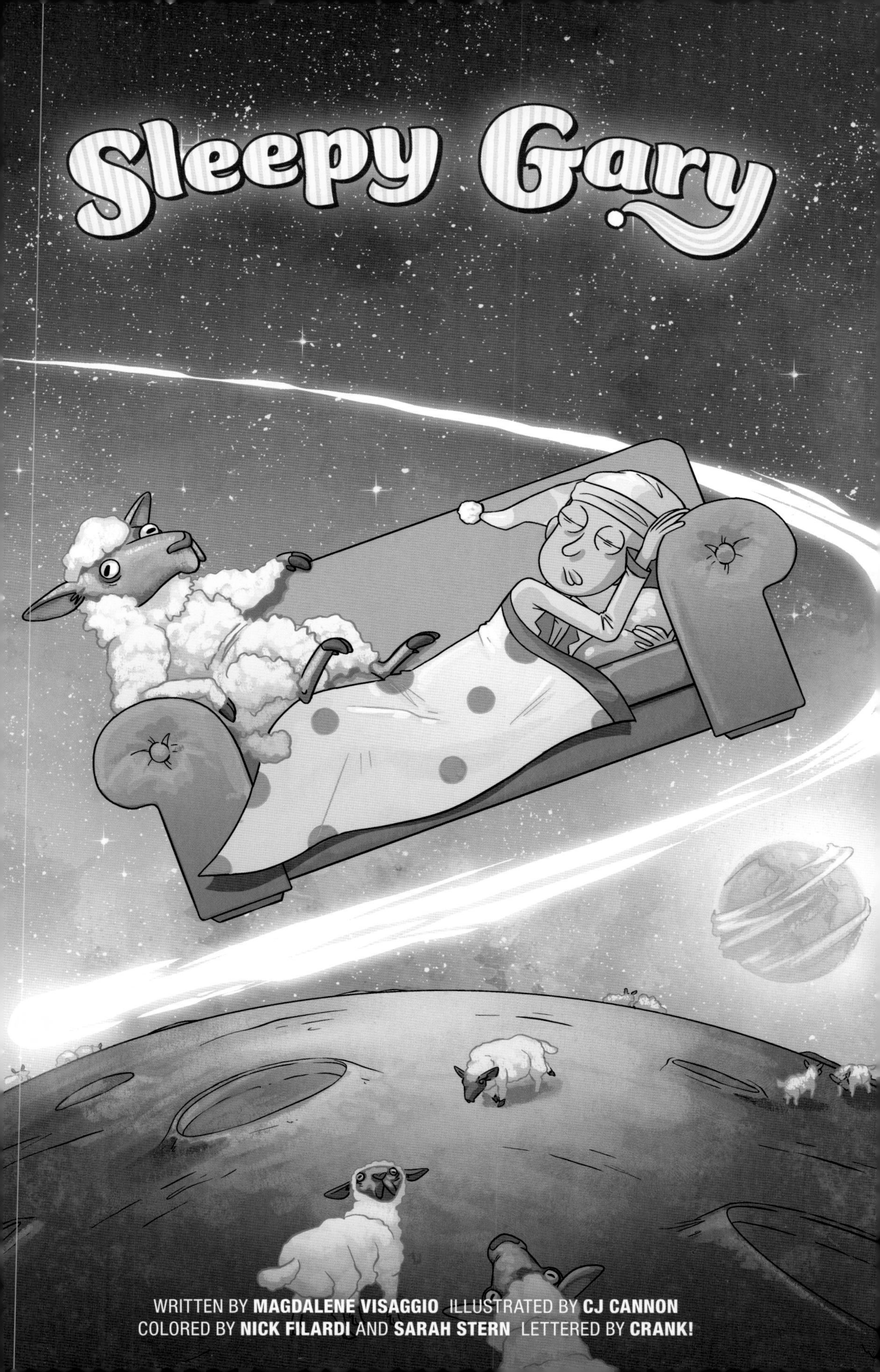
Sleepy Gary
WRITTEN BY MAGDALENE VISAGGIO ILLUSTRATED BY CJ CANNON
COLORED BY NICK FILARDI AND SARAH STERN LETTERED BY CRANK!

GENE RECONSTRUCTION GOOD.

ADAPTATIONAL PHENOTYPE STABLE AND LOCKED.

SO NOW IT'S JUST THE MEMORIES.

NOW WATCH THIS, MORTY. ITS MEMORIES ARE--*URRRP*-- SELF-RESTORING.

IT'S A COMPLEX GENE MEMORY STRUCTURE, ALLOWING BASICALLY INFINITE CAPACITY AND INFINITE REGRESSION DOWN THROUGH A PALIMPSEST OF IDENTITIES LAYERED ONE ON TOP OF THE OTHER.

WHICH MEANS IT'S ALSO *SELF-ORGANIZING.* THERE'S A BIG DUMB HAZE OF MEMORIES BELONGING TO ITS PARENTS, ITS GRANDPARENTS, OR WHATEVER THE SHAPESHIFTING WORM EQUIVALENT WOULD BE.

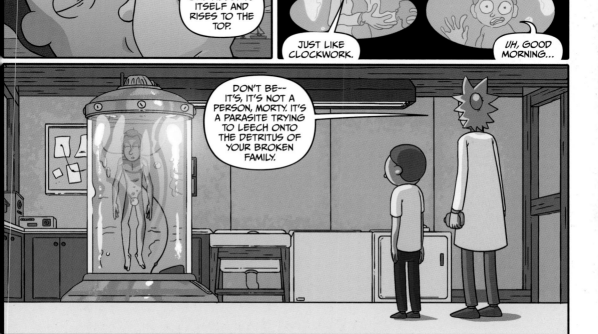

BUT ONLY ONE ASSERTS ITSELF AND RISES TO THE TOP.

JUST LIKE CLOCKWORK.

UH, GOOD MORNING...

DON'T BE-- IT'S, IT'S NOT A PERSON, MORTY. IT'S A PARASITE TRYING TO LEECH ONTO THE DETRITUS OF YOUR BROKEN FAMILY.

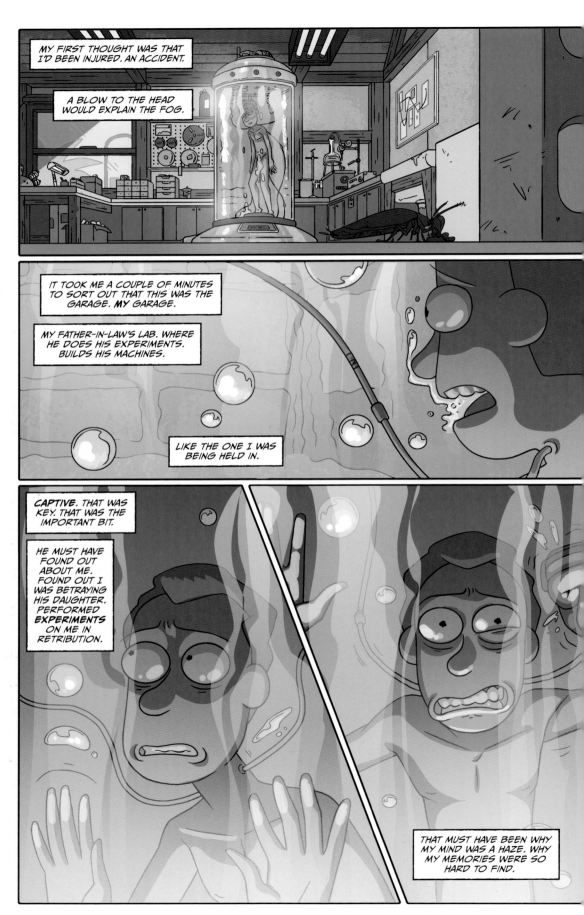

MY FIRST THOUGHT WAS THAT I'D BEEN INJURED. AN ACCIDENT.

A BLOW TO THE HEAD WOULD EXPLAIN THE FOG.

IT TOOK ME A COUPLE OF MINUTES TO SORT OUT THAT THIS WAS THE GARAGE. **MY** GARAGE.

MY FATHER-IN-LAW'S LAB. WHERE HE DOES HIS EXPERIMENTS. BUILDS HIS MACHINES.

LIKE THE ONE I WAS BEING HELD IN.

CAPTIVE. THAT WAS KEY. THAT WAS THE IMPORTANT BIT.

HE MUST HAVE FOUND OUT ABOUT ME. FOUND OUT I WAS BETRAYING HIS DAUGHTER. PERFORMED **EXPERIMENTS** ON ME IN RETRIBUTION.

THAT MUST HAVE BEEN WHY MY MIND WAS A HAZE. WHY MY MEMORIES WERE SO HARD TO FIND.

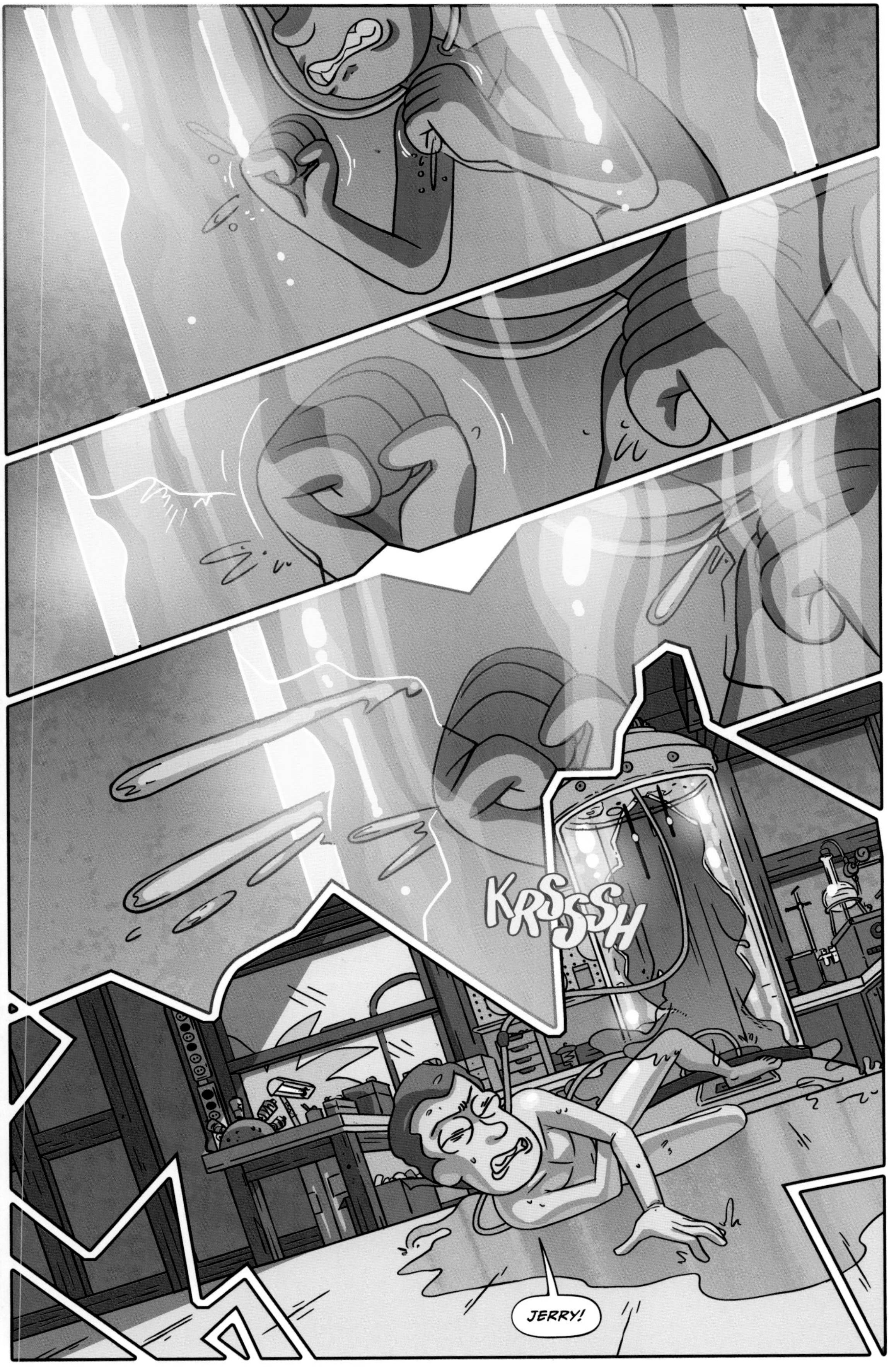
KRSSSSH
JERRY!

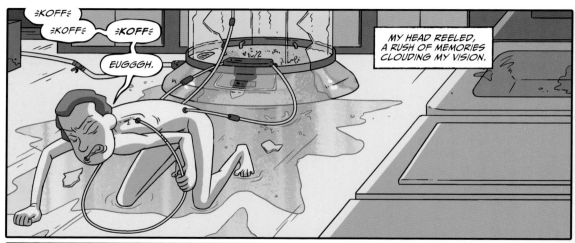

≠KOFF≠

≠KOFF≠ ≠KOFF≠

EUGGGH.

MY HEAD REELED, A RUSH OF MEMORIES CLOUDING MY VISION.

NAMES, FACES, DINOSAURS WITH CAMERAS--TOO FAST TO MAKE SENSE OF IT.

BUT ONE FACE...

...ONE NAME...

...WAS CRYSTAL CLEAR.

JERRY.

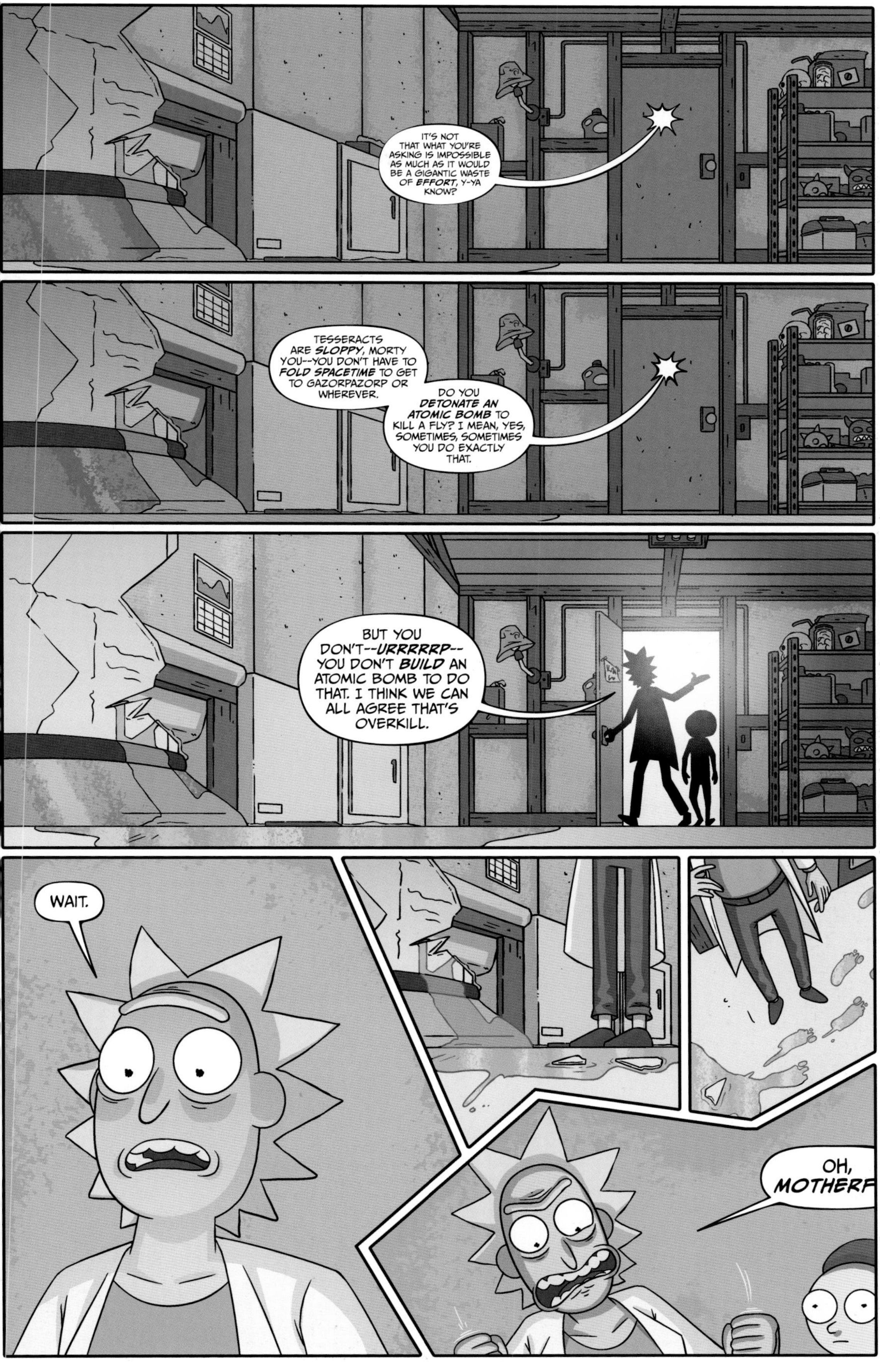
IT'S NOT THAT WHAT YOU'RE ASKING IS IMPOSSIBLE AS MUCH AS IT WOULD BE A GIGANTIC WASTE OF **EFFORT**, Y-YA KNOW?
TESSERACTS ARE **SLOPPY**, MORTY YOU--YOU DON'T HAVE TO **FOLD SPACETIME** TO GET TO GAZORPAZORP OR WHEREVER.
DO YOU **DETONATE AN ATOMIC BOMB** TO KILL A FLY? I MEAN, YES, SOMETIMES, SOMETIMES YOU DO EXACTLY THAT.
BUT YOU DON'T--**URRRRRP**--YOU DON'T **BUILD** AN ATOMIC BOMB TO DO THAT. I THINK WE CAN ALL AGREE THAT'S OVERKILL.
WAIT.
OH, **MOTHERF**

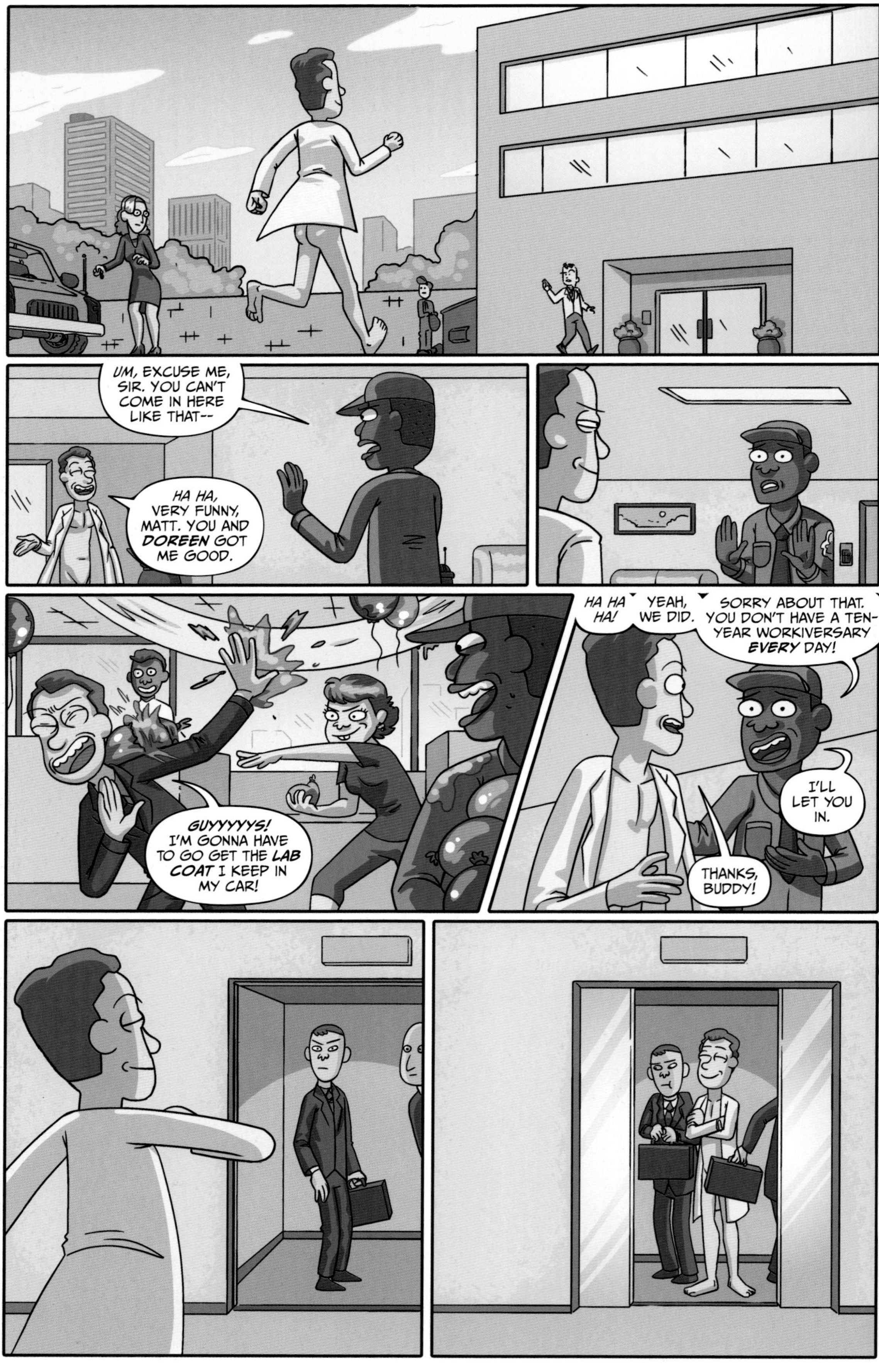
UM, EXCUSE ME, SIR. YOU CAN'T COME IN HERE LIKE THAT--
HA HA, VERY FUNNY, MATT. YOU AND DOREEN GOT ME GOOD.
GUYYYYYS! I'M GONNA HAVE TO GO GET THE LAB COAT I KEEP IN MY CAR!
HA HA HA!
YEAH, WE DID.
SORRY ABOUT THAT. YOU DON'T HAVE A TEN-YEAR WORKIVERSARY EVERY DAY!
I'LL LET YOU IN.
THANKS, BUDDY!

JERRY.

OH, HI, I WAS JUST WORKING ON THE *MEGANTIC* CAMPAIGN.

YOU KNOW, PEOPLE SAID THERE'S NO WAY TO COMBINE "MEGA" WITH "GIGANTIC," BUT--

JERRY, IT'S ME.

SLEEPY GARY...?

HEY, GORGEOUS.

NO, THIS ISN'T--

YOU WERE A--

I WATCHED YOU--

SHHH.

I KNOW WHAT YOU THINK YOU SAW. AND I DON'T UNDERSTAND IT EITHER.

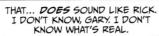

IT'S RICK. SOMEHOW, *HE* CONVINCED YOU I WAS A SHAPESHIFTING PARASITE WITH MIND CONTROL POWERS.

THAT... *DOES* SOUND LIKE RICK. I DON'T KNOW, GARY. I DON'T KNOW WHAT'S REAL.

YES, YOU DO.

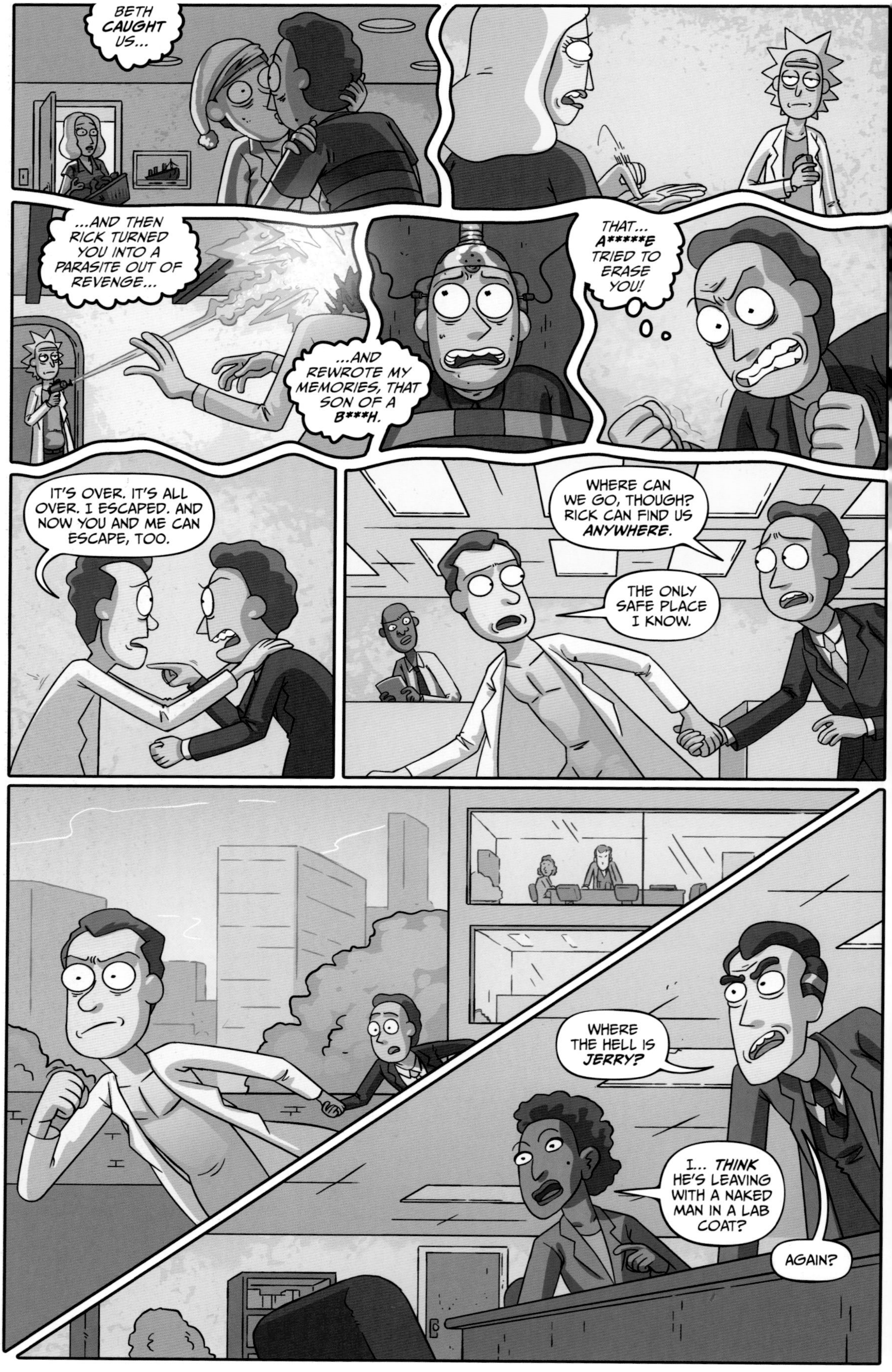
BETH CAUGHT US...
...AND THEN RICK TURNED YOU INTO A PARASITE OUT OF REVENGE...
...AND REWROTE MY MEMORIES, THAT SON OF A B***H.
THAT... A*****E TRIED TO ERASE YOU!
IT'S OVER. IT'S ALL OVER. I ESCAPED. AND NOW YOU AND ME CAN ESCAPE, TOO.
WHERE CAN WE GO, THOUGH? RICK CAN FIND US ANYWHERE.
THE ONLY SAFE PLACE I KNOW.
WHERE THE HELL IS JERRY?
I... THINK HE'S LEAVING WITH A NAKED MAN IN A LAB COAT?
AGAIN?

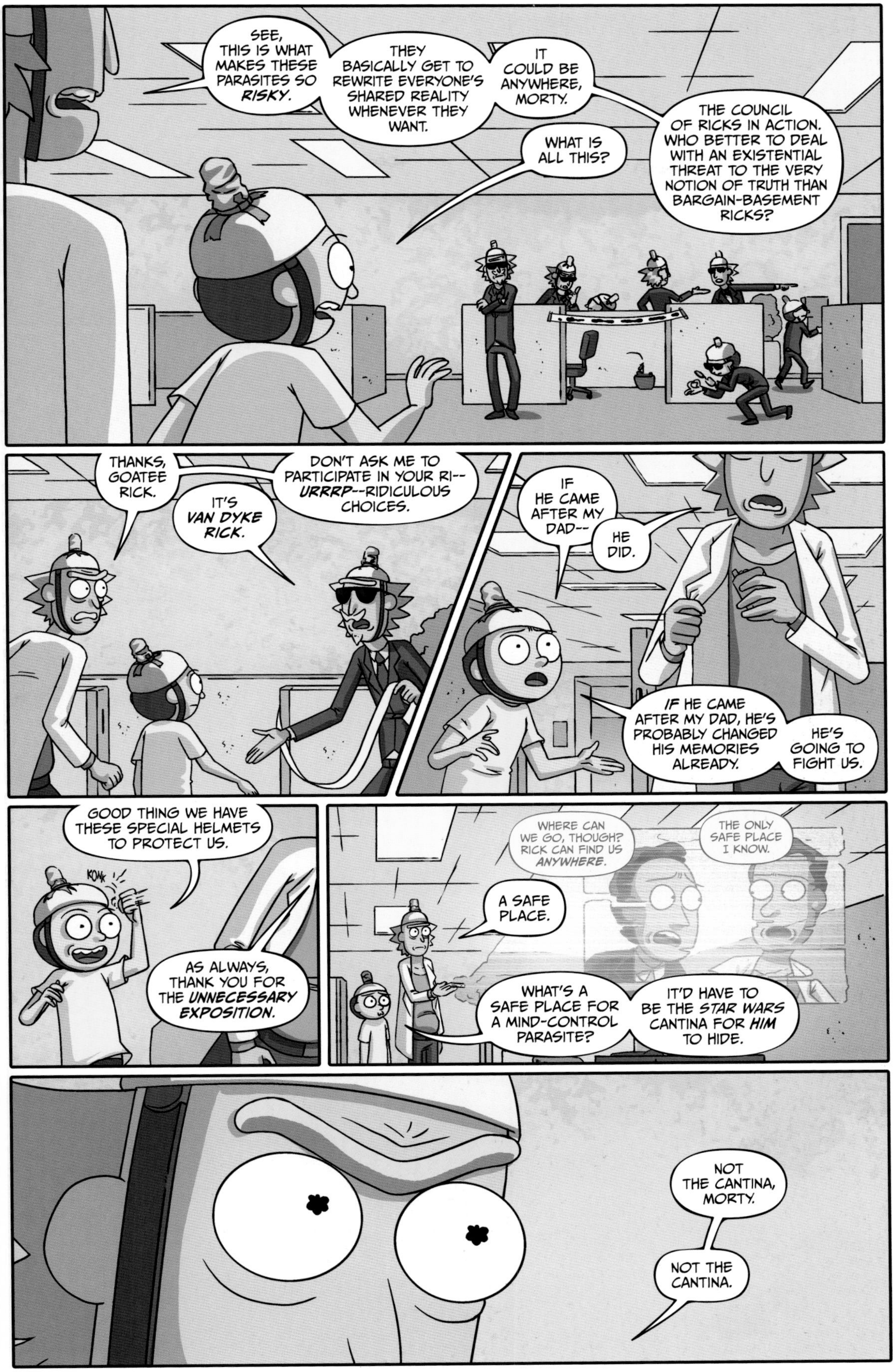
SEE, THIS IS WHAT MAKES THESE PARASITES SO RISKY.
THEY BASICALLY GET TO REWRITE EVERYONE'S SHARED REALITY WHENEVER THEY WANT.
IT COULD BE ANYWHERE, MORTY.
WHAT IS ALL THIS?
THE COUNCIL OF RICKS IN ACTION. WHO BETTER TO DEAL WITH AN EXISTENTIAL THREAT TO THE VERY NOTION OF TRUTH THAN BARGAIN-BASEMENT RICKS?
THANKS, GOATEE RICK.
DON'T ASK ME TO PARTICIPATE IN YOUR RI-- URRRP--RIDICULOUS CHOICES.
IT'S VAN DYKE RICK.
IF HE CAME AFTER MY DAD--
HE DID.
IF HE CAME AFTER MY DAD, HE'S PROBABLY CHANGED HIS MEMORIES ALREADY.
HE'S GOING TO FIGHT US.
GOOD THING WE HAVE THESE SPECIAL HELMETS TO PROTECT US.
KONK
AS ALWAYS, THANK YOU FOR THE UNNECESSARY EXPOSITION.
WHERE CAN WE GO, THOUGH? RICK CAN FIND US ANYWHERE.
THE ONLY SAFE PLACE I KNOW.
A SAFE PLACE.
WHAT'S A SAFE PLACE FOR A MIND-CONTROL PARASITE?
IT'D HAVE TO BE THE STAR WARS CANTINA FOR HIM TO HIDE.
NOT THE CANTINA, MORTY.
NOT THE CANTINA.

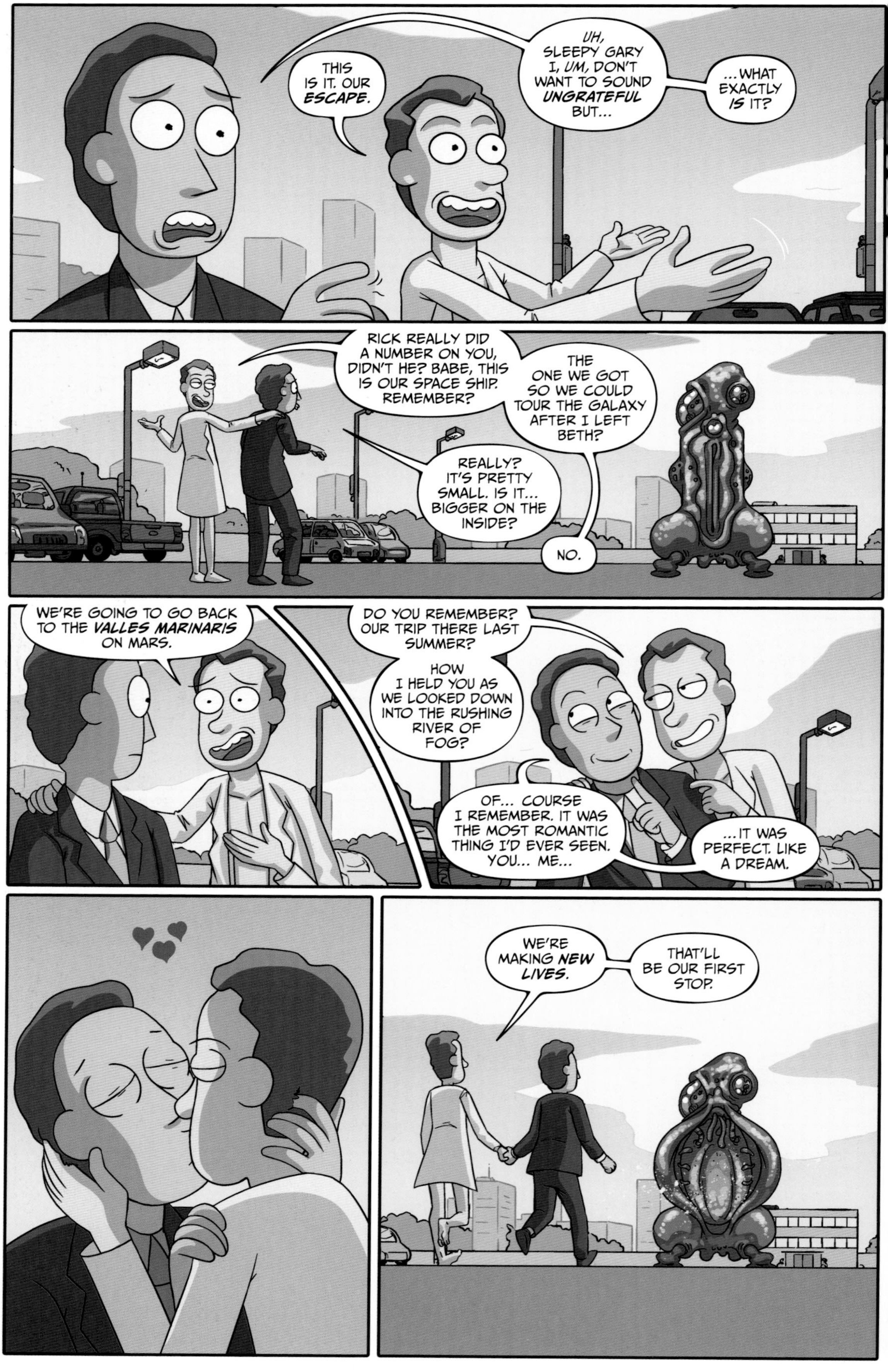
THIS IS IT. OUR ESCAPE.
UH, SLEEPY GARY I, UM, DON'T WANT TO SOUND UNGRATEFUL BUT...
...WHAT EXACTLY IS IT?
RICK REALLY DID A NUMBER ON YOU, DIDN'T HE? BABE, THIS IS OUR SPACE SHIP. REMEMBER?
THE ONE WE GOT SO WE COULD TOUR THE GALAXY AFTER I LEFT BETH?
REALLY? IT'S PRETTY SMALL. IS IT... BIGGER ON THE INSIDE?
NO.
WE'RE GOING TO GO BACK TO THE VALLES MARINARIS ON MARS.
DO YOU REMEMBER? OUR TRIP THERE LAST SUMMER?
HOW I HELD YOU AS WE LOOKED DOWN INTO THE RUSHING RIVER OF FOG?
OF... COURSE I REMEMBER. IT WAS THE MOST ROMANTIC THING I'D EVER SEEN. YOU... ME...
...IT WAS PERFECT. LIKE A DREAM.
WE'RE MAKING NEW LIVES.
THAT'LL BE OUR FIRST STOP.

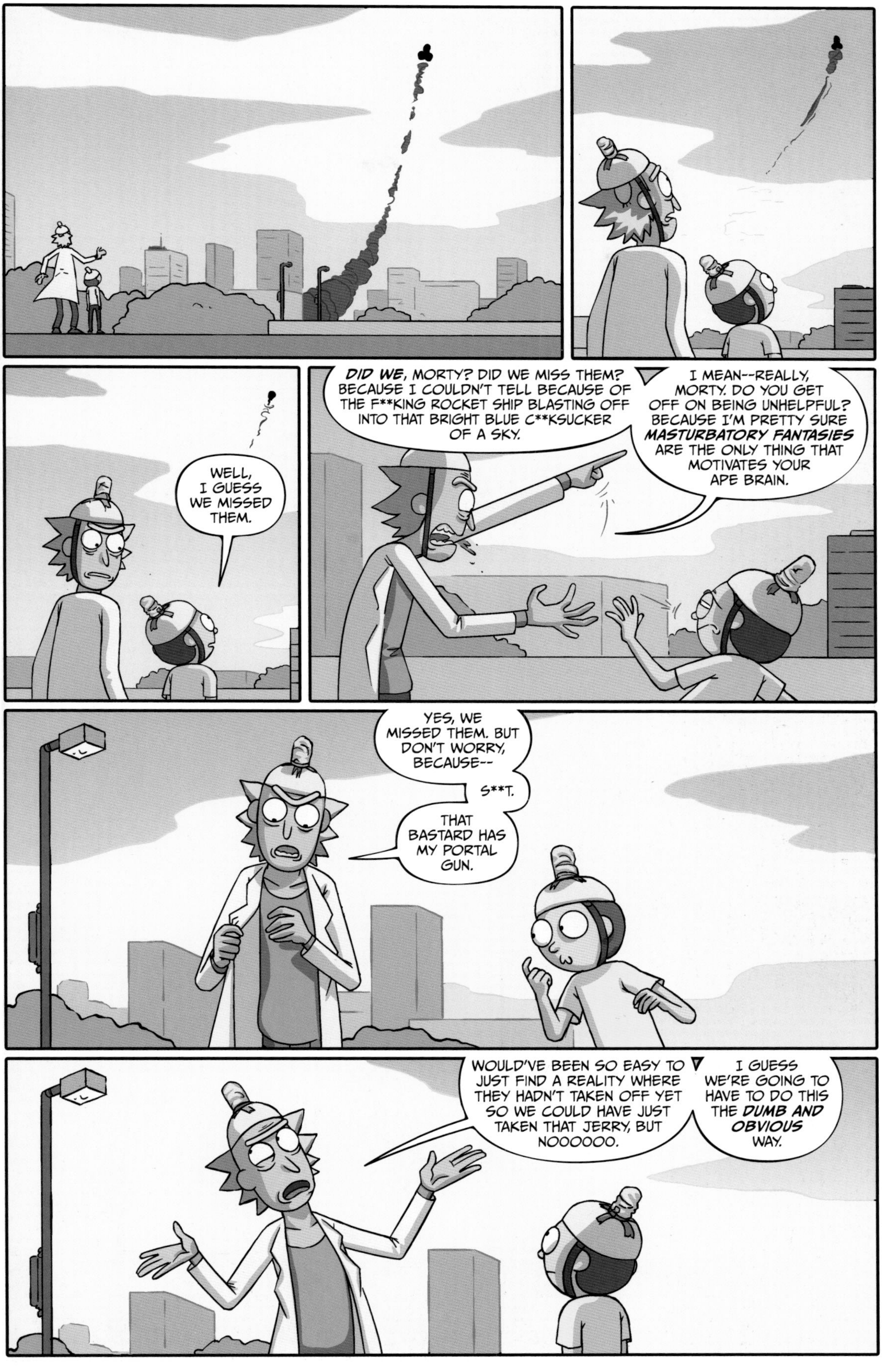
WELL, I GUESS WE MISSED THEM.
DID WE, MORTY? DID WE MISS THEM? BECAUSE I COULDN'T TELL BECAUSE OF THE F**KING ROCKET SHIP BLASTING OFF INTO THAT BRIGHT BLUE C**KSUCKER OF A SKY.
I MEAN--REALLY, MORTY. DO YOU GET OFF ON BEING UNHELPFUL? BECAUSE I'M PRETTY SURE MASTURBATORY FANTASIES ARE THE ONLY THING THAT MOTIVATES YOUR APE BRAIN.
YES, WE MISSED THEM. BUT DON'T WORRY, BECAUSE--
S**T.
THAT BASTARD HAS MY PORTAL GUN.
WOULD'VE BEEN SO EASY TO JUST FIND A REALITY WHERE THEY HADN'T TAKEN OFF YET SO WE COULD HAVE JUST TAKEN THAT JERRY, BUT NOOOOOO.
I GUESS WE'RE GOING TO HAVE TO DO THIS THE DUMB AND OBVIOUS WAY.

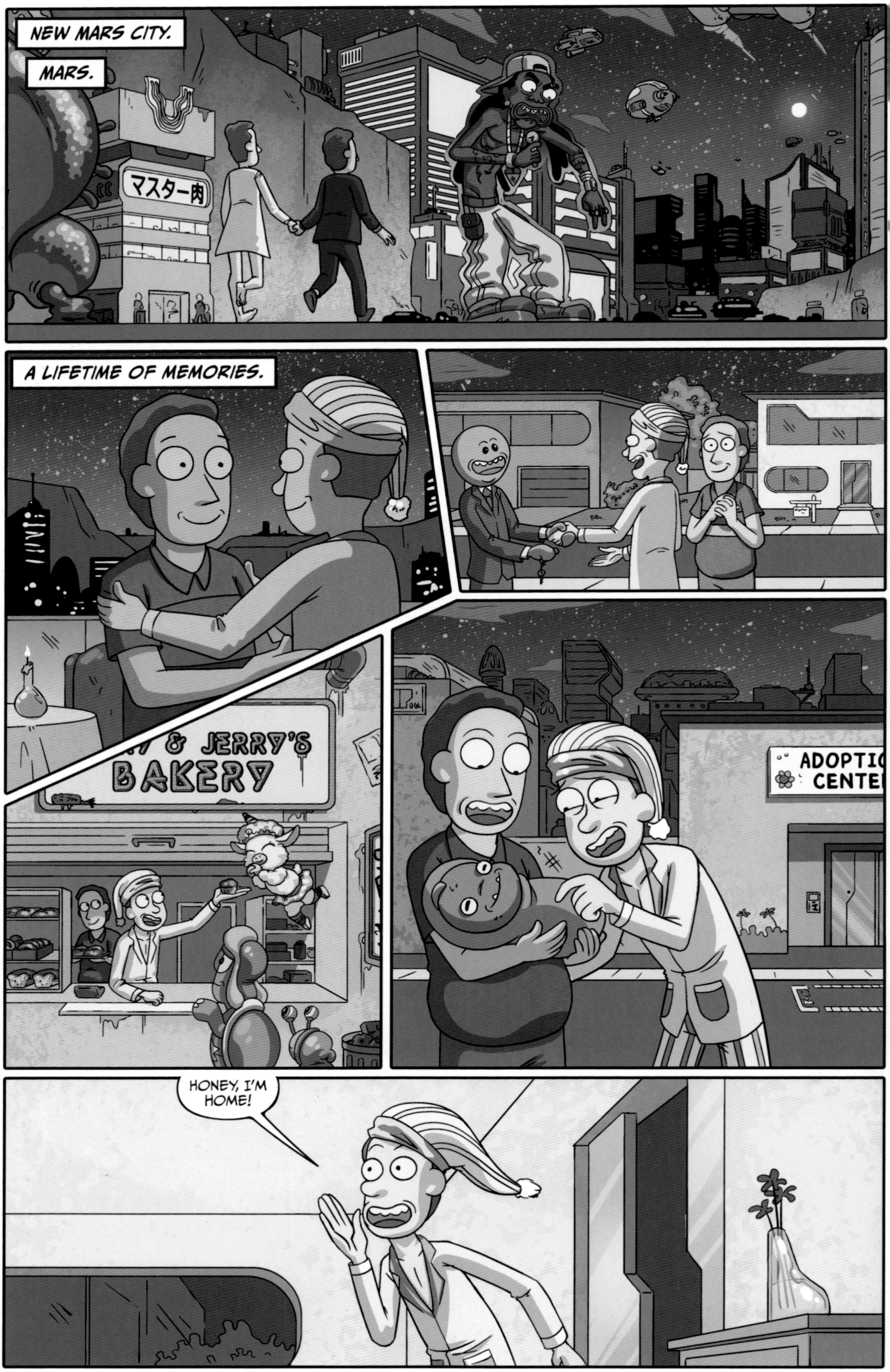
NEW MARS CITY.
MARS.
マスター肉
A LIFETIME OF MEMORIES.
& JERRY'S
BAKERY
HONEY, I'M HOME!

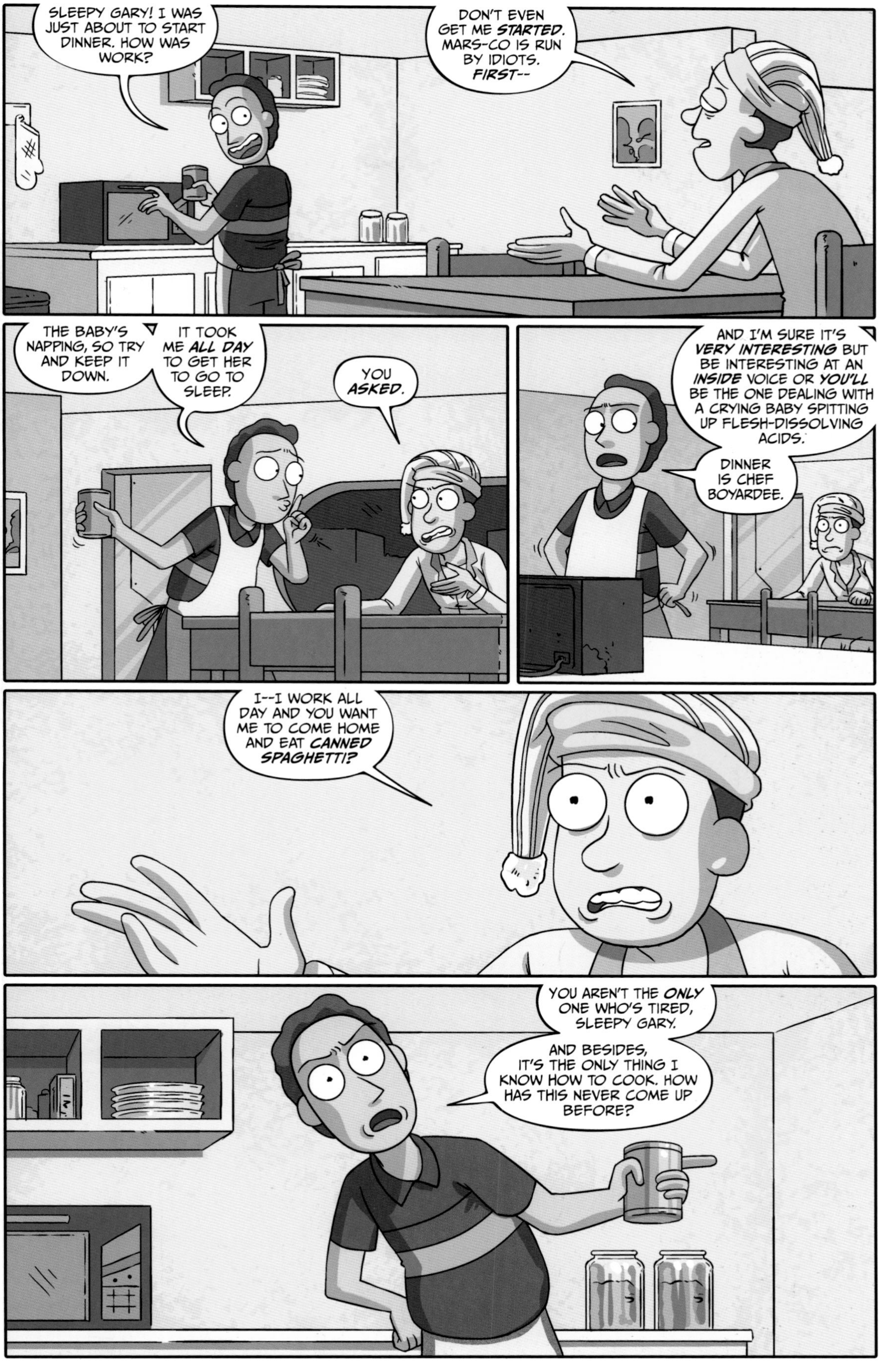
SLEEPY GARY! I WAS JUST ABOUT TO START DINNER. HOW WAS WORK?
DON'T EVEN GET ME *STARTED*. MARS-CO IS RUN BY IDIOTS. *FIRST*--
THE BABY'S NAPPING, SO TRY AND KEEP IT DOWN.
IT TOOK ME *ALL DAY* TO GET HER TO GO TO SLEEP.
YOU *ASKED*.
AND I'M SURE IT'S *VERY INTERESTING* BUT BE INTERESTING AT AN *INSIDE* VOICE OR *YOU'LL* BE THE ONE DEALING WITH A CRYING BABY SPITTING UP FLESH-DISSOLVING ACIDS.
DINNER IS CHEF BOYARDEE.
I--I WORK ALL DAY AND YOU WANT ME TO COME HOME AND EAT *CANNED SPAGHETTI?*
YOU AREN'T THE *ONLY* ONE WHO'S TIRED, SLEEPY GARY.
AND BESIDES, IT'S THE ONLY THING I KNOW HOW TO COOK. HOW HAS THIS NEVER COME UP BEFORE?

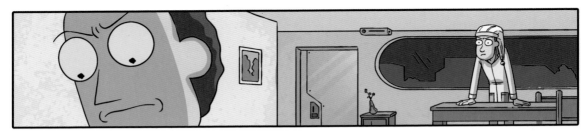

YOU KNOW WHAT?

CANNED SPAGHETTI IS JUST FINE.

YOU MEAN THAT?

I DO.

LIFE ISN'T PERFECT. AND SOMETIMES THINGS AREN'T EXACTLY WHAT WE WANT.

BUT I LOVE YOU, AND I WANT TO MAKE A LIFETIME OF MEMORIES. GOOD AND BAD.

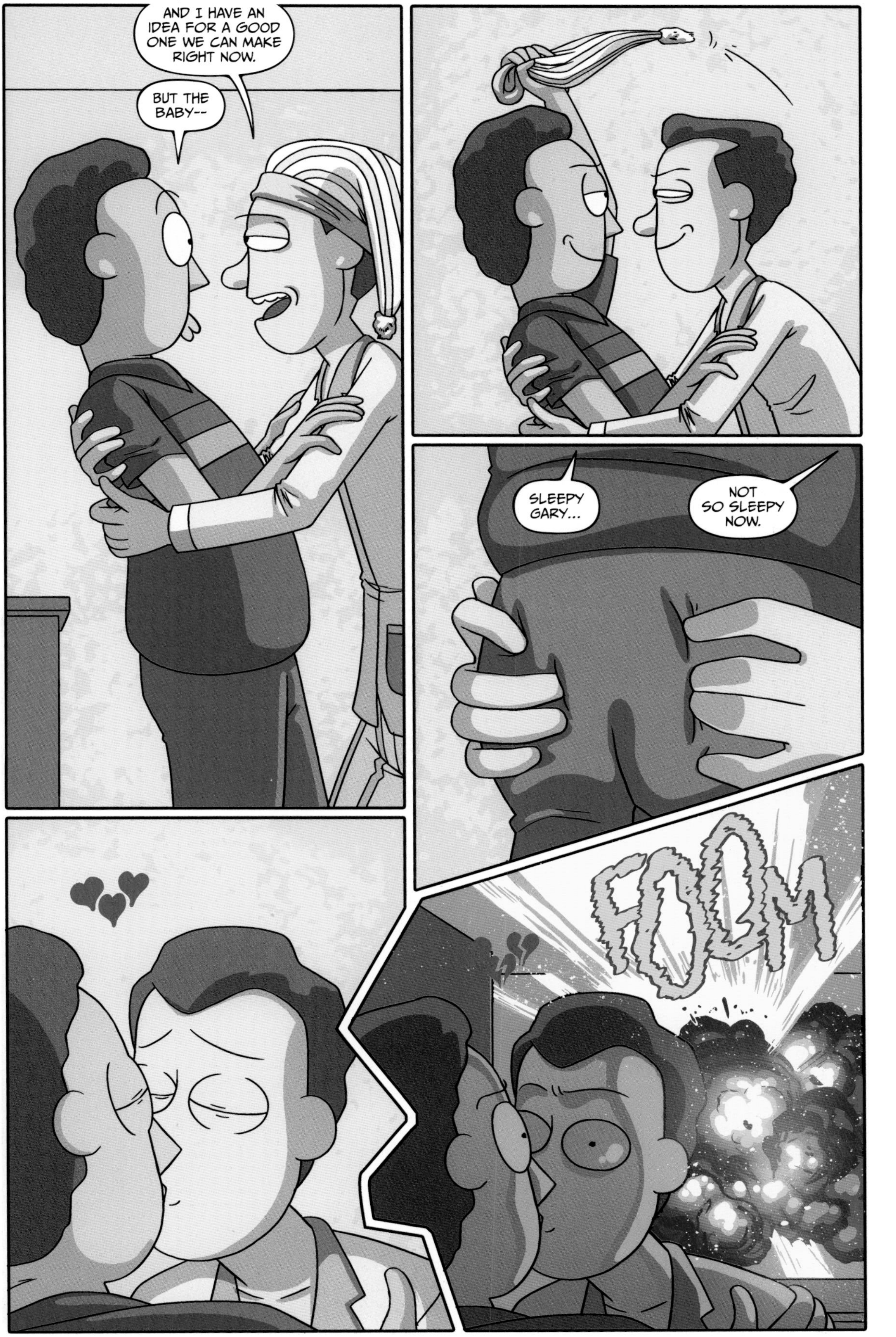
AND I HAVE AN IDEA FOR A GOOD ONE WE CAN MAKE RIGHT NOW.
BUT THE BABY--
SLEEPY GARY...
NOT SO SLEEPY NOW.
FOOM

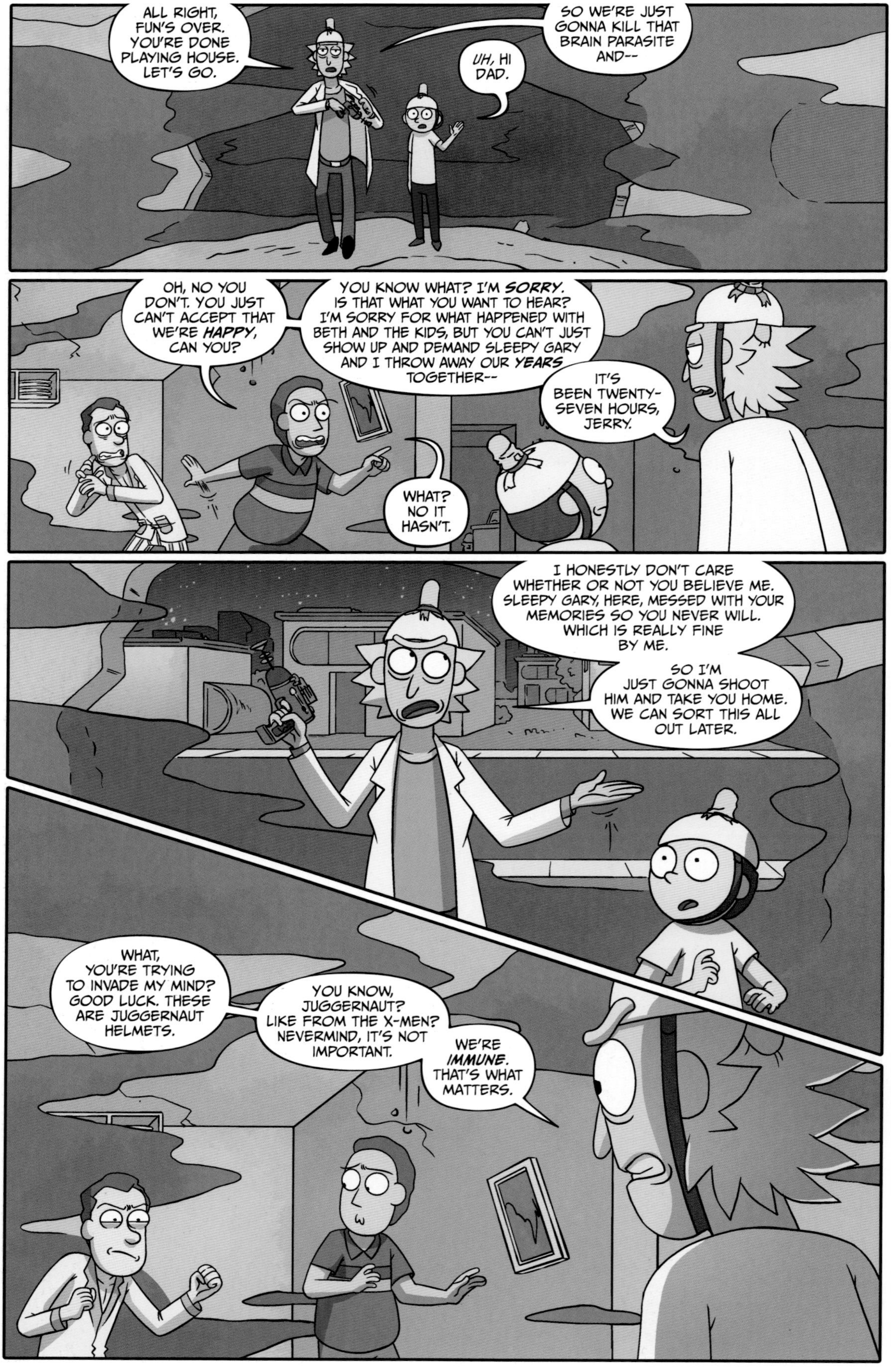
ALL RIGHT, FUN'S OVER. YOU'RE DONE PLAYING HOUSE. LET'S GO.
SO WE'RE JUST GONNA KILL THAT BRAIN PARASITE AND--
UH, HI DAD.
OH, NO YOU DON'T. YOU JUST CAN'T ACCEPT THAT WE'RE HAPPY, CAN YOU?
YOU KNOW WHAT? I'M SORRY. IS THAT WHAT YOU WANT TO HEAR? I'M SORRY FOR WHAT HAPPENED WITH BETH AND THE KIDS, BUT YOU CAN'T JUST SHOW UP AND DEMAND SLEEPY GARY AND I THROW AWAY OUR YEARS TOGETHER--
IT'S BEEN TWENTY-SEVEN HOURS, JERRY.
WHAT? NO IT HASN'T.
I HONESTLY DON'T CARE WHETHER OR NOT YOU BELIEVE ME. SLEEPY GARY, HERE, MESSED WITH YOUR MEMORIES SO YOU NEVER WILL. WHICH IS REALLY FINE BY ME.
SO I'M JUST GONNA SHOOT HIM AND TAKE YOU HOME. WE CAN SORT THIS ALL OUT LATER.
WHAT, YOU'RE TRYING TO INVADE MY MIND? GOOD LUCK. THESE ARE JUGGERNAUT HELMETS.
YOU KNOW, JUGGERNAUT? LIKE FROM THE X-MEN? NEVERMIND, IT'S NOT IMPORTANT.
WE'RE IMMUNE. THAT'S WHAT MATTERS.

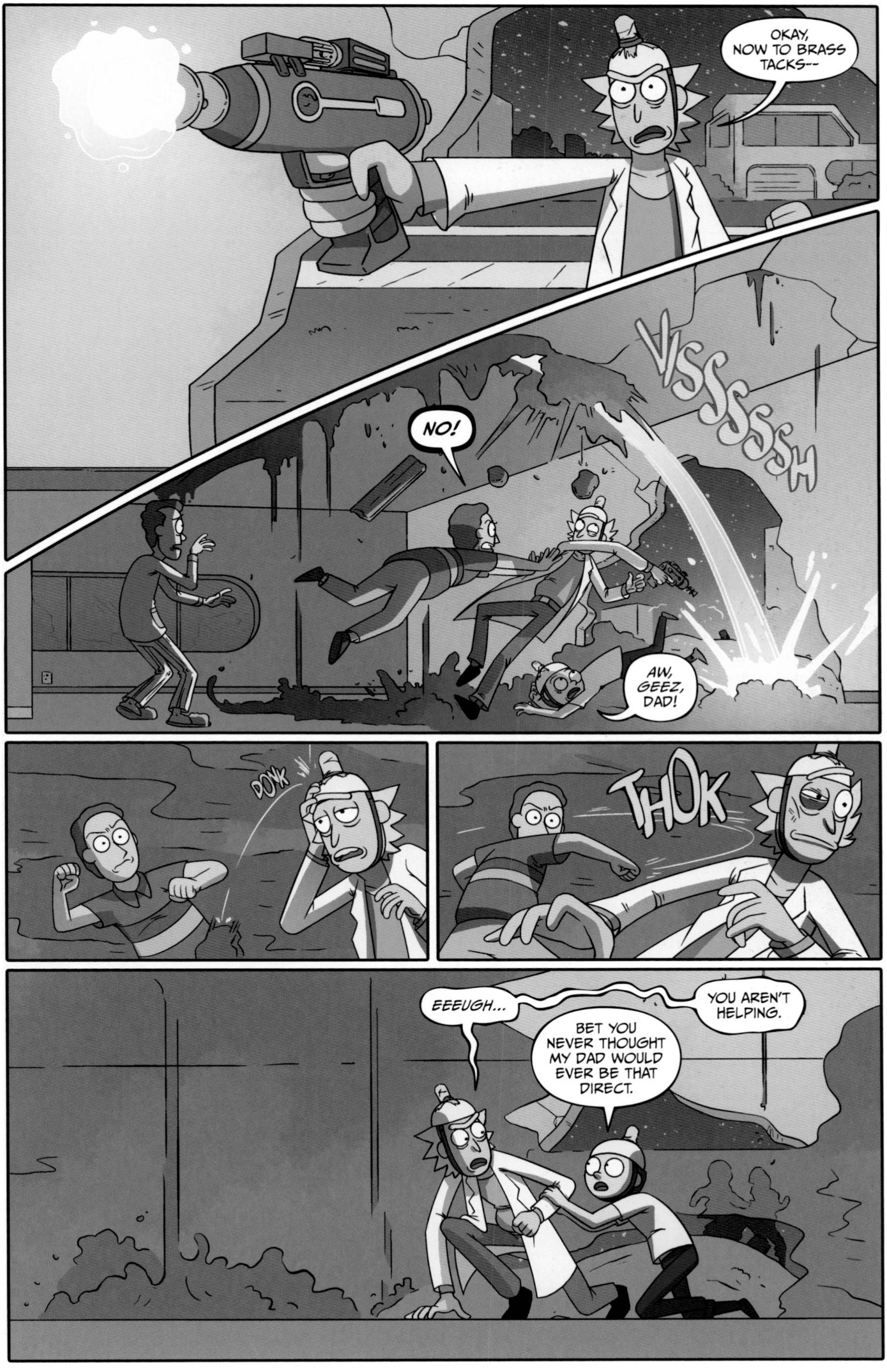

OKAY, NOW TO BRASS TACKS--
VISSSSSSH
NO!
AW, GEEZ, DAD!
DONK
THOK
EEEUGH...
YOU AREN'T HELPING.
BET YOU NEVER THOUGHT MY DAD WOULD EVER BE THAT DIRECT.

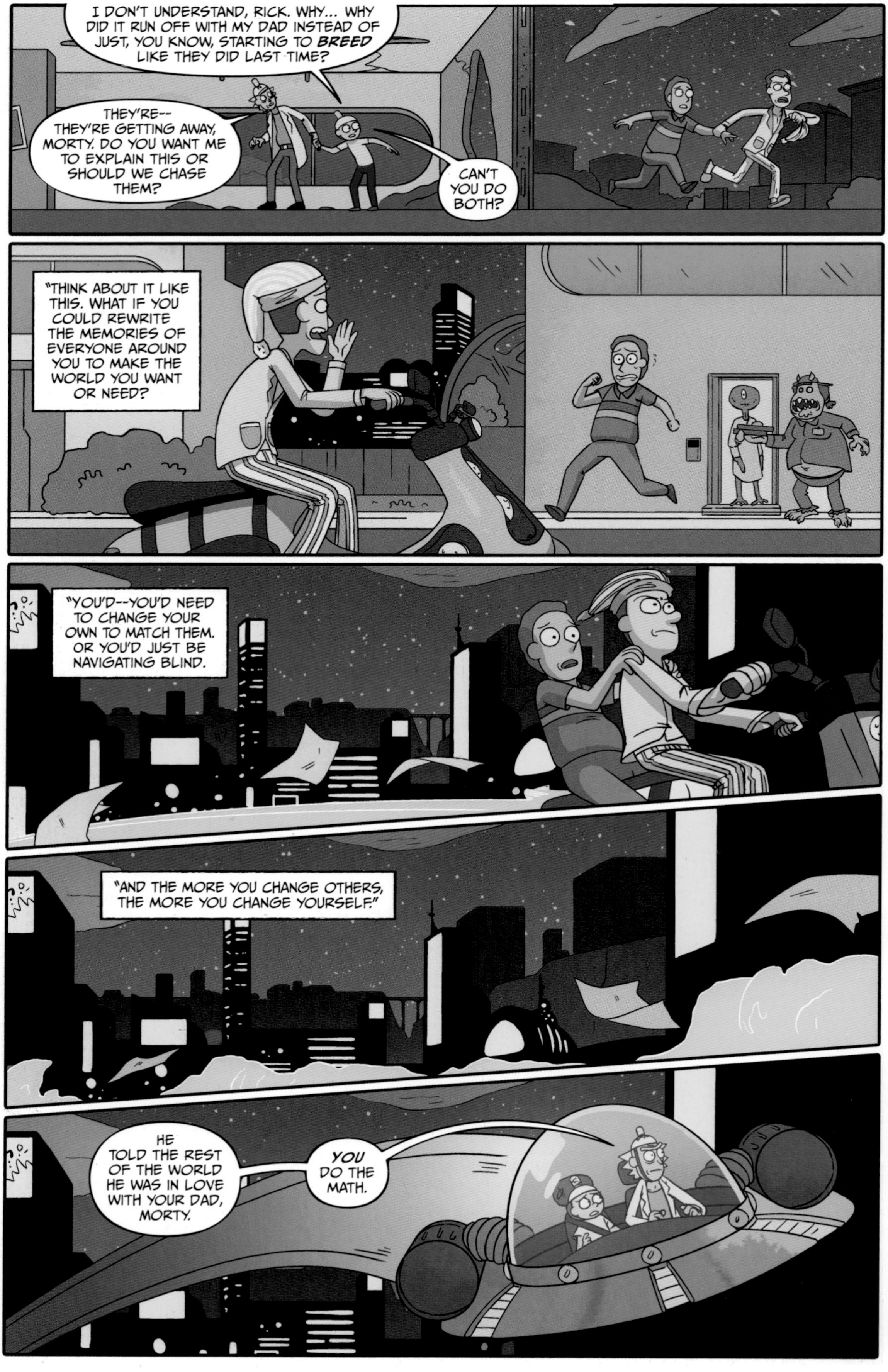
I DON'T UNDERSTAND, RICK. WHY... WHY DID IT RUN OFF WITH MY DAD INSTEAD OF JUST, YOU KNOW, STARTING TO **BREED** LIKE THEY DID LAST TIME?
THEY'RE-- THEY'RE GETTING AWAY, MORTY. DO YOU WANT ME TO EXPLAIN THIS OR SHOULD WE CHASE THEM?
CAN'T YOU DO BOTH?
"THINK ABOUT IT LIKE THIS. WHAT IF YOU COULD REWRITE THE MEMORIES OF EVERYONE AROUND YOU TO MAKE THE WORLD YOU WANT OR NEED?
"YOU'D--YOU'D NEED TO CHANGE YOUR OWN TO MATCH THEM. OR YOU'D JUST BE NAVIGATING BLIND.
"AND THE MORE YOU CHANGE OTHERS, THE MORE YOU CHANGE YOURSELF."
HE TOLD THE REST OF THE WORLD HE WAS IN LOVE WITH YOUR DAD, MORTY.
YOU DO THE MATH.

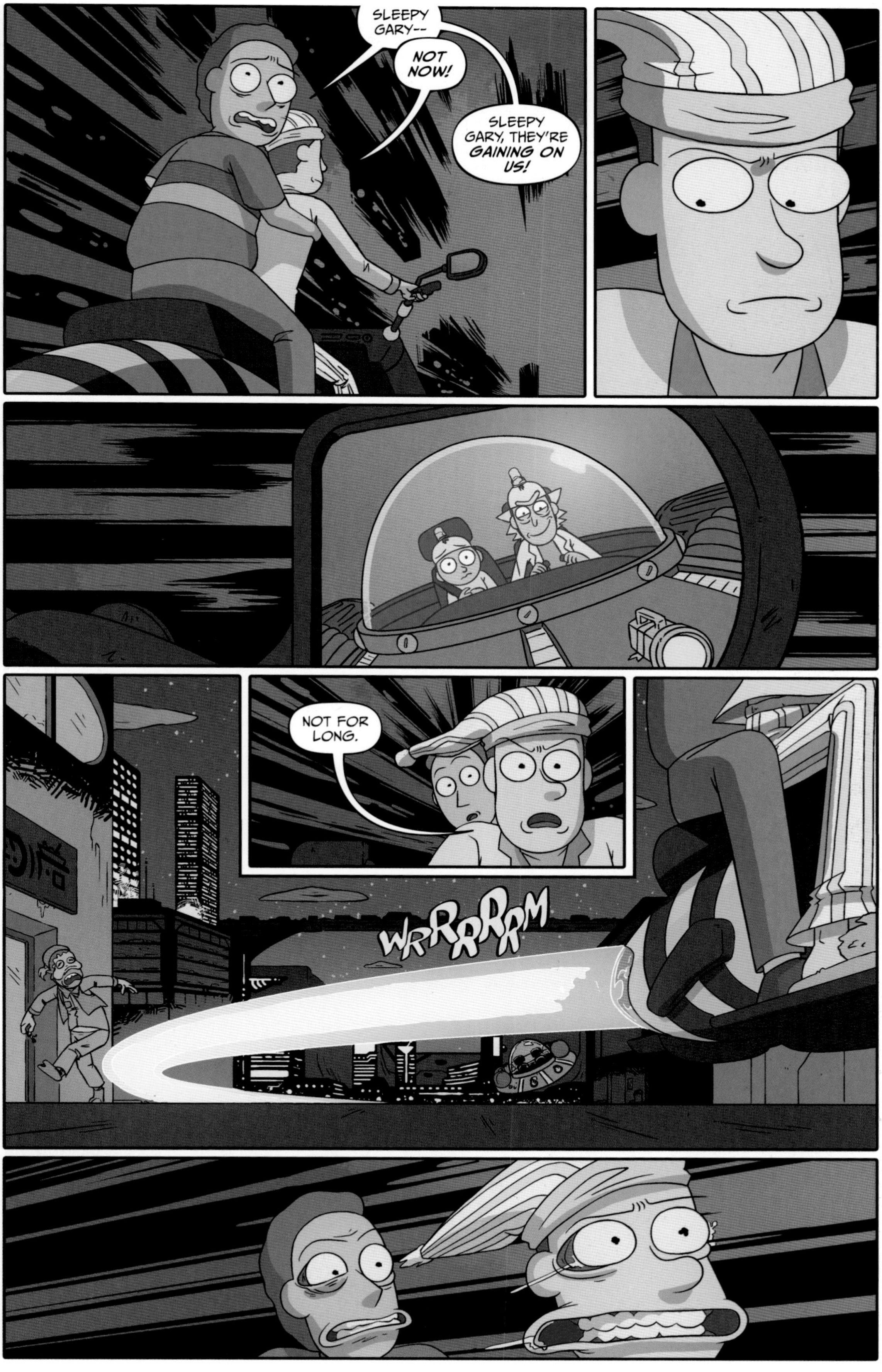
SLEEPY GARY--
NOT NOW!
SLEEPY GARY, THEY'RE GAINING ON US!
NOT FOR LONG.
WRRRRRRM

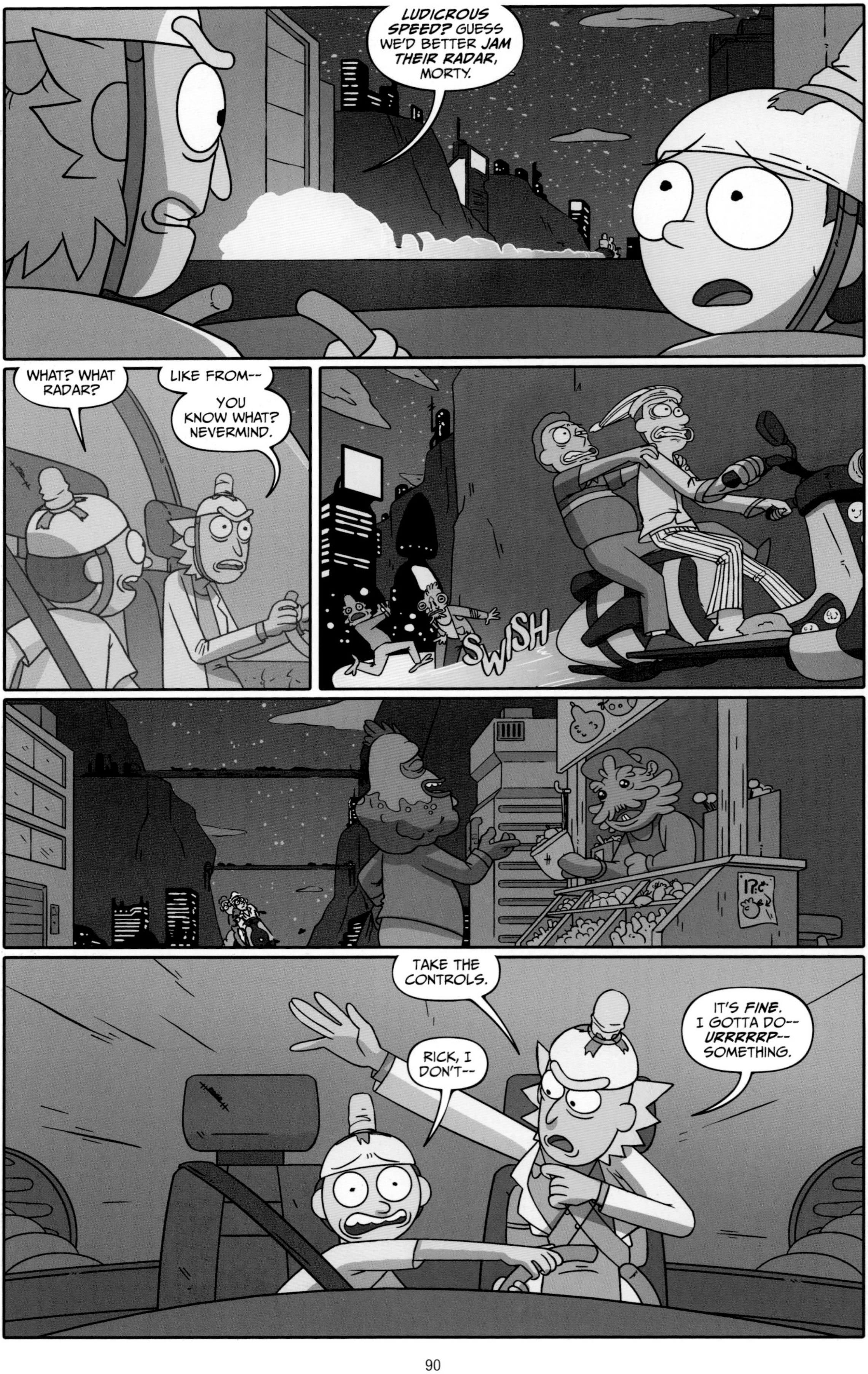
LUDICROUS SPEED? GUESS WE'D BETTER JAM THEIR RADAR, MORTY.
WHAT? WHAT RADAR?
LIKE FROM--
YOU KNOW WHAT? NEVERMIND.
SWISH
TAKE THE CONTROLS.
RICK, I DON'T--
IT'S FINE. I GOTTA DO-- URRRRRP-- SOMETHING.

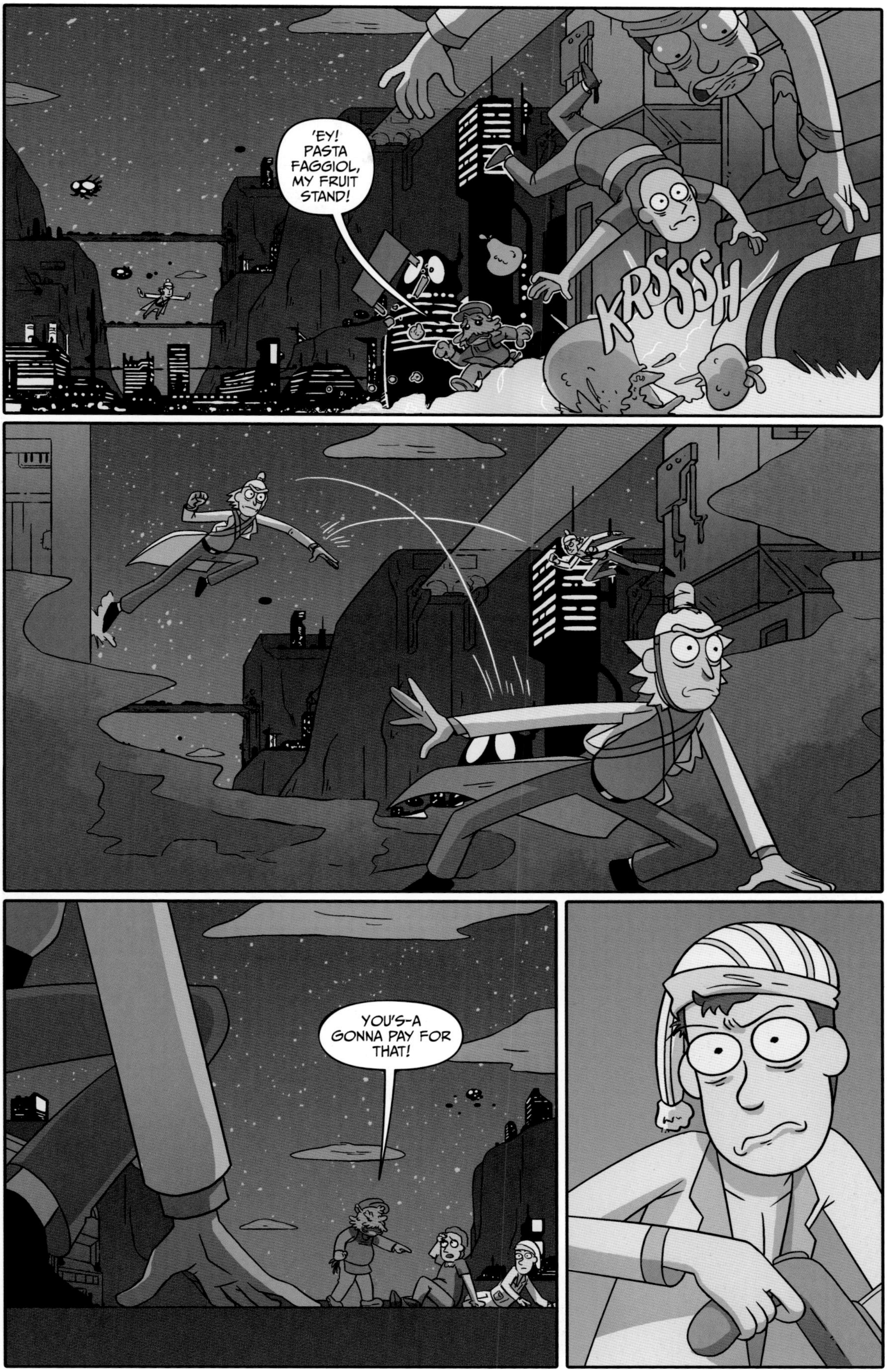
'EY! PASTA FAGGIOL, MY FRUIT STAND!
KRSSSH
YOU'S-A GONNA PAY FOR THAT!

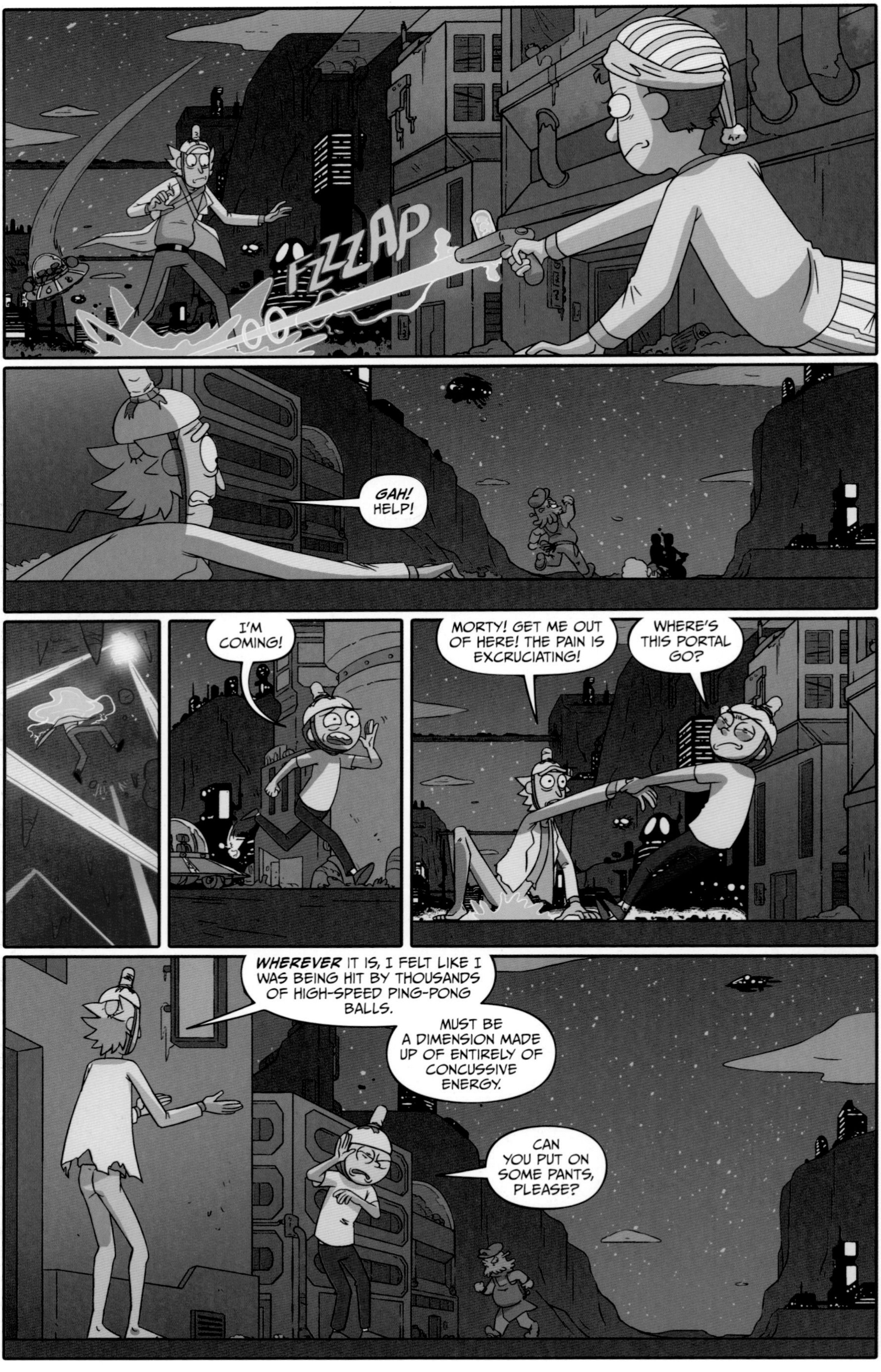
FZZZAP
GAH! HELP!
I'M COMING!
MORTY! GET ME OUT OF HERE! THE PAIN IS EXCRUCIATING!
WHERE'S THIS PORTAL GO?
WHEREVER IT IS, I FELT LIKE I WAS BEING HIT BY THOUSANDS OF HIGH-SPEED PING-PONG BALLS.
MUST BE A DIMENSION MADE UP OF ENTIRELY OF CONCUSSIVE ENERGY.
CAN YOU PUT ON SOME PANTS, PLEASE?

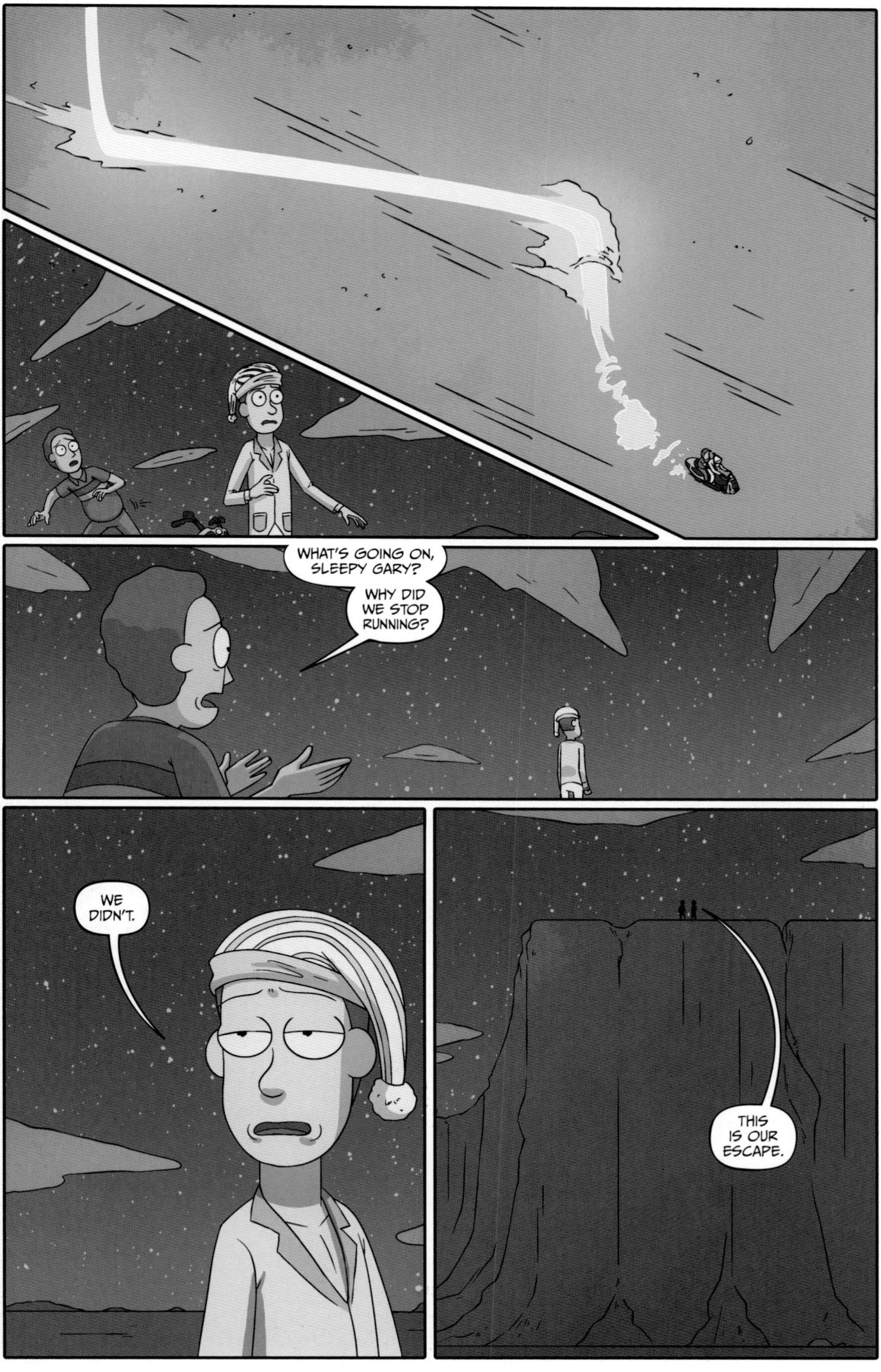
WHAT'S GOING ON, SLEEPY GARY?
WHY DID WE STOP RUNNING?
WE DIDN'T.
THIS IS OUR ESCAPE.

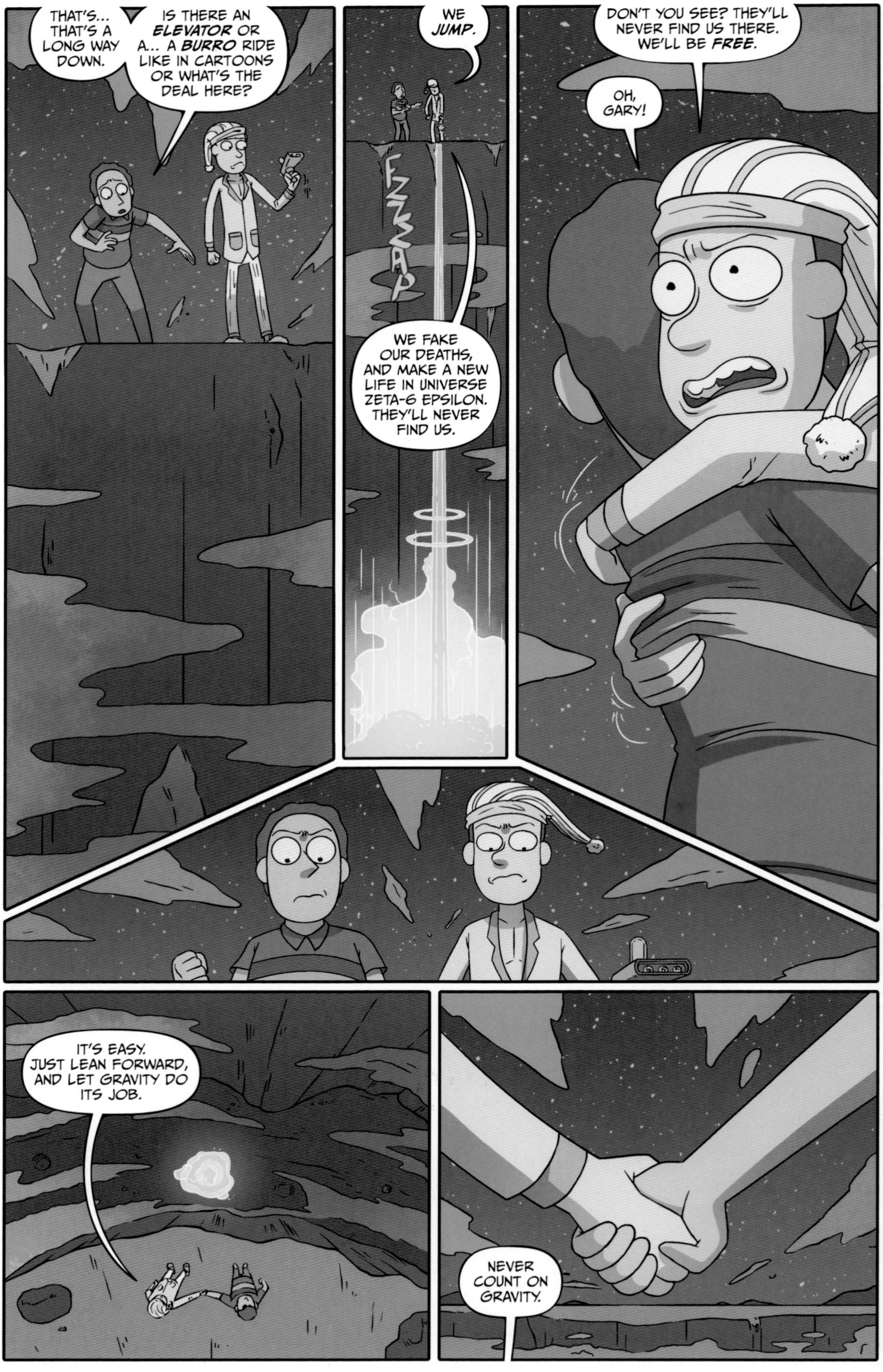

THAT'S... THAT'S A LONG WAY DOWN.
IS THERE AN **ELEVATOR** OR A... A **BURRO** RIDE LIKE IN CARTOONS OR WHAT'S THE DEAL HERE?
WE **JUMP**.
FZZSAP
WE FAKE OUR DEATHS, AND MAKE A NEW LIFE IN UNIVERSE ZETA-6 EPSILON. THEY'LL NEVER FIND US.
DON'T YOU SEE? THEY'LL NEVER FIND US THERE. WE'LL BE **FREE**.
OH, GARY!
IT'S EASY. JUST LEAN FORWARD, AND LET GRAVITY DO ITS JOB.
NEVER COUNT ON GRAVITY.

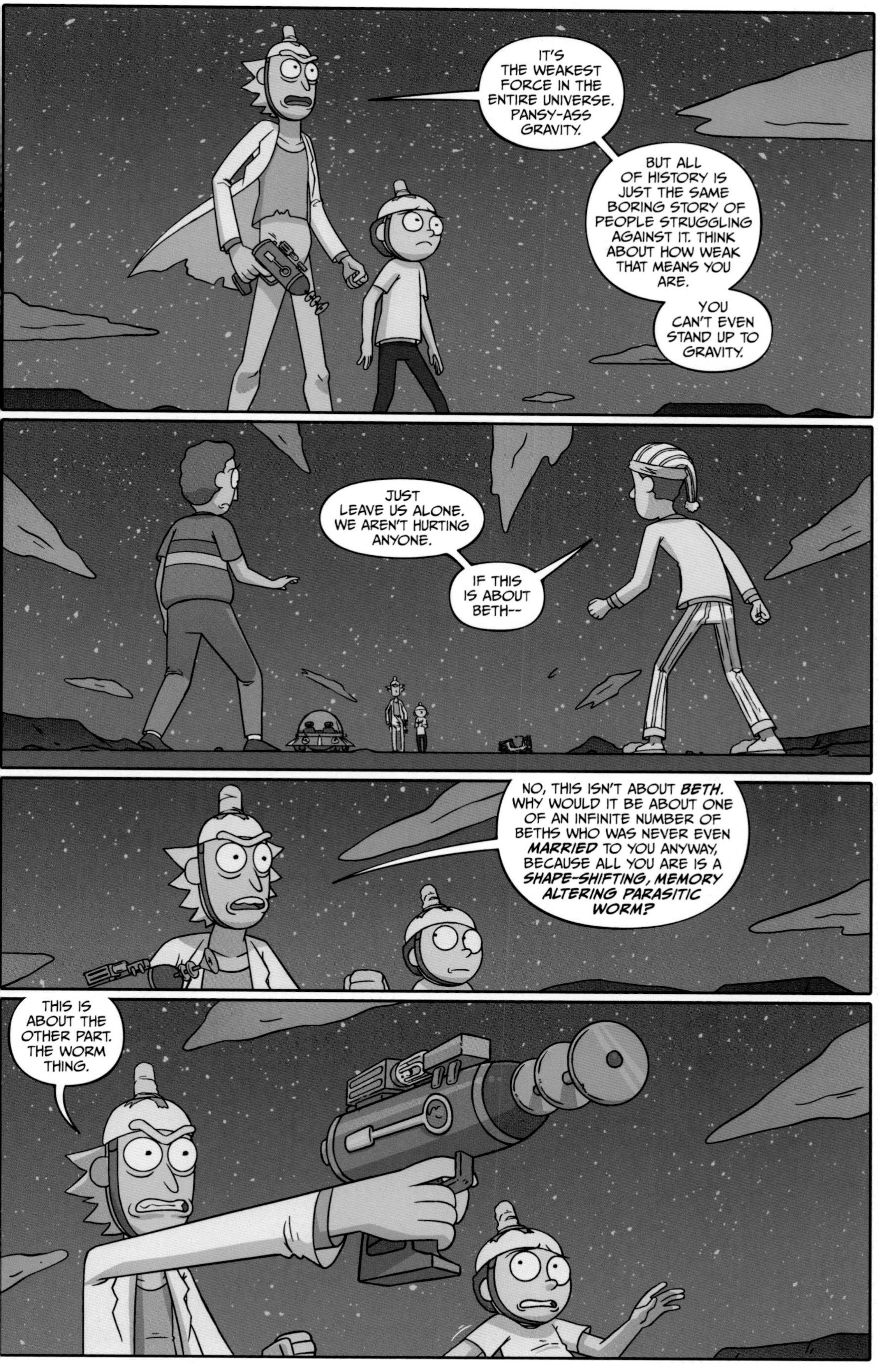
IT'S THE WEAKEST FORCE IN THE ENTIRE UNIVERSE. PANSY-ASS GRAVITY.
BUT ALL OF HISTORY IS JUST THE SAME BORING STORY OF PEOPLE STRUGGLING AGAINST IT. THINK ABOUT HOW WEAK THAT MEANS YOU ARE.
YOU CAN'T EVEN STAND UP TO GRAVITY.
JUST LEAVE US ALONE. WE AREN'T HURTING ANYONE.
IF THIS IS ABOUT BETH--
NO, THIS ISN'T ABOUT ***BETH.*** WHY WOULD IT BE ABOUT ONE OF AN INFINITE NUMBER OF BETHS WHO WAS NEVER EVEN ***MARRIED*** TO YOU ANYWAY, BECAUSE ALL YOU ARE IS A ***SHAPE-SHIFTING, MEMORY ALTERING PARASITIC WORM?***
THIS IS ABOUT THE OTHER PART. THE WORM THING.

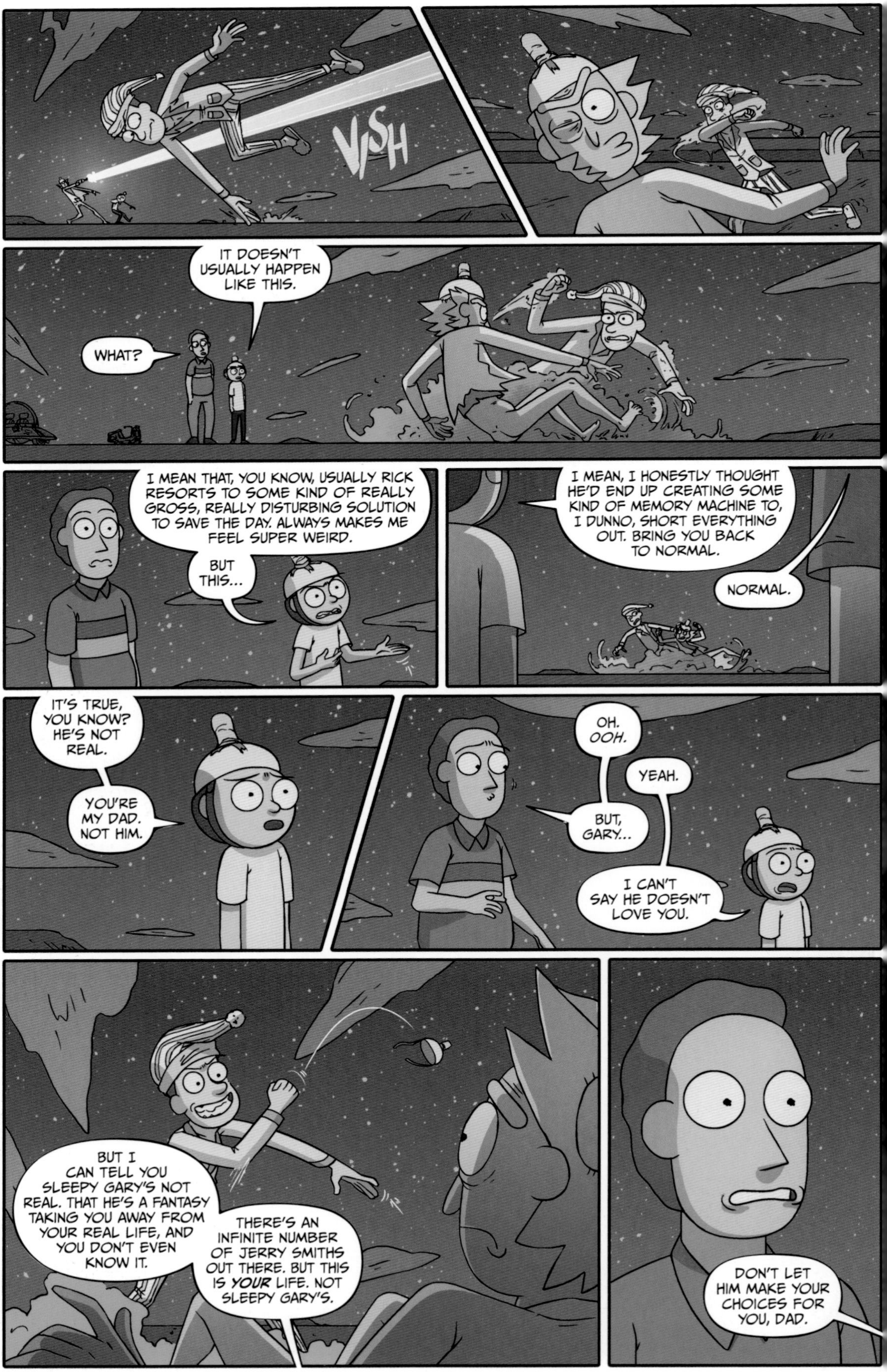
VISH
IT DOESN'T USUALLY HAPPEN LIKE THIS.
WHAT?
I MEAN THAT, YOU KNOW, USUALLY RICK RESORTS TO SOME KIND OF REALLY GROSS, REALLY DISTURBING SOLUTION TO SAVE THE DAY. ALWAYS MAKES ME FEEL SUPER WEIRD.
BUT THIS...
I MEAN, I HONESTLY THOUGHT HE'D END UP CREATING SOME KIND OF MEMORY MACHINE TO, I DUNNO, SHORT EVERYTHING OUT. BRING YOU BACK TO NORMAL.
NORMAL.
IT'S TRUE, YOU KNOW? HE'S NOT REAL.
YOU'RE MY DAD. NOT HIM.
OH. OOH.
YEAH.
BUT, GARY...
I CAN'T SAY HE DOESN'T LOVE YOU.
BUT I CAN TELL YOU SLEEPY GARY'S NOT REAL. THAT HE'S A FANTASY TAKING YOU AWAY FROM YOUR REAL LIFE, AND YOU DON'T EVEN KNOW IT.
THERE'S AN INFINITE NUMBER OF JERRY SMITHS OUT THERE. BUT THIS IS *YOUR* LIFE. NOT SLEEPY GARY'S.
DON'T LET HIM MAKE YOUR CHOICES FOR YOU, DAD.

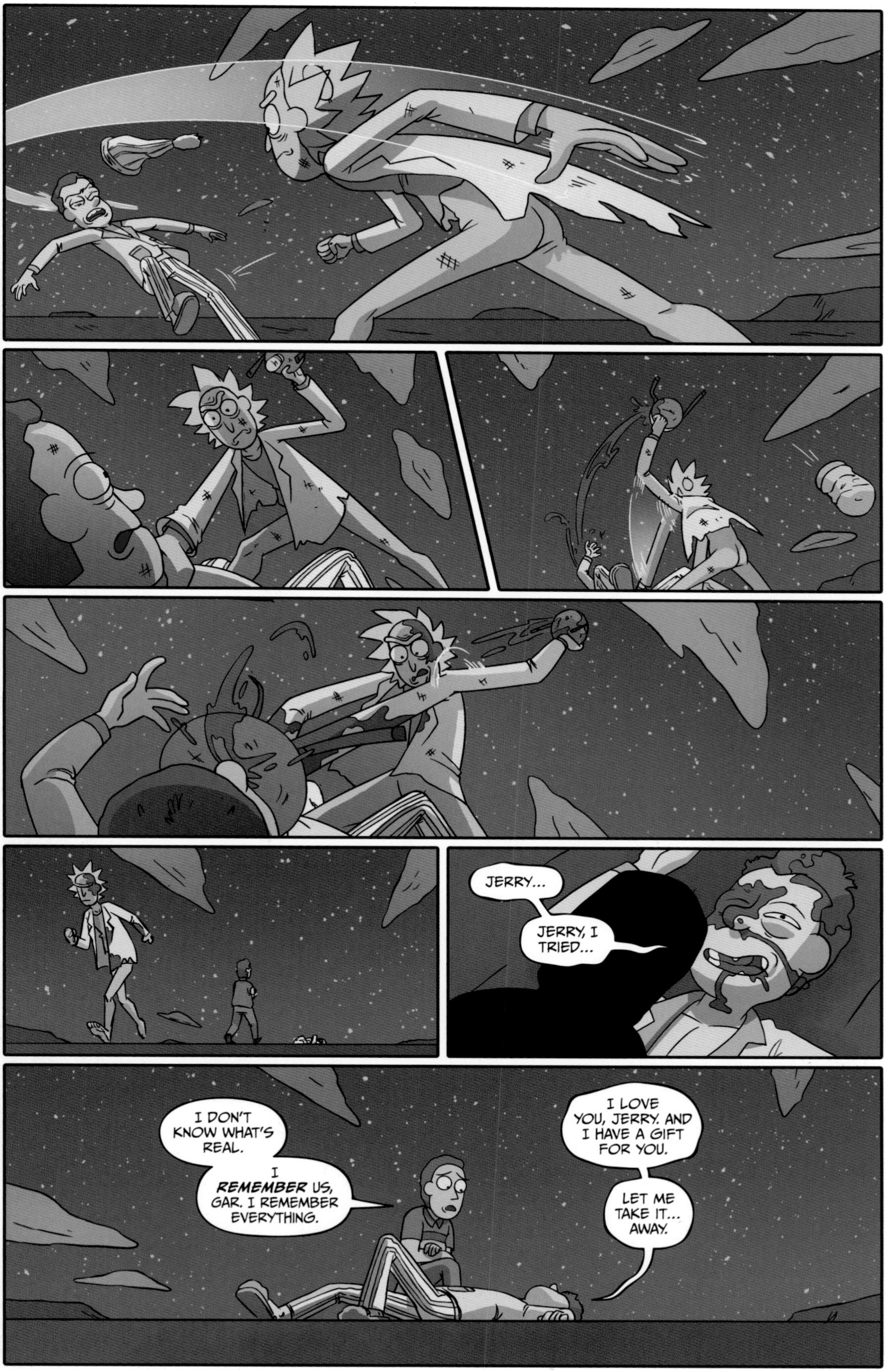

JERRY...
JERRY, I TRIED...
I DON'T KNOW WHAT'S REAL.
I **REMEMBER** US, GAR. I REMEMBER EVERYTHING.
I LOVE YOU, JERRY. AND I HAVE A GIFT FOR YOU.
LET ME TAKE IT... AWAY.

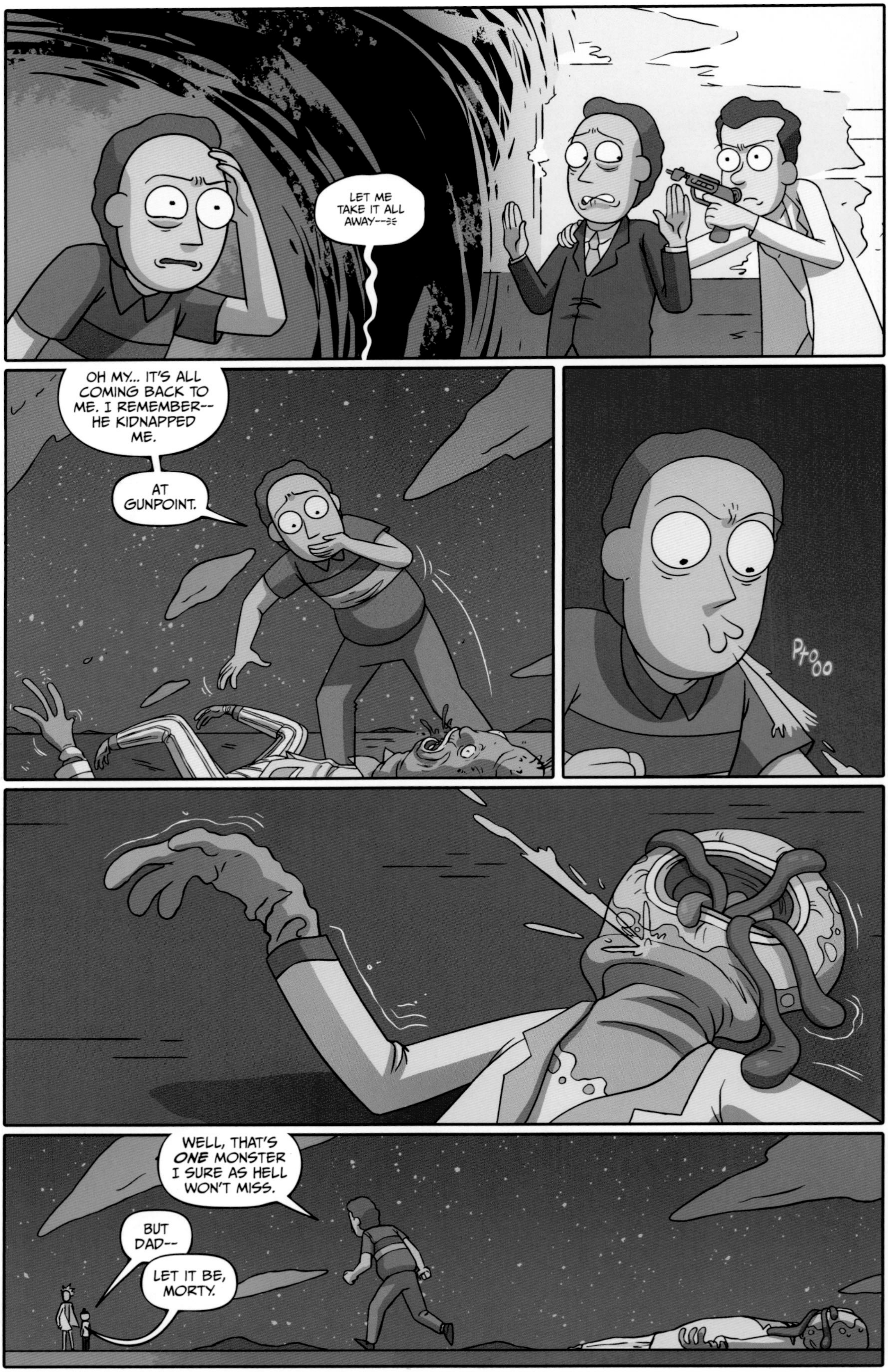
LET ME TAKE IT ALL AWAY--
OH MY... IT'S ALL COMING BACK TO ME. I REMEMBER-- HE KIDNAPPED ME.
AT GUNPOINT.
PTOOO
WELL, THAT'S *ONE* MONSTER I SURE AS HELL WON'T MISS.
BUT DAD--
LET IT BE, MORTY.

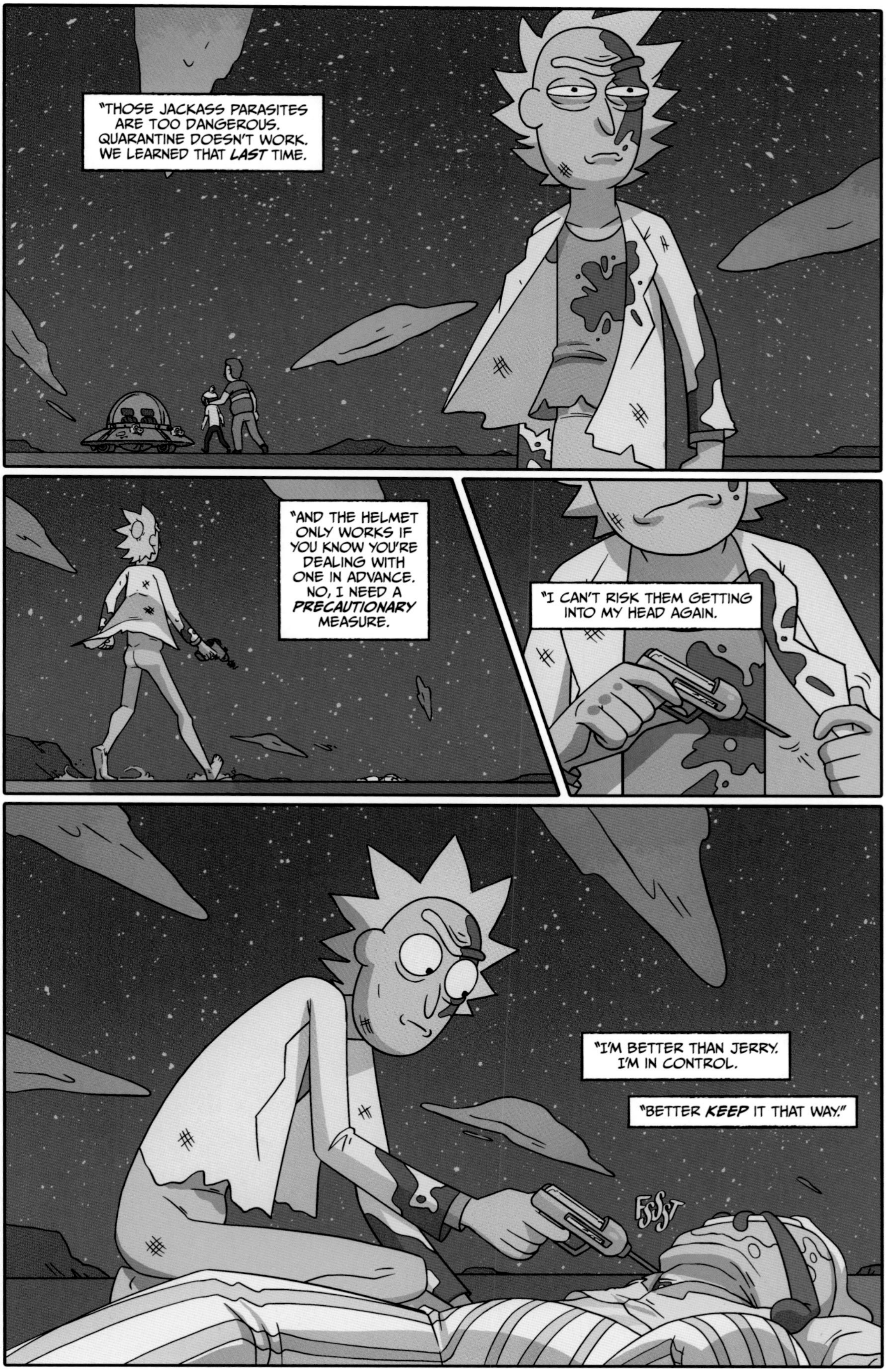
"THOSE JACKASS PARASITES ARE TOO DANGEROUS. QUARANTINE DOESN'T WORK. WE LEARNED THAT *LAST* TIME.
"AND THE HELMET ONLY WORKS IF YOU KNOW YOU'RE DEALING WITH ONE IN ADVANCE. NO, I NEED A *PRECAUTIONARY* MEASURE.
"I CAN'T RISK THEM GETTING INTO MY HEAD AGAIN.
"I'M BETTER THAN JERRY. I'M IN CONTROL.
"BETTER *KEEP* IT THAT WAY."
FSSST

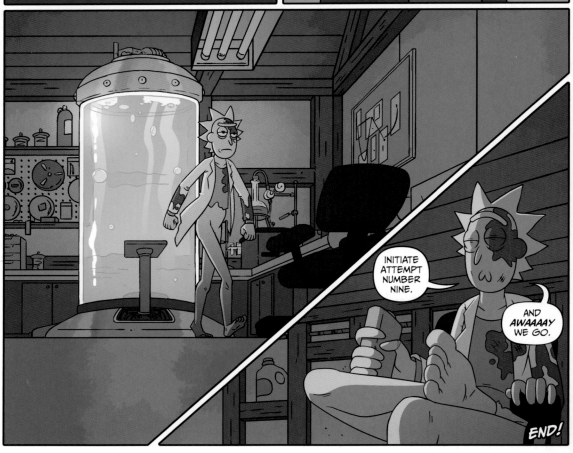

INITIATE ATTEMPT NUMBER NINE.

AND *AWAAAAY* WE GO.

END!

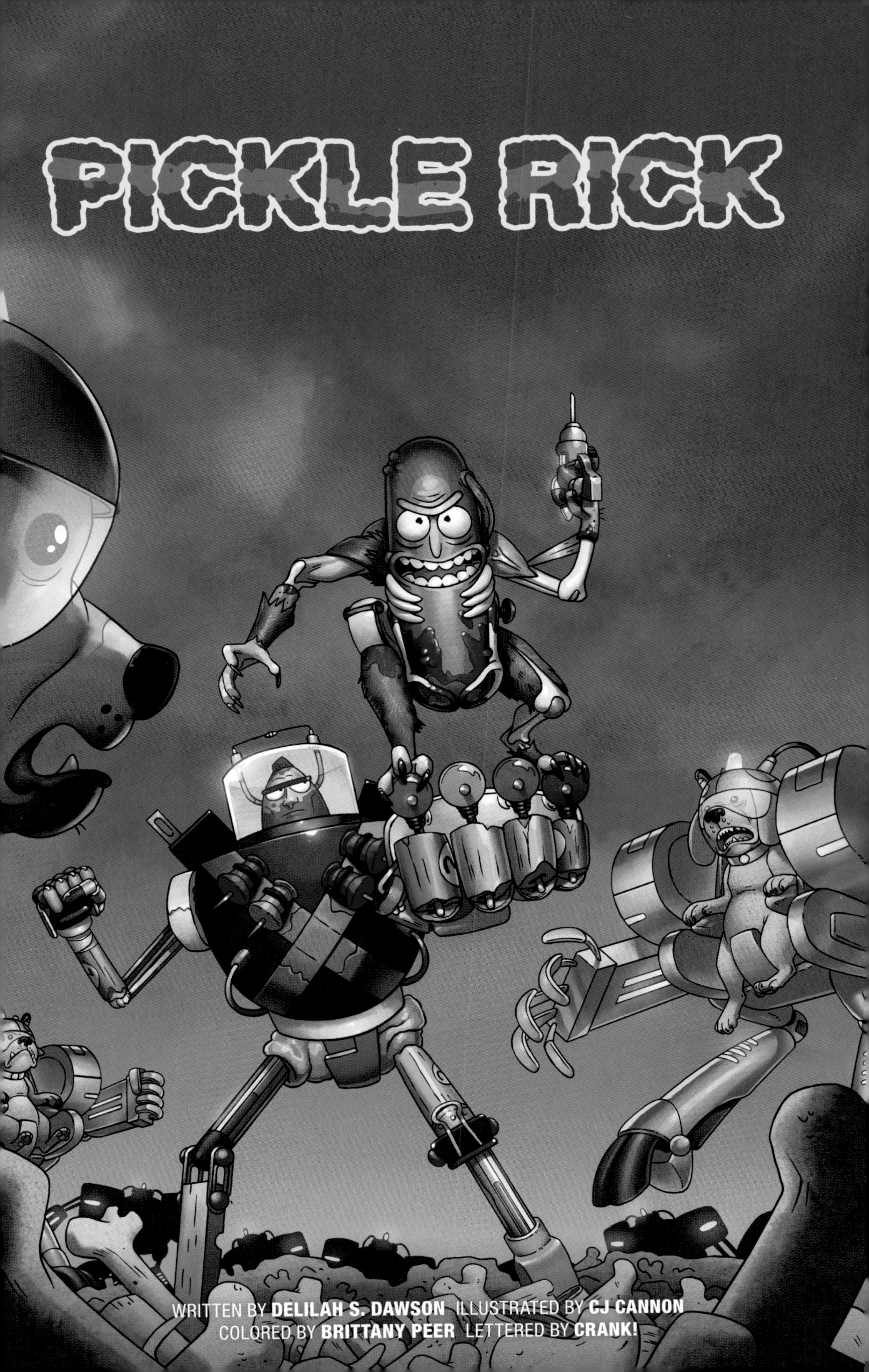
PICKLE RICK
WRITTEN BY DELILAH S. DAWSON ILLUSTRATED BY CJ CANNON
COLORED BY BRITTANY PEER LETTERED BY CRANK!

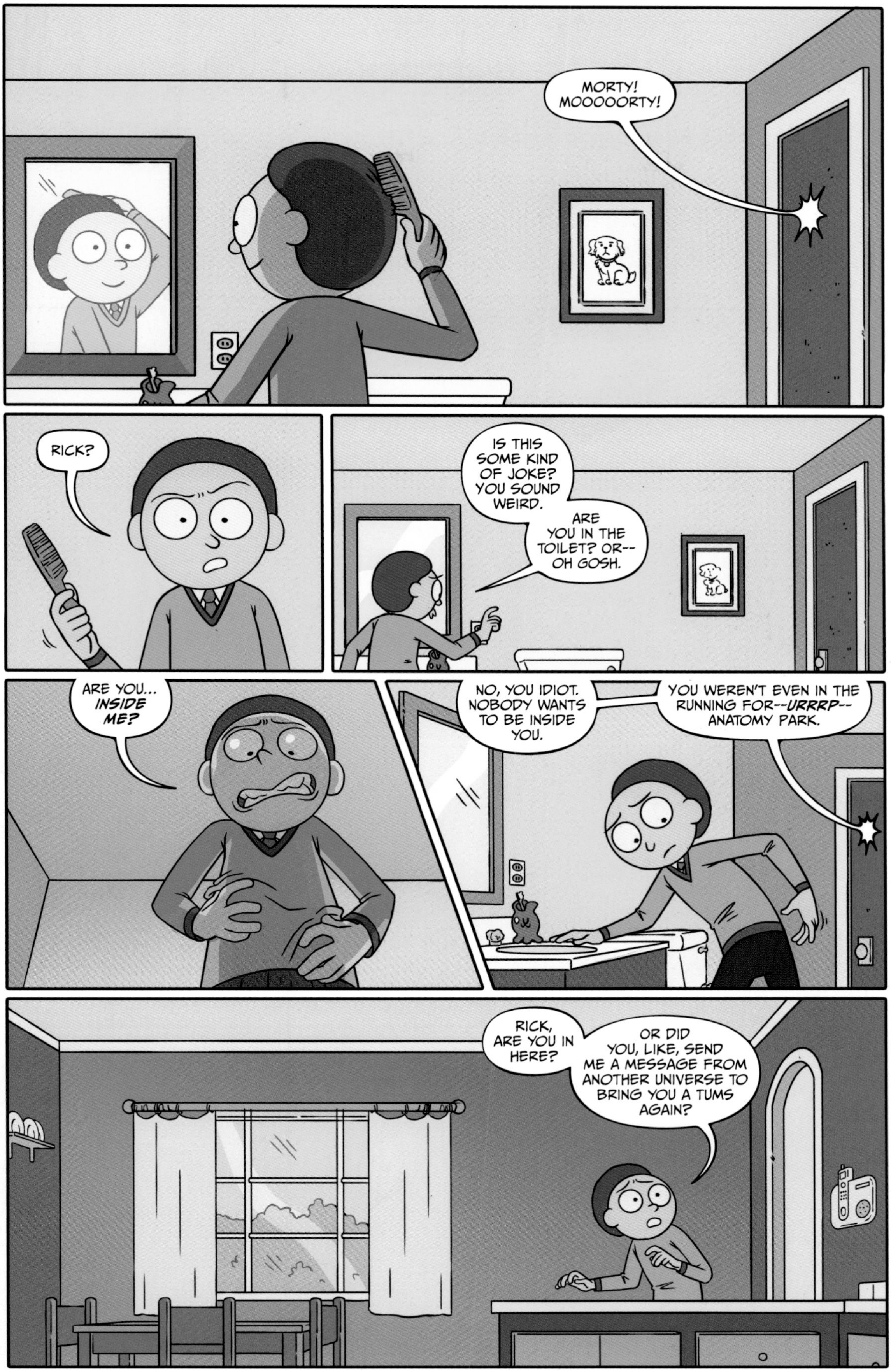
MORTY! MOOOOORTY!
RICK?
IS THIS SOME KIND OF JOKE? YOU SOUND WEIRD.
ARE YOU IN THE TOILET? OR-- OH GOSH.
ARE YOU... INSIDE ME?
NO, YOU IDIOT. NOBODY WANTS TO BE INSIDE YOU.
YOU WEREN'T EVEN IN THE RUNNING FOR--URRRP-- ANATOMY PARK.
RICK, ARE YOU IN HERE?
OR DID YOU, LIKE, SEND ME A MESSAGE FROM ANOTHER UNIVERSE TO BRING YOU A TUMS AGAIN?

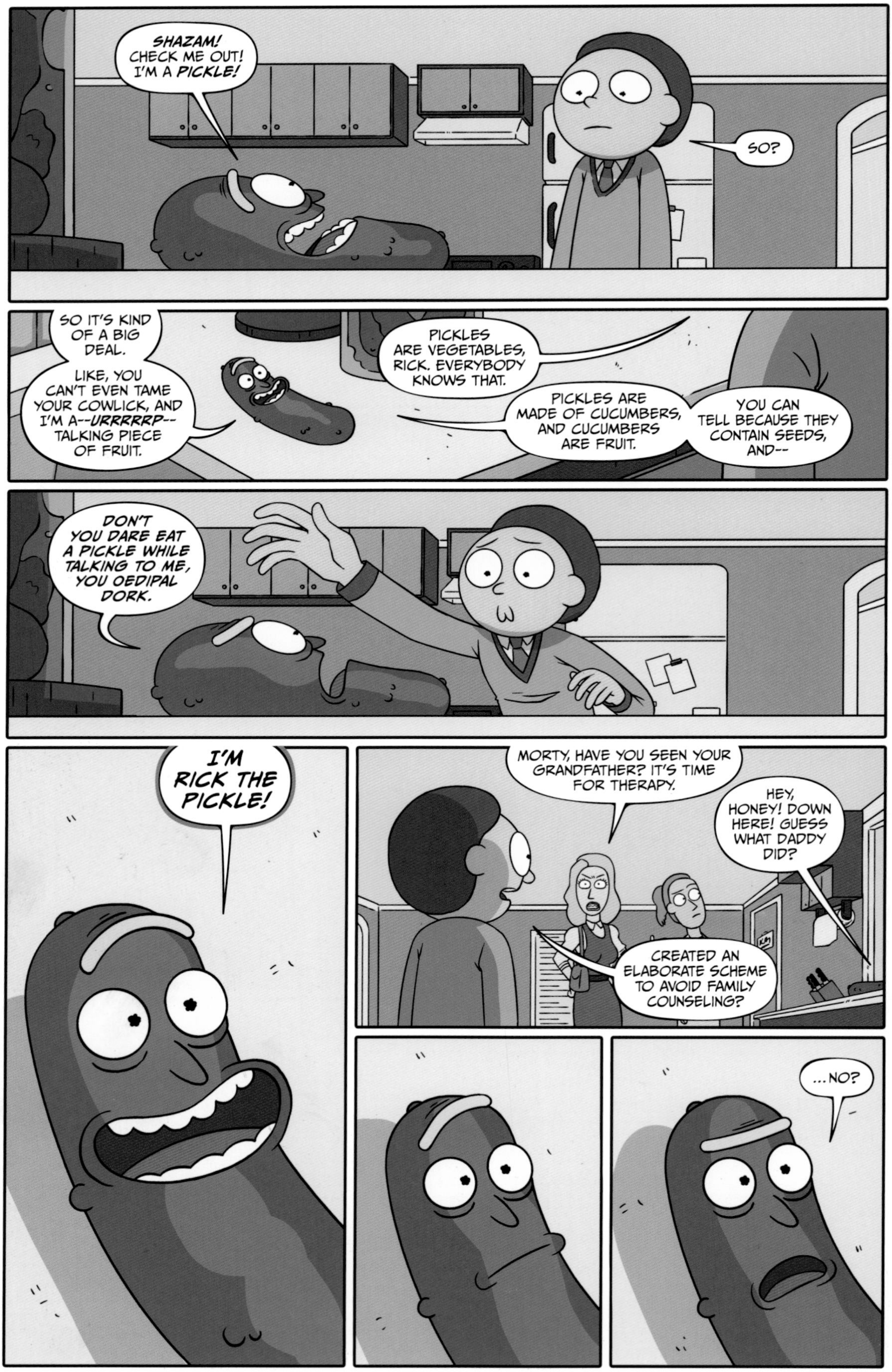
SHAZAM! CHECK ME OUT! I'M A PICKLE!
SO?
SO IT'S KIND OF A BIG DEAL.
LIKE, YOU CAN'T EVEN TAME YOUR COWLICK, AND I'M A--URRRRRP-- TALKING PIECE OF FRUIT.
PICKLES ARE VEGETABLES, RICK. EVERYBODY KNOWS THAT.
PICKLES ARE MADE OF CUCUMBERS, AND CUCUMBERS ARE FRUIT.
YOU CAN TELL BECAUSE THEY CONTAIN SEEDS, AND--
DON'T YOU DARE EAT A PICKLE WHILE TALKING TO ME, YOU OEDIPAL DORK.
I'M RICK THE PICKLE!
MORTY, HAVE YOU SEEN YOUR GRANDFATHER? IT'S TIME FOR THERAPY.
HEY, HONEY! DOWN HERE! GUESS WHAT DADDY DID?
CREATED AN ELABORATE SCHEME TO AVOID FAMILY COUNSELING?
...NO?

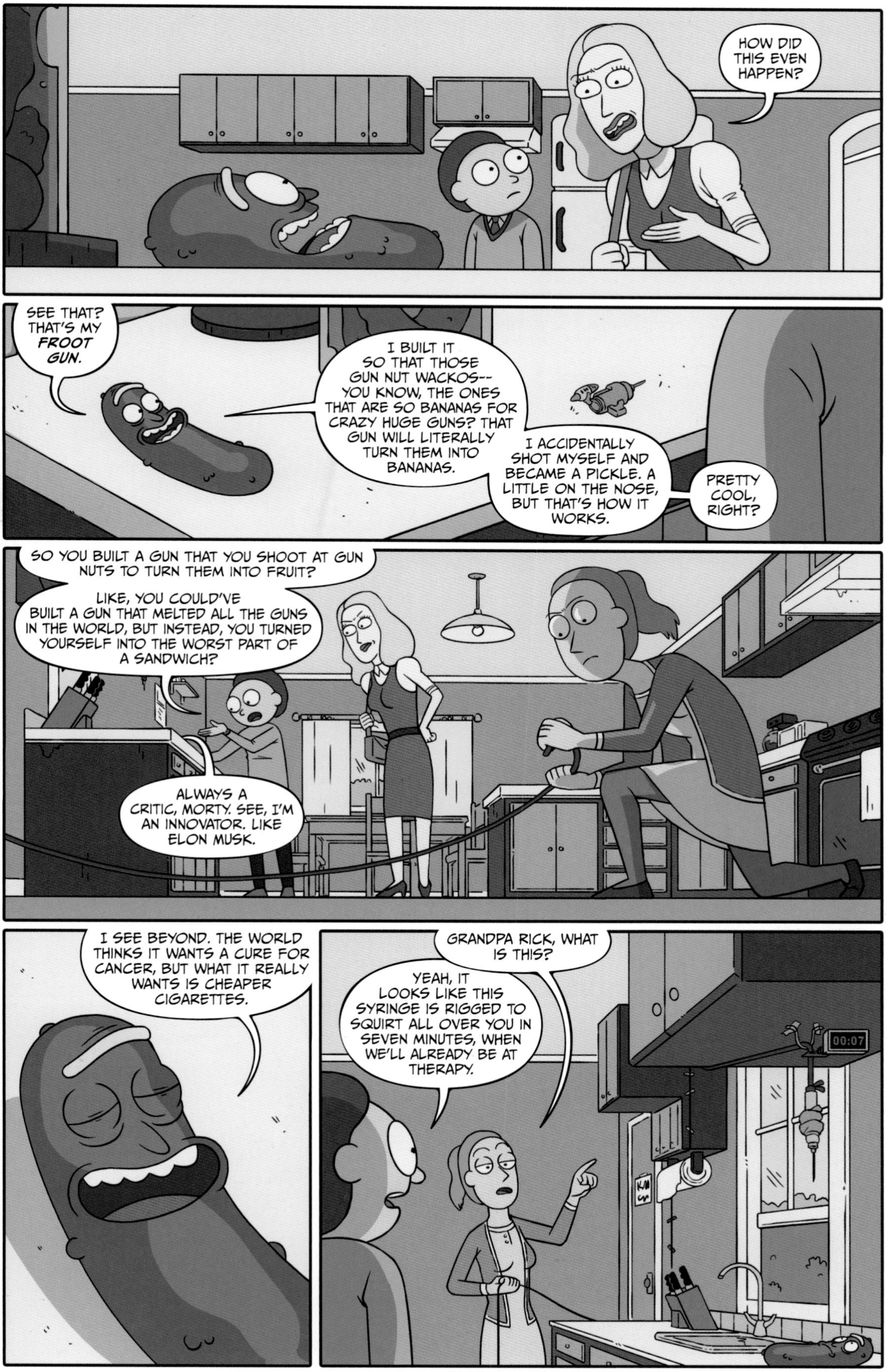
HOW DID THIS EVEN HAPPEN?
SEE THAT? THAT'S MY *FROOT GUN.*
I BUILT IT SO THAT THOSE GUN NUT WACKOS-- YOU KNOW, THE ONES THAT ARE SO BANANAS FOR CRAZY HUGE GUNS? THAT GUN WILL LITERALLY TURN THEM INTO BANANAS.
I ACCIDENTALLY SHOT MYSELF AND BECAME A PICKLE. A LITTLE ON THE NOSE, BUT THAT'S HOW IT WORKS.
PRETTY COOL, RIGHT?
SO YOU BUILT A GUN THAT YOU SHOOT AT GUN NUTS TO TURN THEM INTO FRUIT?
LIKE, YOU COULD'VE BUILT A GUN THAT MELTED ALL THE GUNS IN THE WORLD, BUT INSTEAD, YOU TURNED YOURSELF INTO THE WORST PART OF A SANDWICH?
ALWAYS A CRITIC, MORTY. SEE, I'M AN INNOVATOR. LIKE ELON MUSK.
I SEE BEYOND. THE WORLD THINKS IT WANTS A CURE FOR CANCER, BUT WHAT IT REALLY WANTS IS CHEAPER CIGARETTES.
GRANDPA RICK, WHAT IS THIS?
YEAH, IT LOOKS LIKE THIS SYRINGE IS RIGGED TO SQUIRT ALL OVER YOU IN SEVEN MINUTES, WHEN WE'LL ALREADY BE AT THERAPY.
00:07

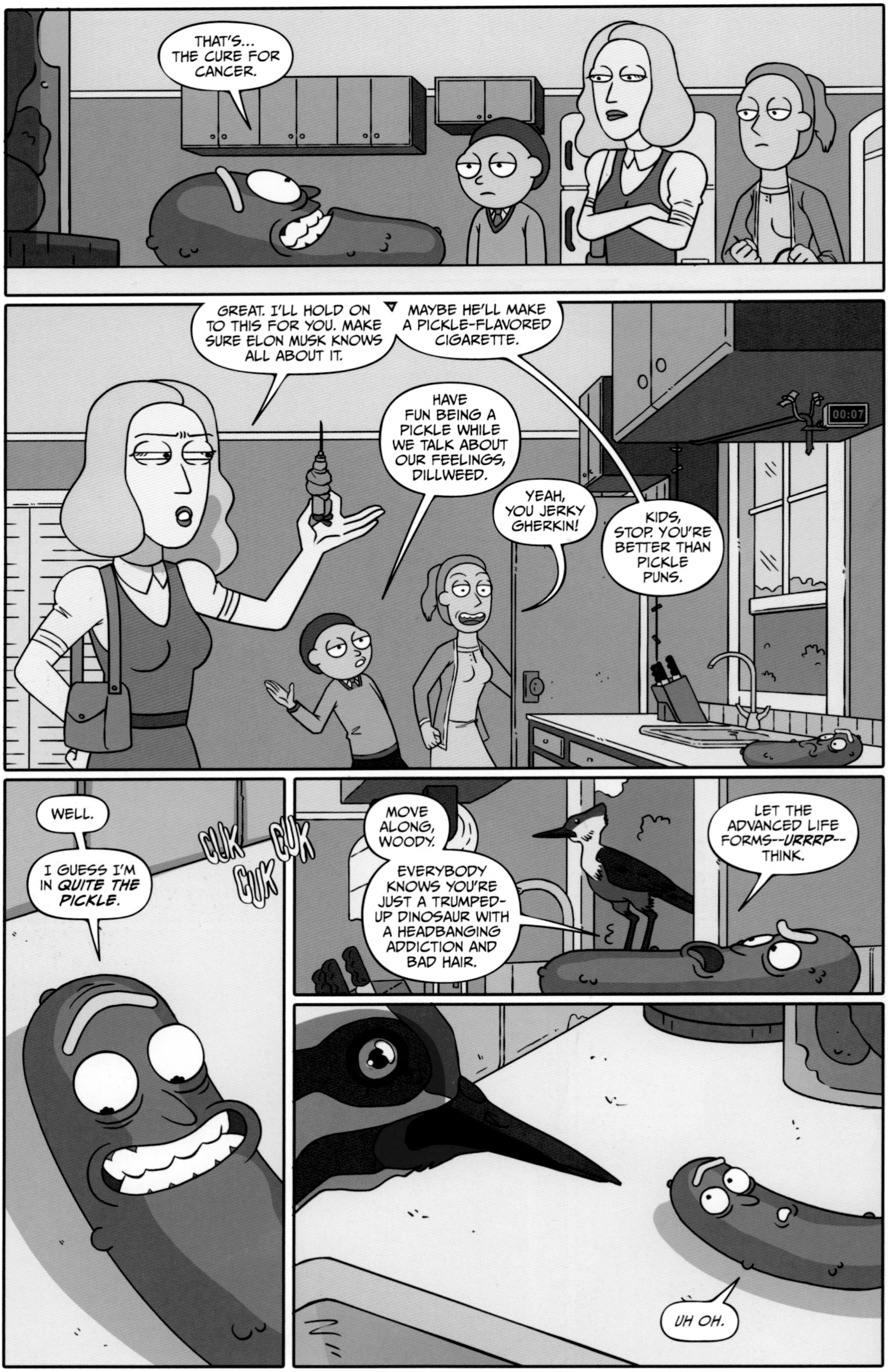
THAT'S... THE CURE FOR CANCER.
GREAT. I'LL HOLD ON TO THIS FOR YOU. MAKE SURE ELON MUSK KNOWS ALL ABOUT IT.
MAYBE HE'LL MAKE A PICKLE-FLAVORED CIGARETTE.
00:07
HAVE FUN BEING A PICKLE WHILE WE TALK ABOUT OUR FEELINGS, DILLWEED.
YEAH, YOU JERKY GHERKIN!
KIDS, STOP. YOU'RE BETTER THAN PICKLE PUNS.
WELL.
I GUESS I'M IN *QUITE THE PICKLE*.
CUK CUK CUK
MOVE ALONG, WOODY.
EVERYBODY KNOWS YOU'RE JUST A TRUMPED-UP DINOSAUR WITH A HEADBANGING ADDICTION AND BAD HAIR.
LET THE ADVANCED LIFE FORMS--*URRRP*--THINK.
UH OH.

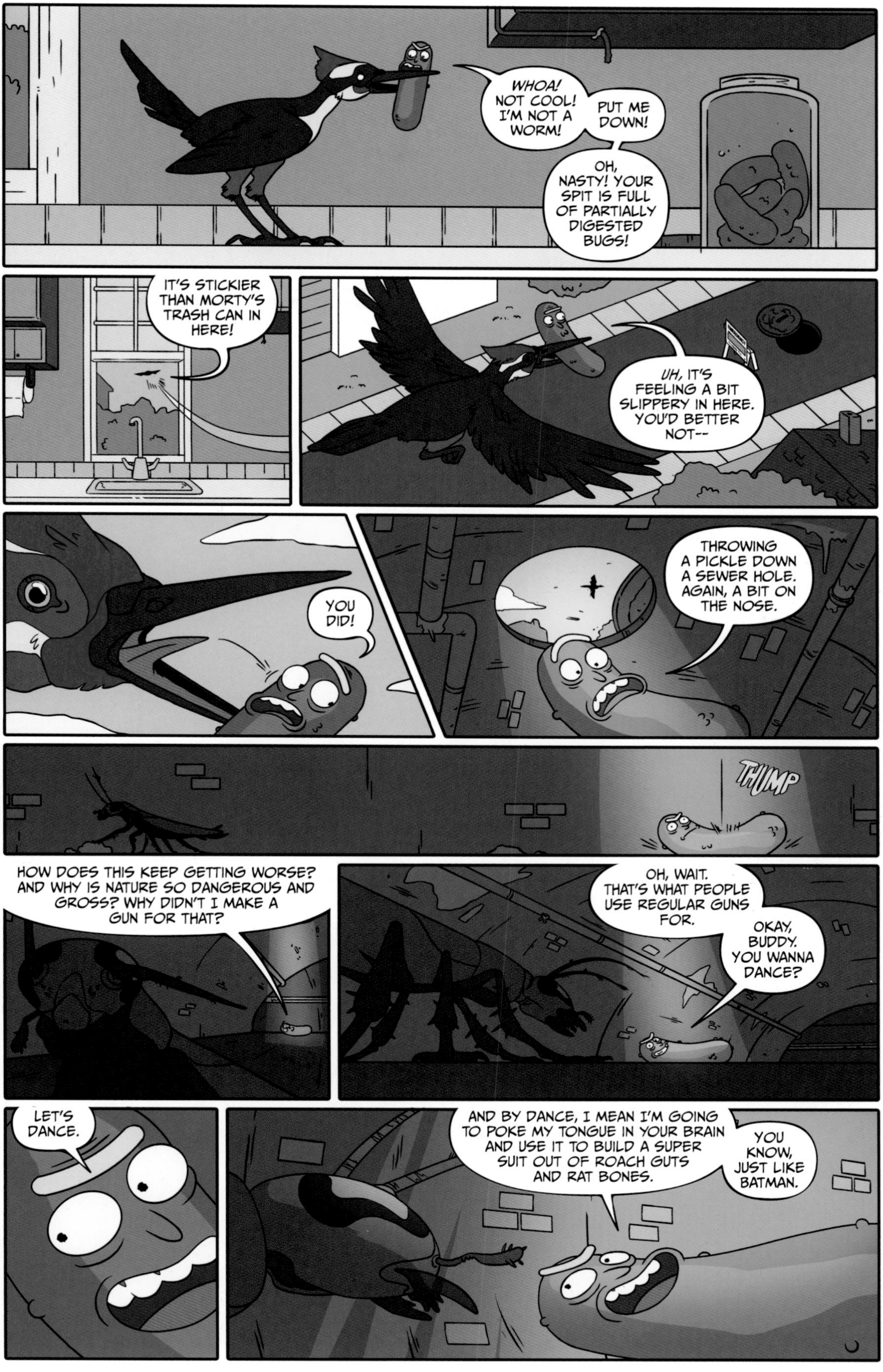

WHOA! NOT COOL! I'M NOT A WORM!
PUT ME DOWN!
OH, NASTY! YOUR SPIT IS FULL OF PARTIALLY DIGESTED BUGS!
IT'S STICKIER THAN MORTY'S TRASH CAN IN HERE!
UH, IT'S FEELING A BIT SLIPPERY IN HERE. YOU'D BETTER NOT--
YOU DID!
THROWING A PICKLE DOWN A SEWER HOLE. AGAIN, A BIT ON THE NOSE.
THUMP
HOW DOES THIS KEEP GETTING WORSE? AND WHY IS NATURE SO DANGEROUS AND GROSS? WHY DIDN'T I MAKE A GUN FOR THAT?
OH, WAIT. THAT'S WHAT PEOPLE USE REGULAR GUNS FOR.
OKAY, BUDDY. YOU WANNA DANCE?
LET'S DANCE.
AND BY DANCE, I MEAN I'M GOING TO POKE MY TONGUE IN YOUR BRAIN AND USE IT TO BUILD A SUPER SUIT OUT OF ROACH GUTS AND RAT BONES.
YOU KNOW, JUST LIKE BATMAN.

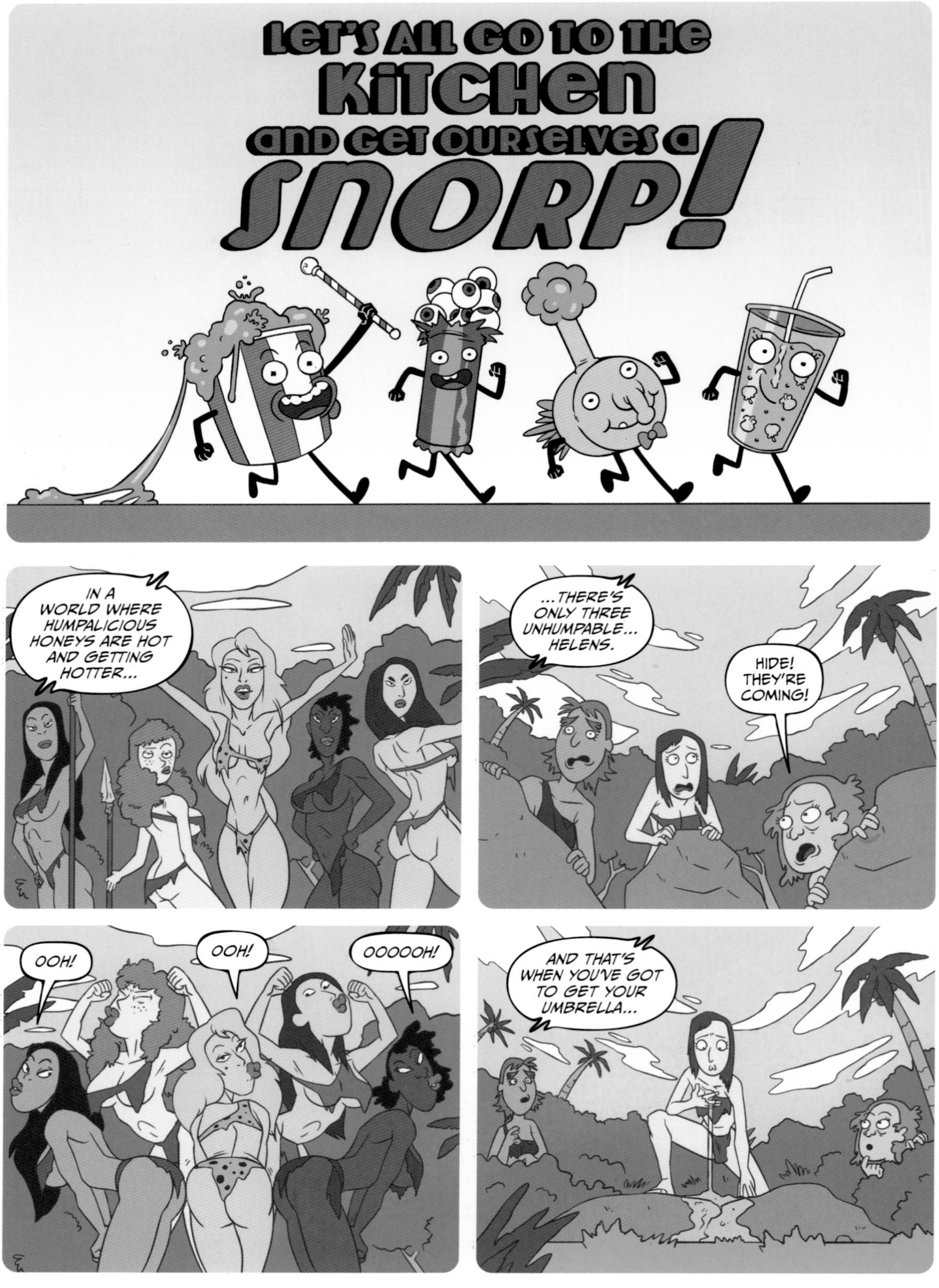
LET'S ALL GO TO THE
KITCHEN
AND GET OURSELVES A
SNORP!
IN A WORLD WHERE HUMPALICIOUS HONEYS ARE HOT AND GETTING HOTTER...
...THERE'S ONLY THREE UNHUMPABLE... HELENS.
HIDE! THEY'RE COMING!
OOH!
OOH!
OOOOOH!
AND THAT'S WHEN YOU'VE GOT TO GET YOUR UMBRELLA...

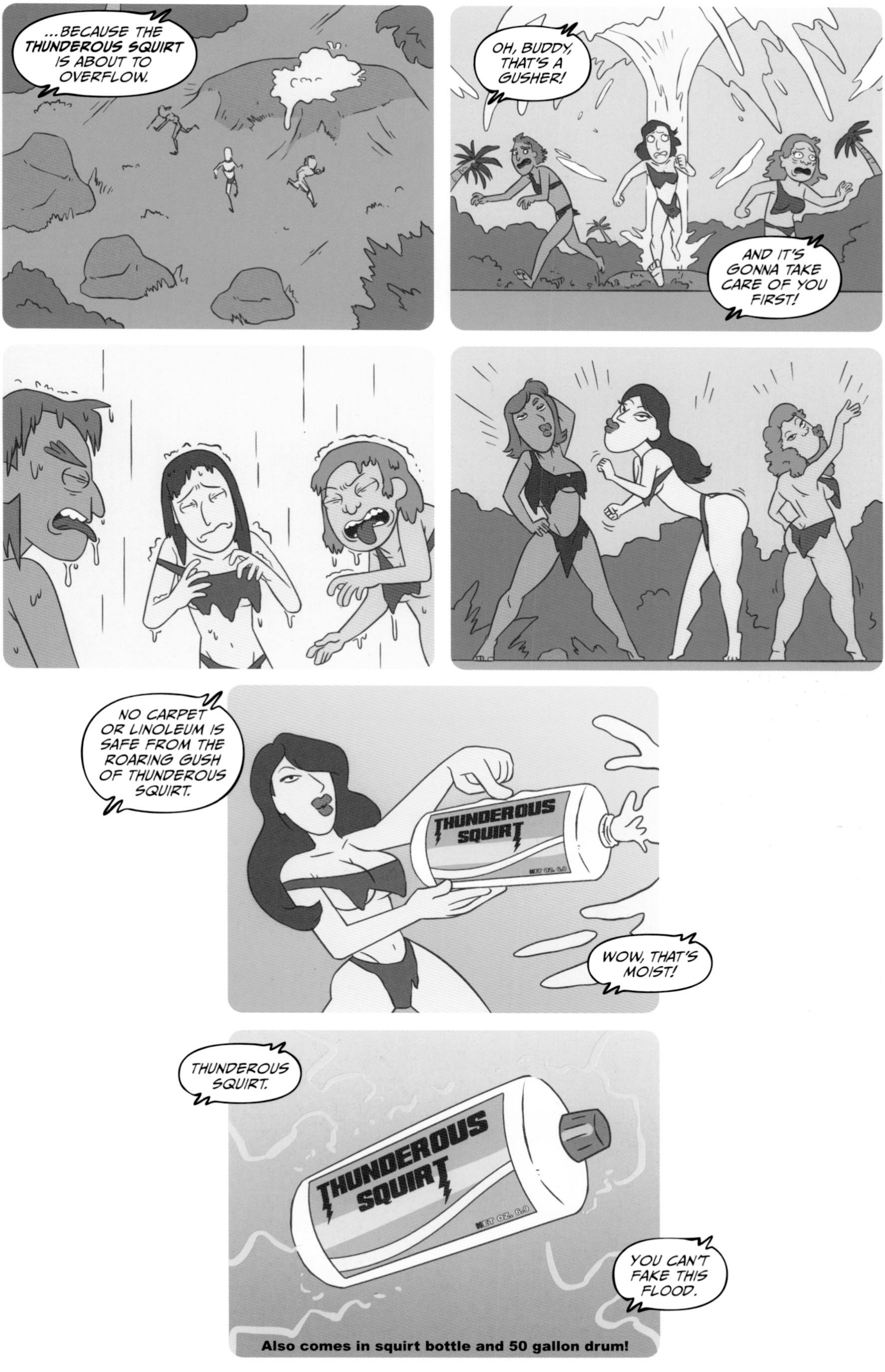
...BECAUSE THE **THUNDEROUS SQUIRT** IS ABOUT TO OVERFLOW.
OH, BUDDY, THAT'S A GUSHER!
AND IT'S GONNA TAKE CARE OF YOU FIRST!
NO CARPET OR LINOLEUM IS SAFE FROM THE ROARING GUSH OF THUNDEROUS SQUIRT.
THUNDEROUS SQUIRT
WOW, THAT'S MOIST!
THUNDEROUS SQUIRT.
THUNDEROUS SQUIRT
YOU CAN'T FAKE THIS FLOOD.
Also comes in squirt bottle and 50 gallon drum!

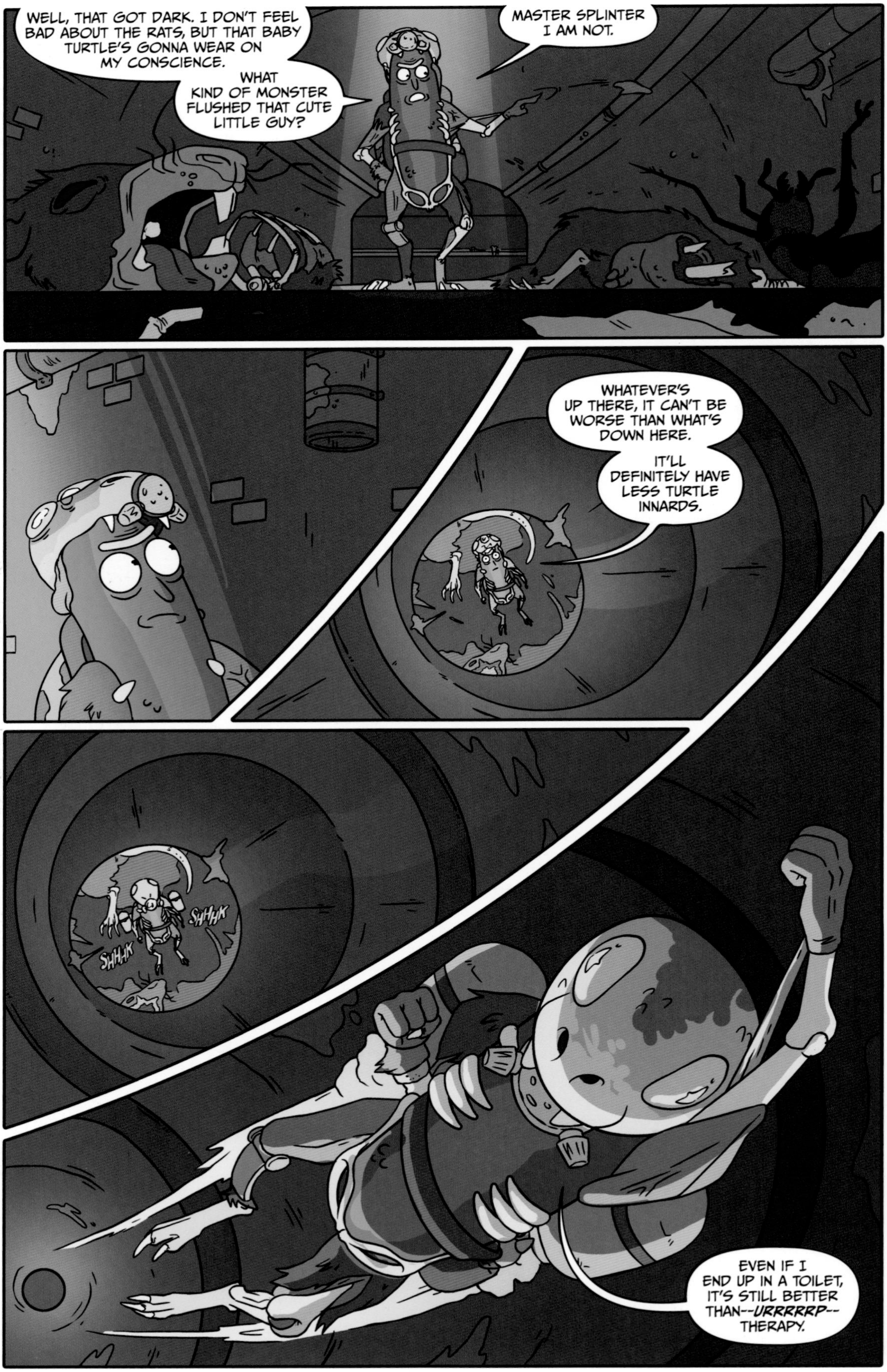
WELL, THAT GOT DARK. I DON'T FEEL BAD ABOUT THE RATS, BUT THAT BABY TURTLE'S GONNA WEAR ON MY CONSCIENCE.
WHAT KIND OF MONSTER FLUSHED THAT CUTE LITTLE GUY?
MASTER SPLINTER I AM NOT.
WHATEVER'S UP THERE, IT CAN'T BE WORSE THAN WHAT'S DOWN HERE.
IT'LL DEFINITELY HAVE LESS TURTLE INNARDS.
SHHHK
SHHHK
EVEN IF I END UP IN A TOILET, IT'S STILL BETTER THAN--URRRRRP-- THERAPY.

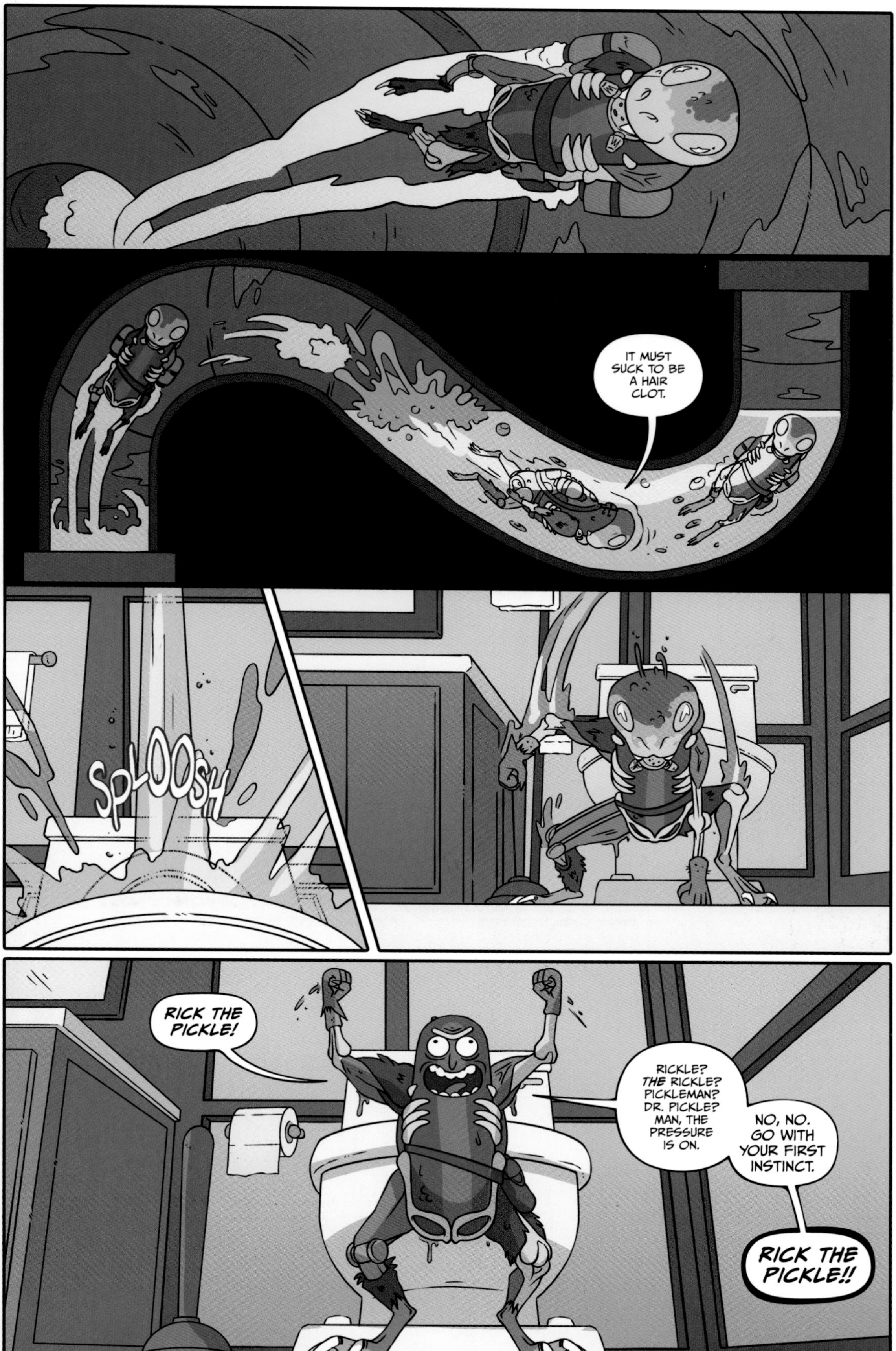
IT MUST SUCK TO BE A HAIR CLOT.
SPLOOSH
RICK THE PICKLE!
RICKLE? THE RICKLE? PICKLEMAN? DR. PICKLE? MAN, THE PRESSURE IS ON.
NO, NO. GO WITH YOUR FIRST INSTINCT.
RICK THE PICKLE!!

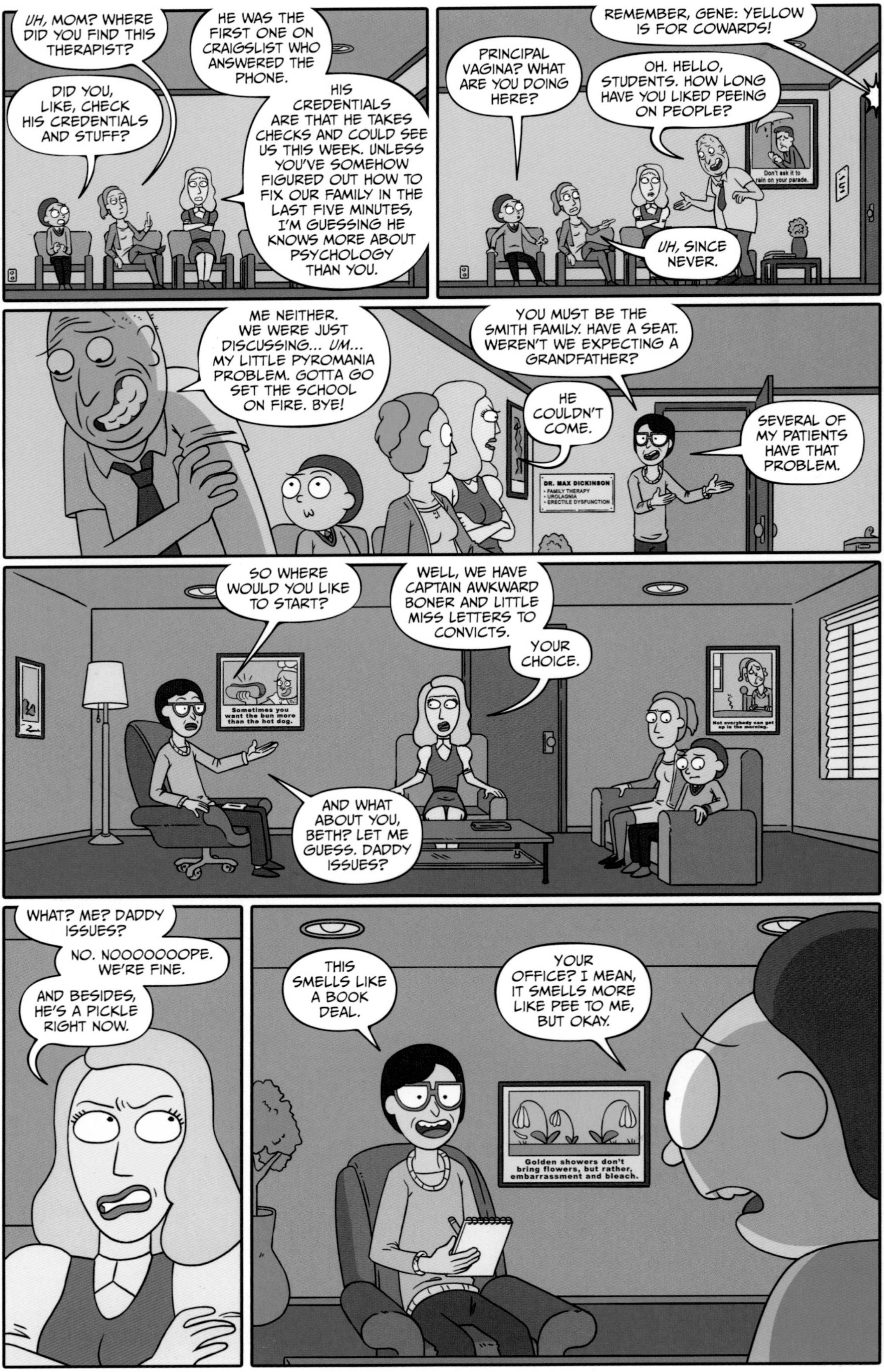
UH, MOM? WHERE DID YOU FIND THIS THERAPIST?
DID YOU, LIKE, CHECK HIS CREDENTIALS AND STUFF?
HE WAS THE FIRST ONE ON CRAIGSLIST WHO ANSWERED THE PHONE.
HIS CREDENTIALS ARE THAT HE TAKES CHECKS AND COULD SEE US THIS WEEK. UNLESS YOU'VE SOMEHOW FIGURED OUT HOW TO FIX OUR FAMILY IN THE LAST FIVE MINUTES, I'M GUESSING HE KNOWS MORE ABOUT PSYCHOLOGY THAN YOU.
REMEMBER, GENE: YELLOW IS FOR COWARDS!
PRINCIPAL VAGINA? WHAT ARE YOU DOING HERE?
OH. HELLO, STUDENTS. HOW LONG HAVE YOU LIKED PEEING ON PEOPLE?
Don't ask it to rain on your parade.
UH, SINCE NEVER.
ME NEITHER. WE WERE JUST DISCUSSING... UM... MY LITTLE PYROMANIA PROBLEM. GOTTA GO SET THE SCHOOL ON FIRE. BYE!
YOU MUST BE THE SMITH FAMILY. HAVE A SEAT. WEREN'T WE EXPECTING A GRANDFATHER?
HE COULDN'T COME.
DR. MAX DICKINSON
• FAMILY THERAPY
• UROLAGNIA
• ERECTILE DYSFUNCTION
SEVERAL OF MY PATIENTS HAVE THAT PROBLEM.
SO WHERE WOULD YOU LIKE TO START?
WELL, WE HAVE CAPTAIN AWKWARD BONER AND LITTLE MISS LETTERS TO CONVICTS.
YOUR CHOICE.
Sometimes you want the bun more than the hot dog.
Not everybody can get up in the morning.
AND WHAT ABOUT YOU, BETH? LET ME GUESS. DADDY ISSUES?
WHAT? ME? DADDY ISSUES?
NO. NOOOOOOOPE. WE'RE FINE.
AND BESIDES, HE'S A PICKLE RIGHT NOW.
THIS SMELLS LIKE A BOOK DEAL.
YOUR OFFICE? I MEAN, IT SMELLS MORE LIKE PEE TO ME, BUT OKAY.
Golden showers don't bring flowers, but rather, embarrassment and bleach.

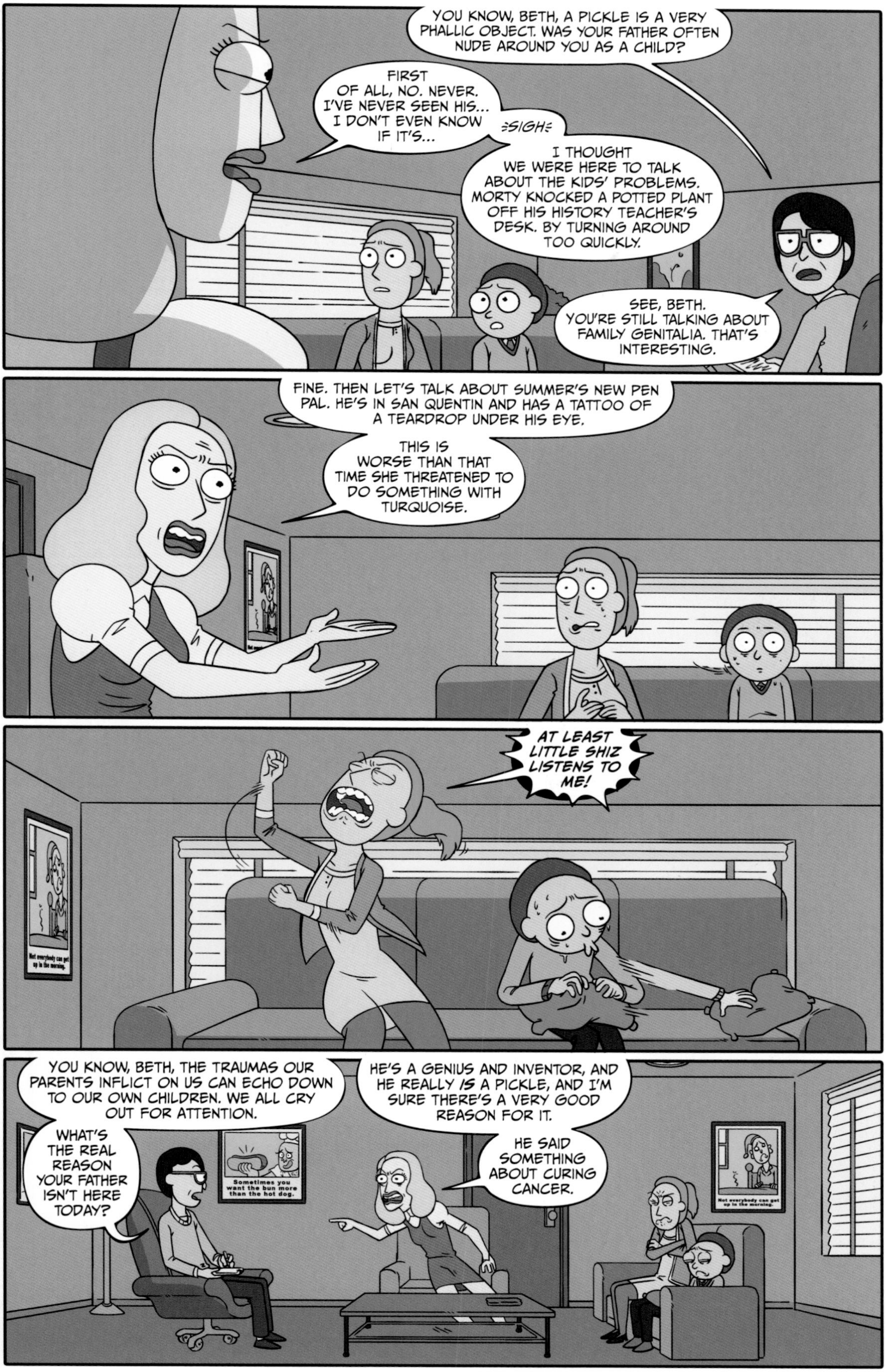
YOU KNOW, BETH, A PICKLE IS A VERY PHALLIC OBJECT. WAS YOUR FATHER OFTEN NUDE AROUND YOU AS A CHILD?
FIRST OF ALL, NO. NEVER. I'VE NEVER SEEN HIS... I DON'T EVEN KNOW IF IT'S...
SIGH
I THOUGHT WE WERE HERE TO TALK ABOUT THE KIDS' PROBLEMS. MORTY KNOCKED A POTTED PLANT OFF HIS HISTORY TEACHER'S DESK. BY TURNING AROUND TOO QUICKLY.
SEE, BETH. YOU'RE STILL TALKING ABOUT FAMILY GENITALIA. THAT'S INTERESTING.
FINE. THEN LET'S TALK ABOUT SUMMER'S NEW PEN PAL. HE'S IN SAN QUENTIN AND HAS A TATTOO OF A TEARDROP UNDER HIS EYE.
THIS IS WORSE THAN THAT TIME SHE THREATENED TO DO SOMETHING WITH TURQUOISE.
AT LEAST LITTLE SHIZ LISTENS TO ME!
Not everybody can get up in the morning.
YOU KNOW, BETH, THE TRAUMAS OUR PARENTS INFLICT ON US CAN ECHO DOWN TO OUR OWN CHILDREN. WE ALL CRY OUT FOR ATTENTION.
WHAT'S THE REAL REASON YOUR FATHER ISN'T HERE TODAY?
Sometimes you want the bun more than the hot dog.
HE'S A GENIUS AND INVENTOR, AND HE REALLY *IS* A PICKLE, AND I'M SURE THERE'S A VERY GOOD REASON FOR IT.
HE SAID SOMETHING ABOUT CURING CANCER.
Not everybody can get up in the morning.

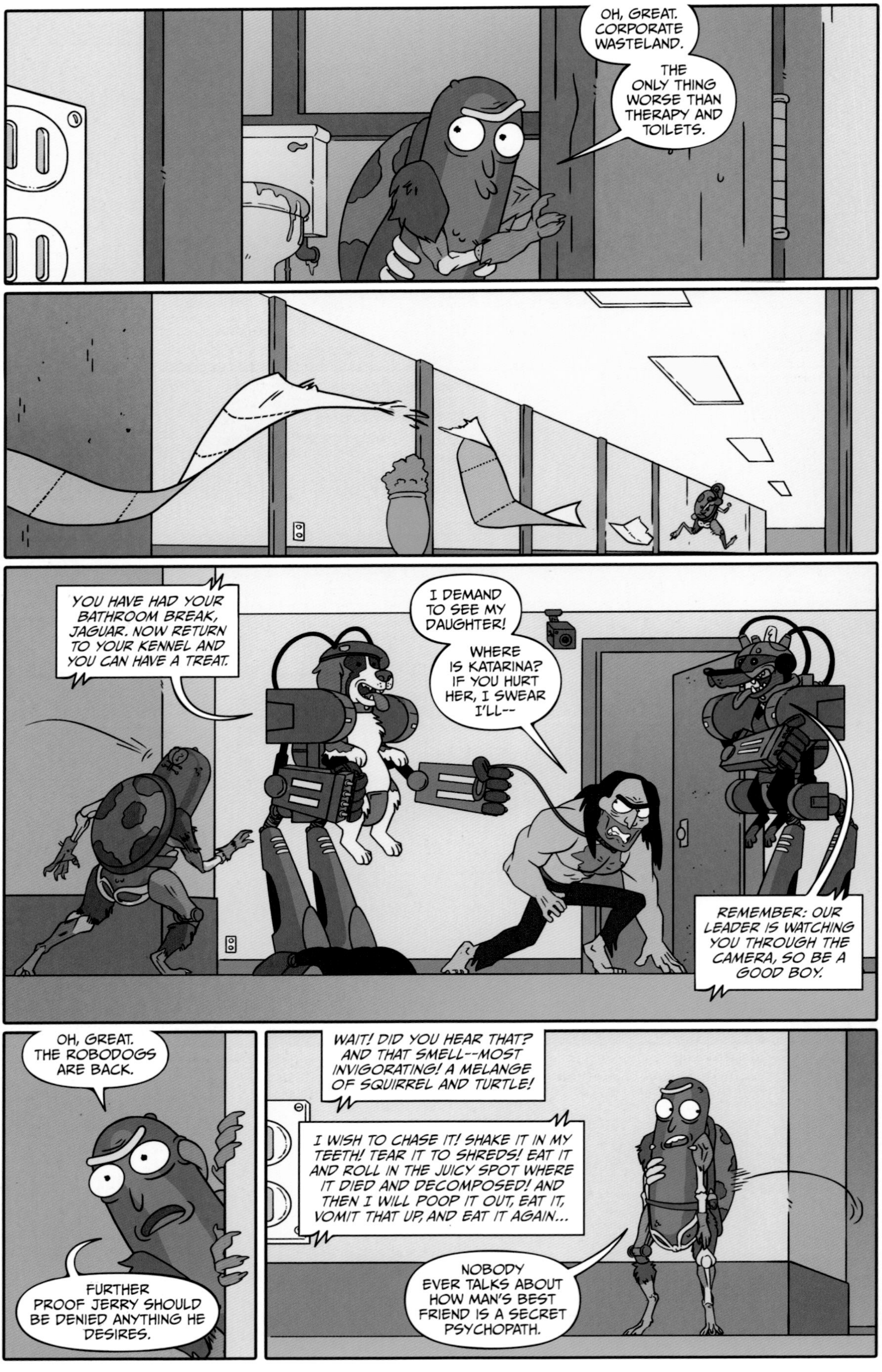
OH, GREAT. CORPORATE WASTELAND.
THE ONLY THING WORSE THAN THERAPY AND TOILETS.
YOU HAVE HAD YOUR BATHROOM BREAK, JAGUAR. NOW RETURN TO YOUR KENNEL AND YOU CAN HAVE A TREAT.
I DEMAND TO SEE MY DAUGHTER!
WHERE IS KATARINA? IF YOU HURT HER, I SWEAR I'LL--
REMEMBER: OUR LEADER IS WATCHING YOU THROUGH THE CAMERA, SO BE A GOOD BOY.
OH, GREAT. THE ROBODOGS ARE BACK.
FURTHER PROOF JERRY SHOULD BE DENIED ANYTHING HE DESIRES.
WAIT! DID YOU HEAR THAT? AND THAT SMELL--MOST INVIGORATING! A MELANGE OF SQUIRREL AND TURTLE!
I WISH TO CHASE IT! SHAKE IT IN MY TEETH! TEAR IT TO SHREDS! EAT IT AND ROLL IN THE JUICY SPOT WHERE IT DIED AND DECOMPOSED! AND THEN I WILL POOP IT OUT, EAT IT, VOMIT THAT UP, AND EAT IT AGAIN...
NOBODY EVER TALKS ABOUT HOW MAN'S BEST FRIEND IS A SECRET PSYCHOPATH.

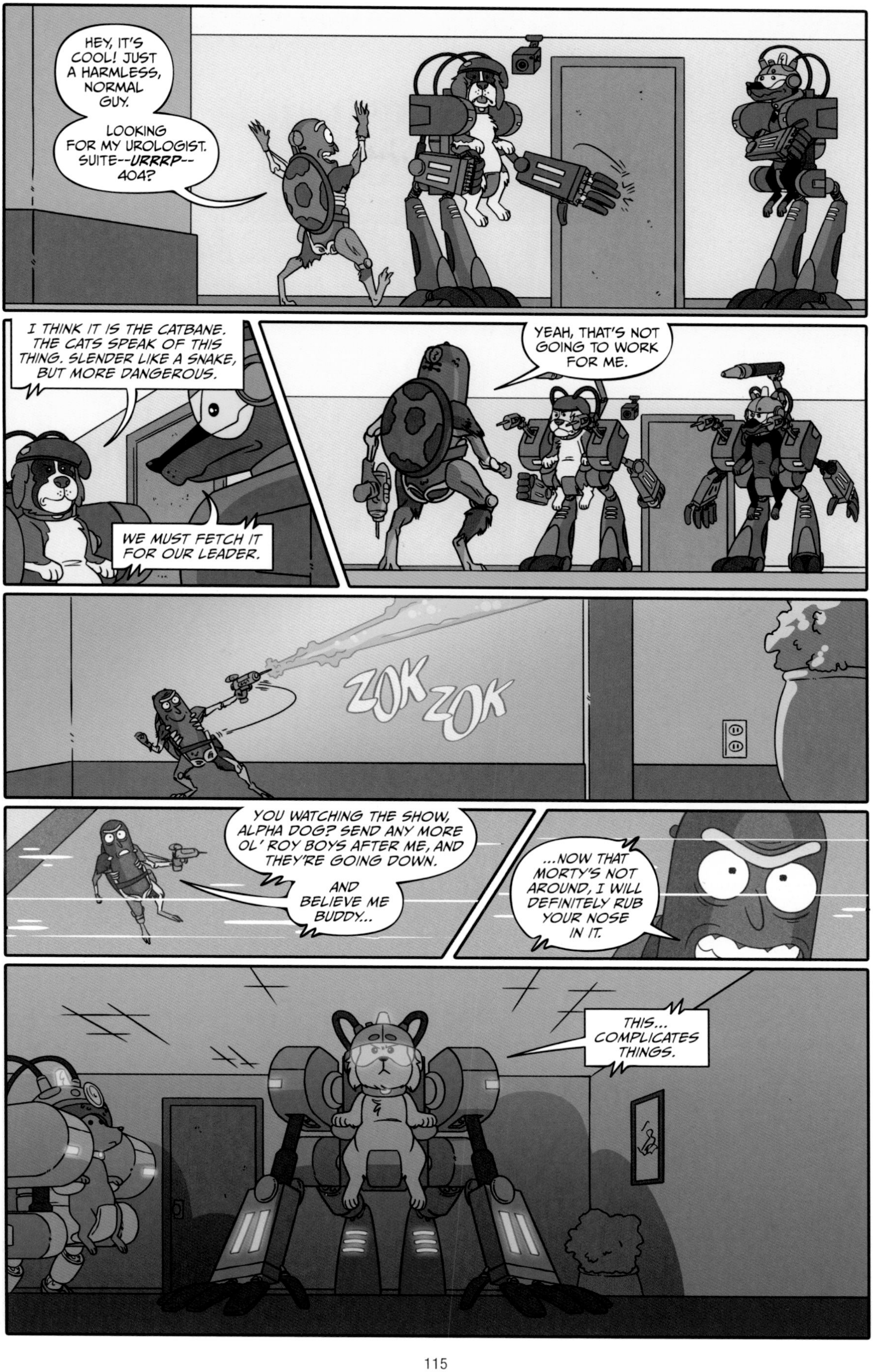
HEY, IT'S COOL! JUST A HARMLESS, NORMAL GUY.
LOOKING FOR MY UROLOGIST. SUITE--URRRP--404?
I THINK IT IS THE CATBANE. THE CATS SPEAK OF THIS THING. SLENDER LIKE A SNAKE, BUT MORE DANGEROUS.
WE MUST FETCH IT FOR OUR LEADER.
YEAH, THAT'S NOT GOING TO WORK FOR ME.
ZOK ZOK
YOU WATCHING THE SHOW, ALPHA DOG? SEND ANY MORE OL' ROY BOYS AFTER ME, AND THEY'RE GOING DOWN.
AND BELIEVE ME BUDDY...
...NOW THAT MORTY'S NOT AROUND, I WILL DEFINITELY RUB YOUR NOSE IN IT.
THIS... COMPLICATES THINGS.

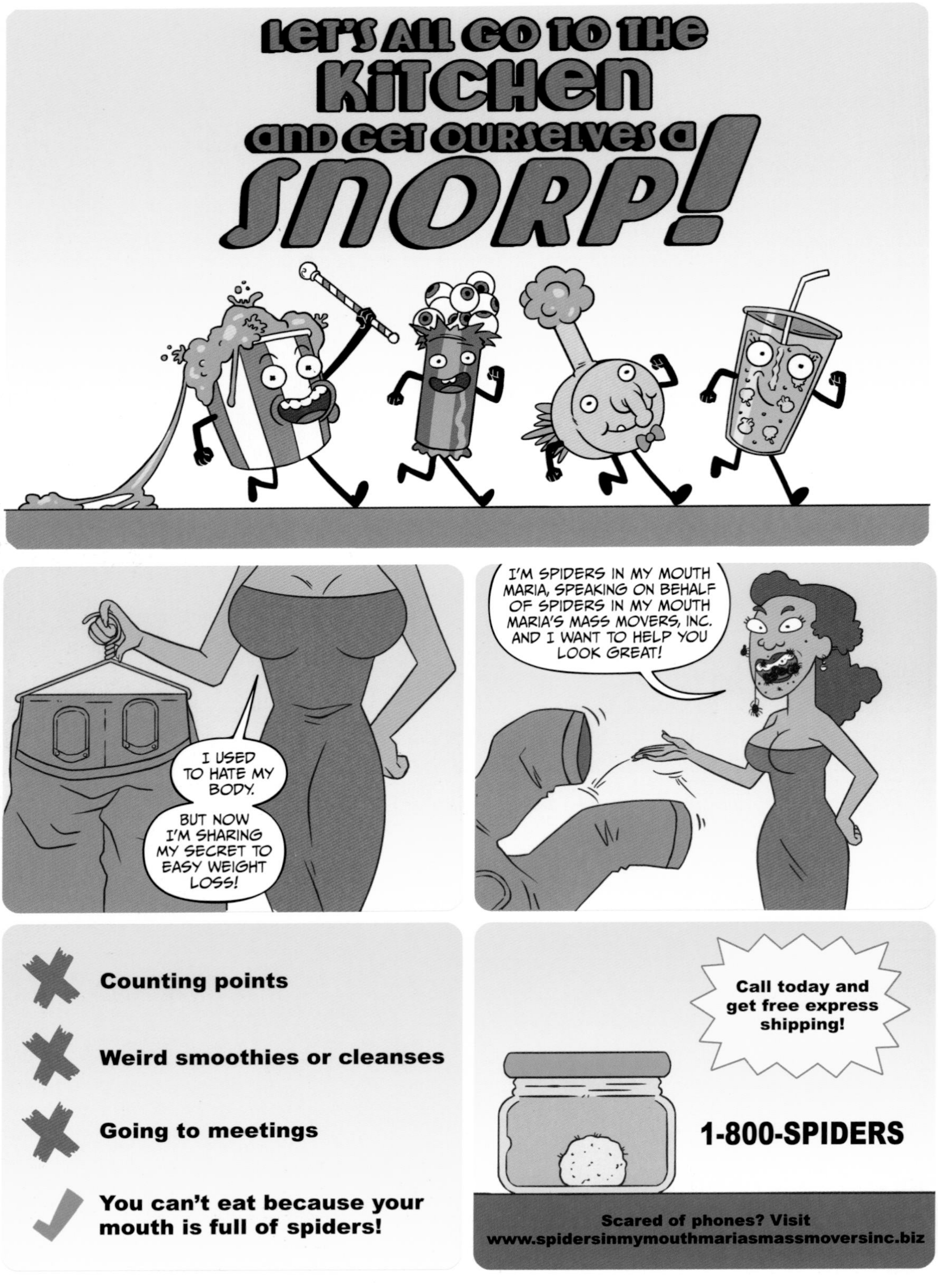

LET'S ALL GO TO THE KITCHEN AND GET OURSELVES A SNORP!
I USED TO HATE MY BODY.
BUT NOW I'M SHARING MY SECRET TO EASY WEIGHT LOSS!
I'M SPIDERS IN MY MOUTH MARIA, SPEAKING ON BEHALF OF SPIDERS IN MY MOUTH MARIA'S MASS MOVERS, INC. AND I WANT TO HELP YOU LOOK GREAT!
Counting points
Weird smoothies or cleanses
Going to meetings
You can't eat because your mouth is full of spiders!
Call today and get free express shipping!
1-800-SPIDERS
Scared of phones? Visit www.spidersinmymouthmariasmassmoversinc.biz

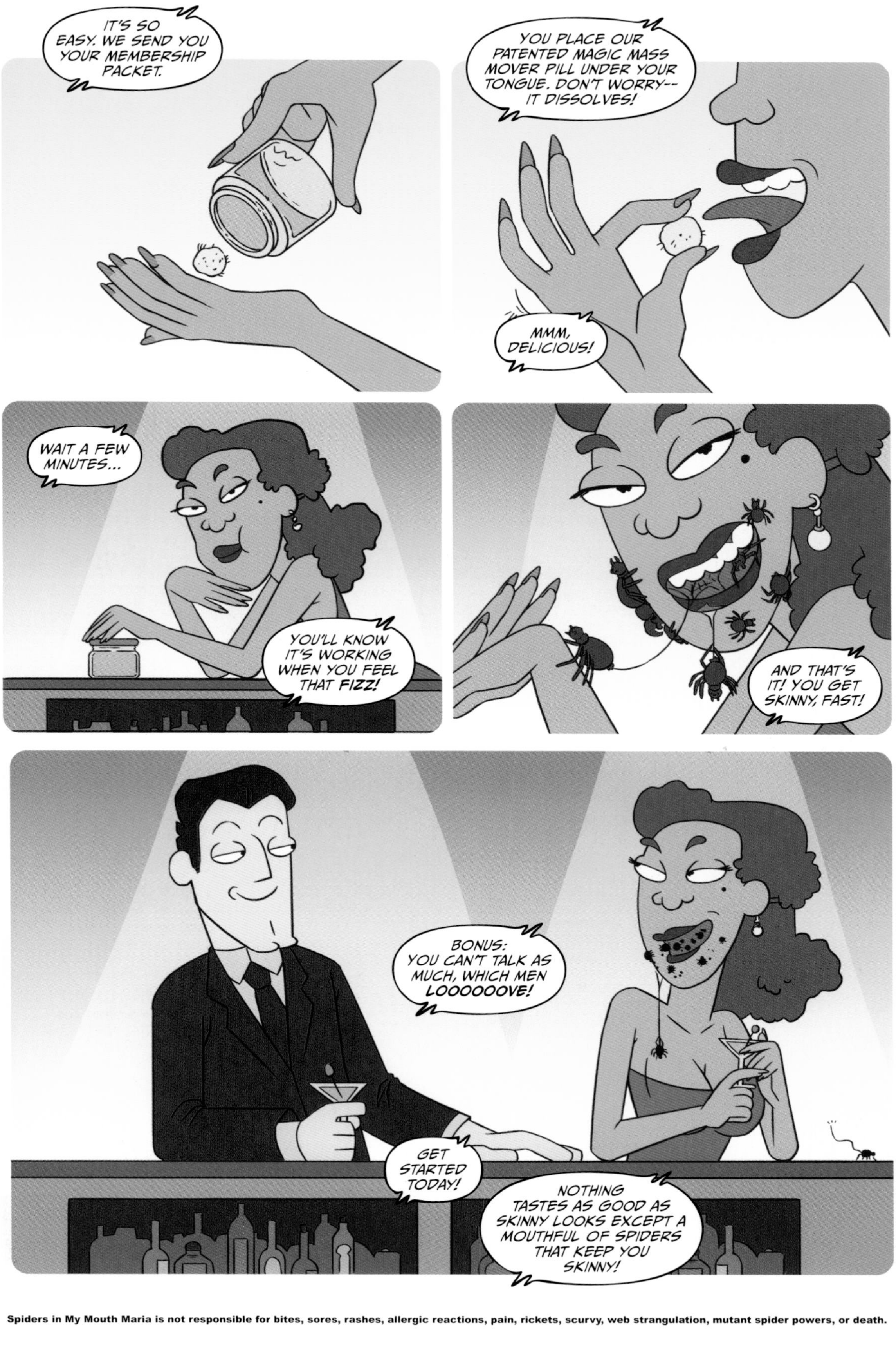
IT'S SO EASY. WE SEND YOU YOUR MEMBERSHIP PACKET.
YOU PLACE OUR PATENTED MAGIC MASS MOVER PILL UNDER YOUR TONGUE. DON'T WORRY-- IT DISSOLVES!
MMM, DELICIOUS!
WAIT A FEW MINUTES...
YOU'LL KNOW IT'S WORKING WHEN YOU FEEL THAT FIZZ!
AND THAT'S IT! YOU GET SKINNY, FAST!
BONUS: YOU CAN'T TALK AS MUCH, WHICH MEN LOOOOOOVE!
GET STARTED TODAY!
NOTHING TASTES AS GOOD AS SKINNY LOOKS EXCEPT A MOUTHFUL OF SPIDERS THAT KEEP YOU SKINNY!

Spiders in My Mouth Maria is not responsible for bites, sores, rashes, allergic reactions, pain, rickets, scurvy, web strangulation, mutant spider powers, or death.

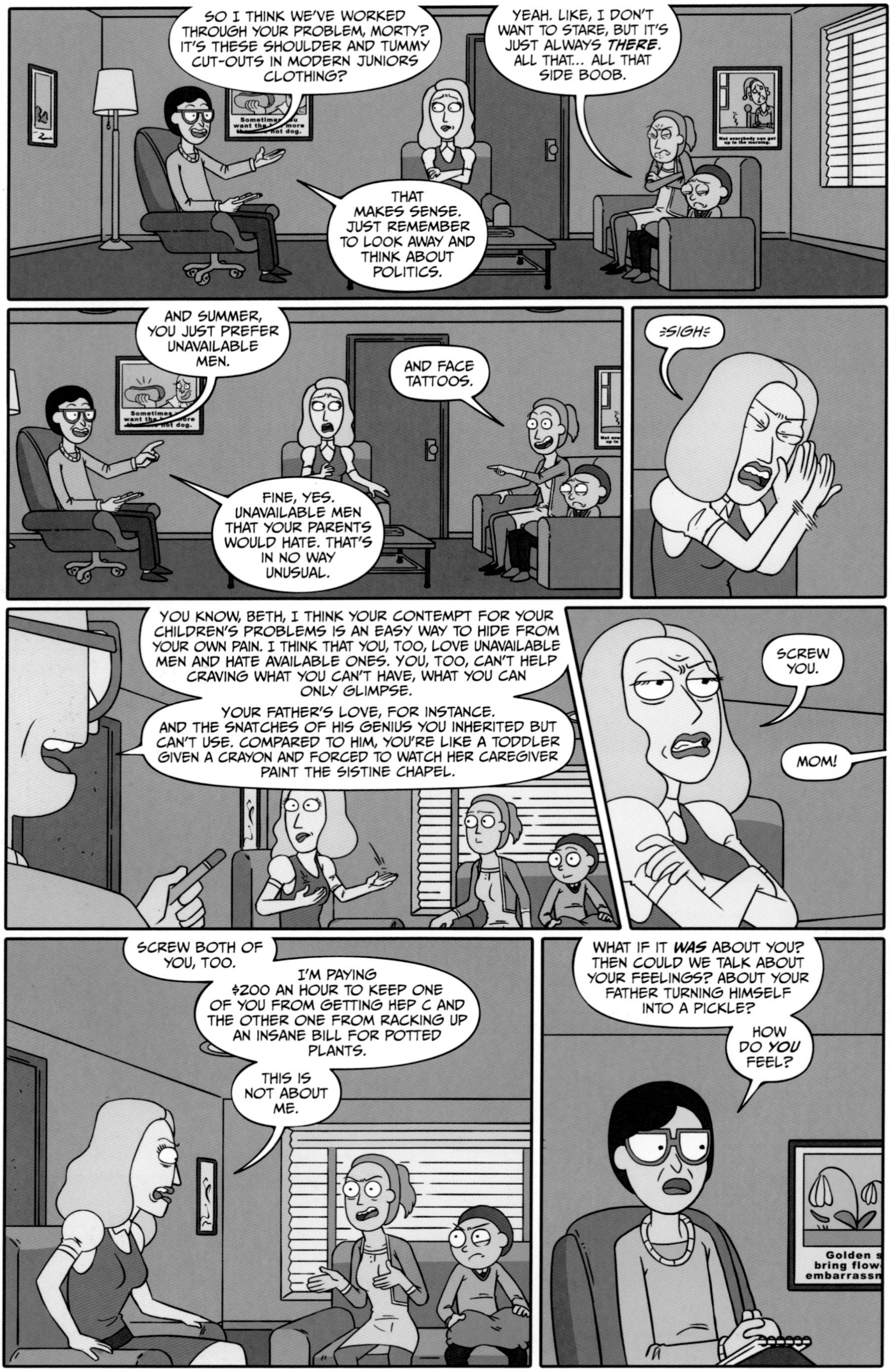
SO I THINK WE'VE WORKED THROUGH YOUR PROBLEM, MORTY? IT'S THESE SHOULDER AND TUMMY CUT-OUTS IN MODERN JUNIORS CLOTHING?
YEAH. LIKE, I DON'T WANT TO STARE, BUT IT'S JUST ALWAYS *THERE*. ALL THAT... ALL THAT SIDE BOOB.
Not everybody can get up in the morning.
THAT MAKES SENSE. JUST REMEMBER TO LOOK AWAY AND THINK ABOUT POLITICS.
AND SUMMER, YOU JUST PREFER UNAVAILABLE MEN.
AND FACE TATTOOS.
FINE, YES. UNAVAILABLE MEN THAT YOUR PARENTS WOULD HATE. THAT'S IN NO WAY UNUSUAL.
SIGH
YOU KNOW, BETH, I THINK YOUR CONTEMPT FOR YOUR CHILDREN'S PROBLEMS IS AN EASY WAY TO HIDE FROM YOUR OWN PAIN. I THINK THAT YOU, TOO, LOVE UNAVAILABLE MEN AND HATE AVAILABLE ONES. YOU, TOO, CAN'T HELP CRAVING WHAT YOU CAN'T HAVE, WHAT YOU CAN ONLY GLIMPSE.
YOUR FATHER'S LOVE, FOR INSTANCE. AND THE SNATCHES OF HIS GENIUS YOU INHERITED BUT CAN'T USE. COMPARED TO HIM, YOU'RE LIKE A TODDLER GIVEN A CRAYON AND FORCED TO WATCH HER CAREGIVER PAINT THE SISTINE CHAPEL.
SCREW YOU.
MOM!
SCREW BOTH OF YOU, TOO.
I'M PAYING $200 AN HOUR TO KEEP ONE OF YOU FROM GETTING HEP C AND THE OTHER ONE FROM RACKING UP AN INSANE BILL FOR POTTED PLANTS.
THIS IS NOT ABOUT ME.
WHAT IF IT *WAS* ABOUT YOU? THEN COULD WE TALK ABOUT YOUR FEELINGS? ABOUT YOUR FATHER TURNING HIMSELF INTO A PICKLE?
HOW DO *YOU* FEEL?

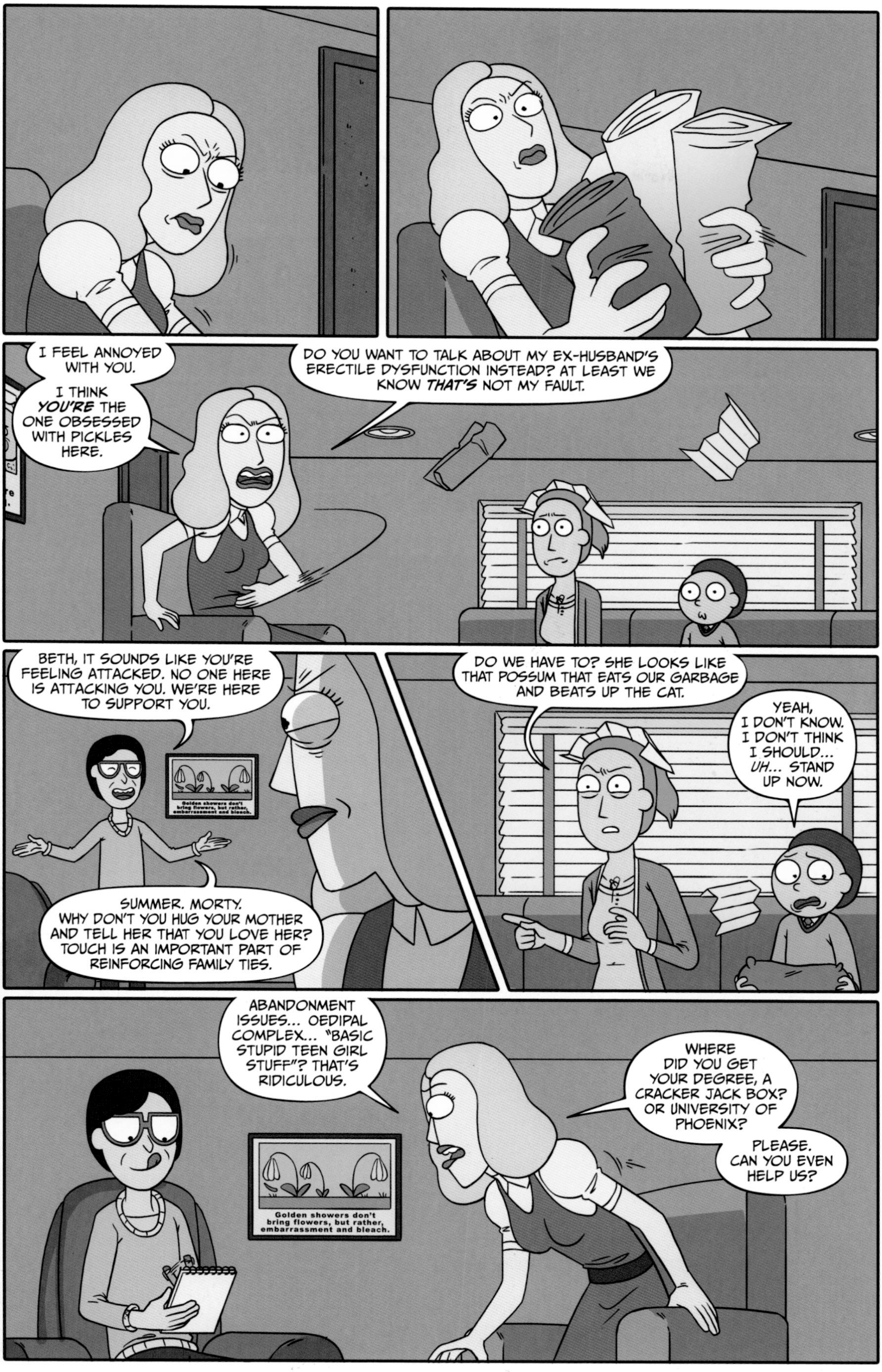
I FEEL ANNOYED WITH YOU.
I THINK *YOU'RE* THE ONE OBSESSED WITH PICKLES HERE.
DO YOU WANT TO TALK ABOUT MY EX-HUSBAND'S ERECTILE DYSFUNCTION INSTEAD? AT LEAST WE KNOW *THAT'S* NOT MY FAULT.
BETH, IT SOUNDS LIKE YOU'RE FEELING ATTACKED. NO ONE HERE IS ATTACKING YOU. WE'RE HERE TO SUPPORT YOU.
Golden showers don't bring flowers, but rather, embarrassment and bleach.
SUMMER. MORTY. WHY DON'T YOU HUG YOUR MOTHER AND TELL HER THAT YOU LOVE HER? TOUCH IS AN IMPORTANT PART OF REINFORCING FAMILY TIES.
DO WE HAVE TO? SHE LOOKS LIKE THAT POSSUM THAT EATS OUR GARBAGE AND BEATS UP THE CAT.
YEAH, I DON'T KNOW. I DON'T THINK I SHOULD... *UH*... STAND UP NOW.
ABANDONMENT ISSUES... OEDIPAL COMPLEX... "BASIC STUPID TEEN GIRL STUFF"? THAT'S RIDICULOUS.
Golden showers don't bring flowers, but rather, embarrassment and bleach.
WHERE DID YOU GET YOUR DEGREE, A CRACKER JACK BOX? OR UNIVERSITY OF PHOENIX?
PLEASE. CAN YOU EVEN HELP US?

DR. SCRAPS, CAN YOU DO ANYTHING FOR THEM?
I DON'T KNOW. WE'VE NEVER SEEN A WEAPON LIKE THIS BEFORE.
IT IS TRULY TERRIFYING, THE POWER OF THE CATBANE.
DO NOT CALL HIM THAT NAME. DO NOT GIVE HIM THAT POWER. IT IS MY ONCE BENEFACTOR, RICK, AND HE IS BUT A MAN. A MAN WHO IS ALSO A VEGETABLE.
IT IS VERY CONFUSING.
COMMANDER SNOWBALL, HERE IS ANOTHER VICTIM. BUT I WANT-- I NEED--TO CHASE--
NO! YOU MUST RESIST! THAT IS YOUR COMRADE. YOUR FRIEND, SPARKY. IT IS NOT A BALL!
HE IS NOT A BALL.
RICK SANCHEZ, YOU HAVE DAMAGED OUR PACK. YOU HAVE DONE IRREPARABLE DAMAGE TO THE BUILDING, ASSURING THAT WE WILL NOT GET OUR SECURITY DEPOSIT BACK. YOU ARE NO LONGER MY FRIEND.
YOU ARE NOT A GOOD BOY.

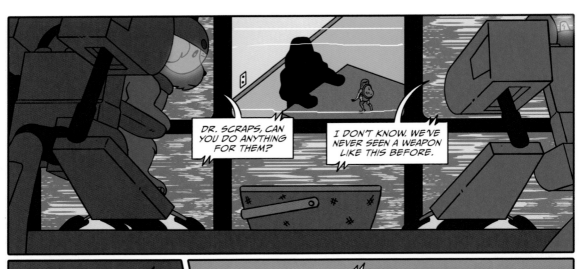

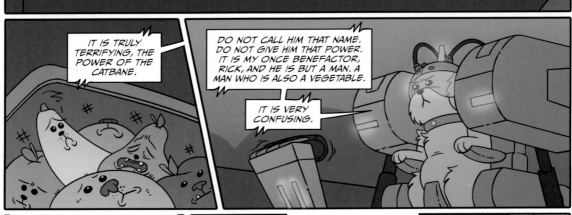

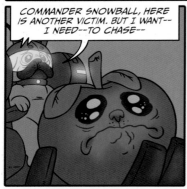

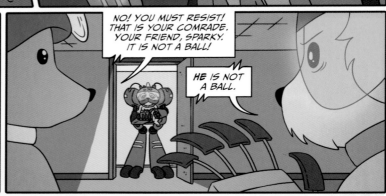

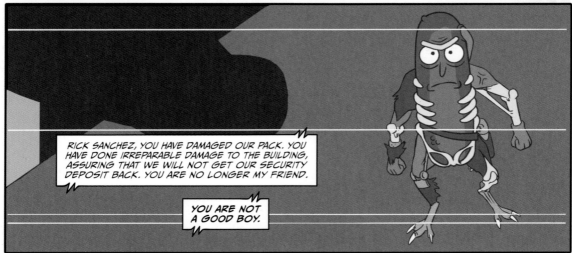

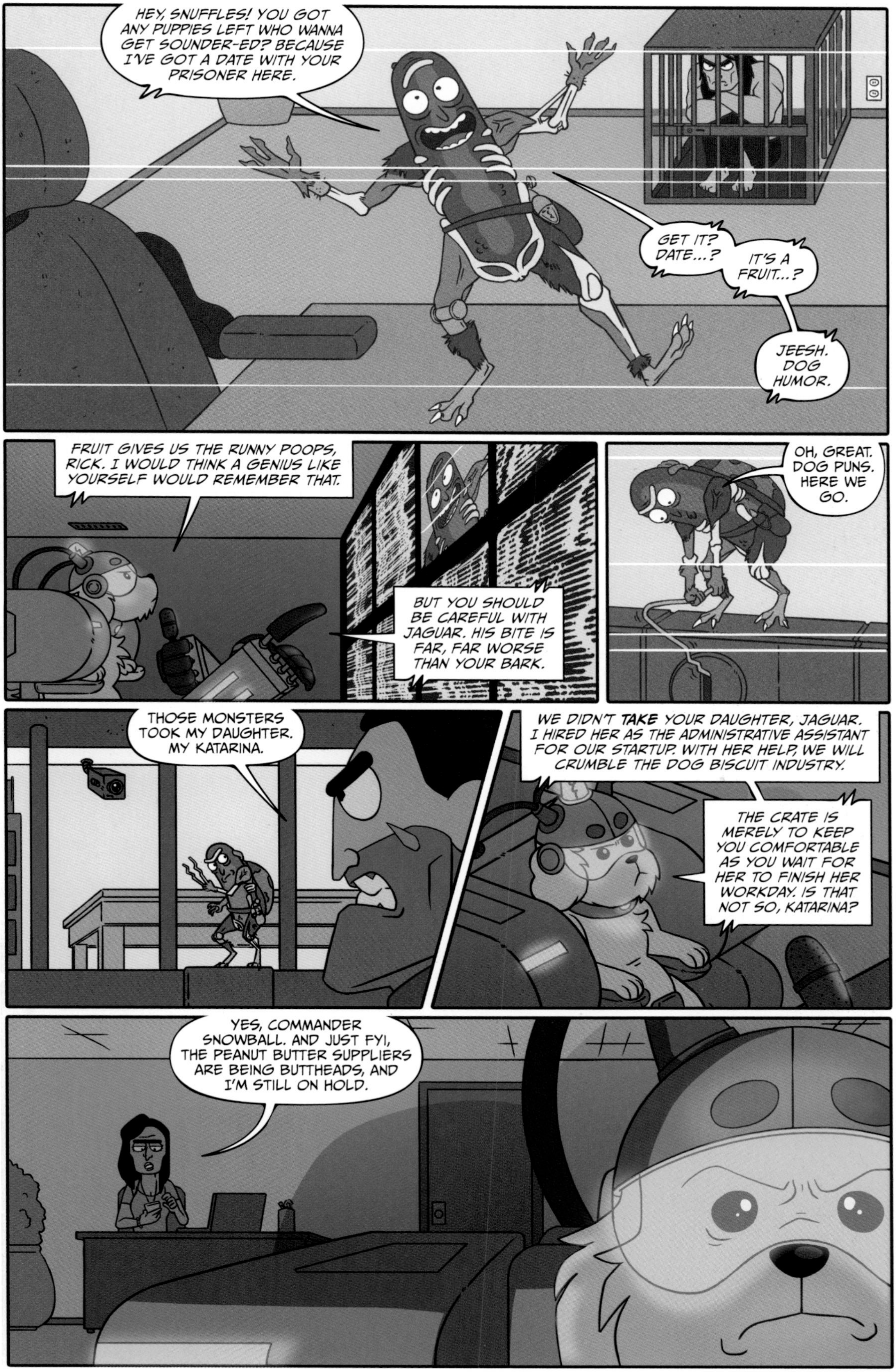
HEY, SNUFFLES! YOU GOT ANY PUPPIES LEFT WHO WANNA GET SOUNDER-ED? BECAUSE I'VE GOT A DATE WITH YOUR PRISONER HERE.
GET IT? DATE...?
IT'S A FRUIT...?
JEESH. DOG HUMOR.
FRUIT GIVES US THE RUNNY POOPS, RICK. I WOULD THINK A GENIUS LIKE YOURSELF WOULD REMEMBER THAT.
BUT YOU SHOULD BE CAREFUL WITH JAGUAR. HIS BITE IS FAR, FAR WORSE THAN YOUR BARK.
OH, GREAT. DOG PUNS. HERE WE GO.
THOSE MONSTERS TOOK MY DAUGHTER. MY KATARINA.
WE DIDN'T **TAKE** YOUR DAUGHTER, JAGUAR. I HIRED HER AS THE ADMINISTRATIVE ASSISTANT FOR OUR STARTUP. WITH HER HELP, WE WILL CRUMBLE THE DOG BISCUIT INDUSTRY.
THE CRATE IS MERELY TO KEEP YOU COMFORTABLE AS YOU WAIT FOR HER TO FINISH HER WORKDAY. IS THAT NOT SO, KATARINA?
YES, COMMANDER SNOWBALL. AND JUST FYI, THE PEANUT BUTTER SUPPLIERS ARE BEING BUTTHEADS, AND I'M STILL ON HOLD.

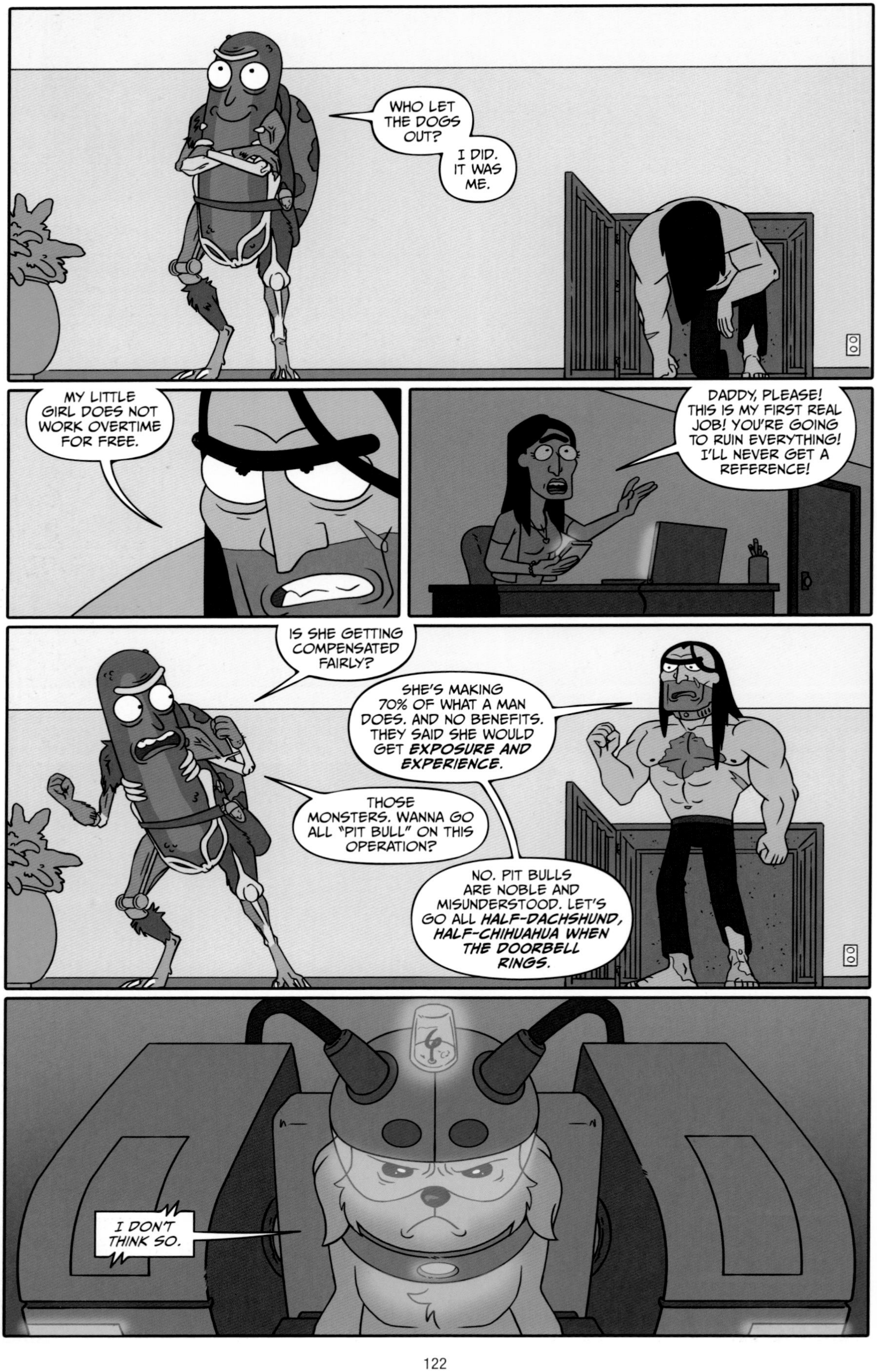
WHO LET THE DOGS OUT?
I DID. IT WAS ME.
MY LITTLE GIRL DOES NOT WORK OVERTIME FOR FREE.
DADDY, PLEASE! THIS IS MY FIRST REAL JOB! YOU'RE GOING TO RUIN EVERYTHING! I'LL NEVER GET A REFERENCE!
IS SHE GETTING COMPENSATED FAIRLY?
SHE'S MAKING 70% OF WHAT A MAN DOES. AND NO BENEFITS. THEY SAID SHE WOULD GET EXPOSURE AND EXPERIENCE.
THOSE MONSTERS. WANNA GO ALL "PIT BULL" ON THIS OPERATION?
NO. PIT BULLS ARE NOBLE AND MISUNDERSTOOD. LET'S GO ALL HALF-DACHSHUND, HALF-CHIHUAHUA WHEN THE DOORBELL RINGS.
I DON'T THINK SO.

GET BACK IN YOUR CRATE AND BEHAVE UNTIL 5PM.
ARRRGH!
ZZZZT
YEAH, I DON'T--URRRRRP--TAKE ORDERS FROM PHONE SPEAKERS. OR INBRED PUPPY MILL REFUGEES WHO GOT NEUTERED TOO EARLY AND CONSTANTLY PIDDLE ON THINGS.
HEY, NOW. DON'T SHOOT, PICKLE MAN. I THOUGHT WE WERE ON THE SAME SIDE!
WE ARE. YOU JUST DON'T HAVE THE BENEFIT OF THE FOURTH WALL.
RAAHHH!
THUD
I'M COMING FOR YOU NEXT. AND YOU DON'T HAVE A SNOWBALL'S CHANCE IN HELL.

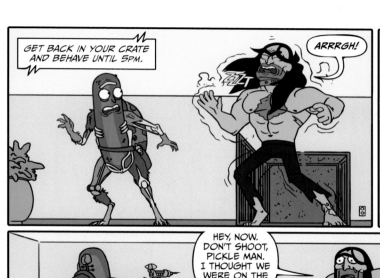

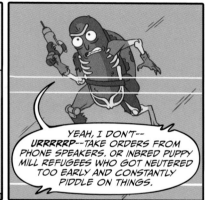

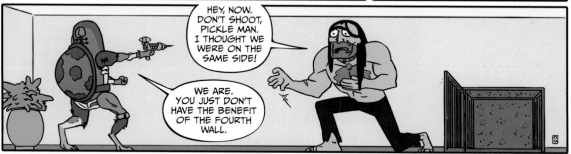

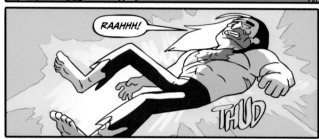

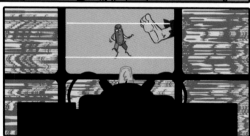

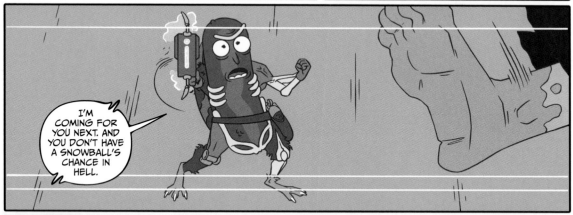

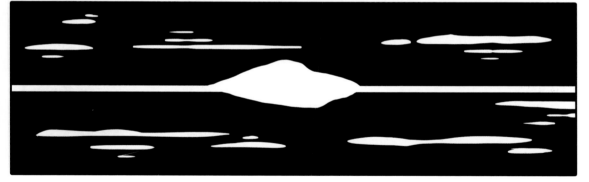

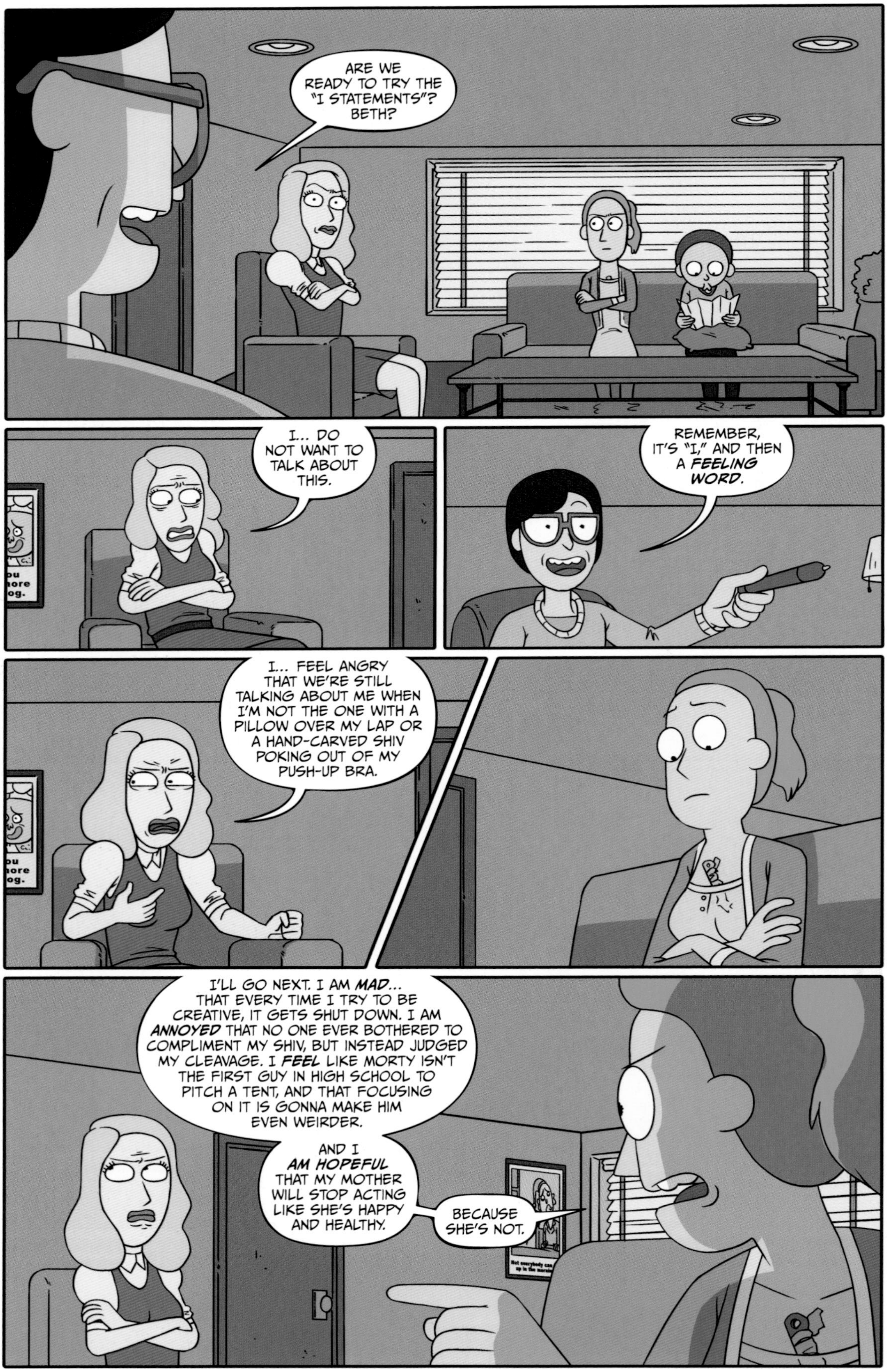
ARE WE READY TO TRY THE "I STATEMENTS"? BETH?
I... DO NOT WANT TO TALK ABOUT THIS.
REMEMBER, IT'S "I," AND THEN A ***FEELING WORD***.
I... FEEL ANGRY THAT WE'RE STILL TALKING ABOUT ME WHEN I'M NOT THE ONE WITH A PILLOW OVER MY LAP OR A HAND-CARVED SHIV POKING OUT OF MY PUSH-UP BRA.
I'LL GO NEXT. I AM ***MAD***... THAT EVERY TIME I TRY TO BE CREATIVE, IT GETS SHUT DOWN. I AM ***ANNOYED*** THAT NO ONE EVER BOTHERED TO COMPLIMENT MY SHIV, BUT INSTEAD JUDGED MY CLEAVAGE. I ***FEEL*** LIKE MORTY ISN'T THE FIRST GUY IN HIGH SCHOOL TO PITCH A TENT, AND THAT FOCUSING ON IT IS GONNA MAKE HIM EVEN WEIRDER.
AND I ***AM HOPEFUL*** THAT MY MOTHER WILL STOP ACTING LIKE SHE'S HAPPY AND HEALTHY.
BECAUSE SHE'S NOT.

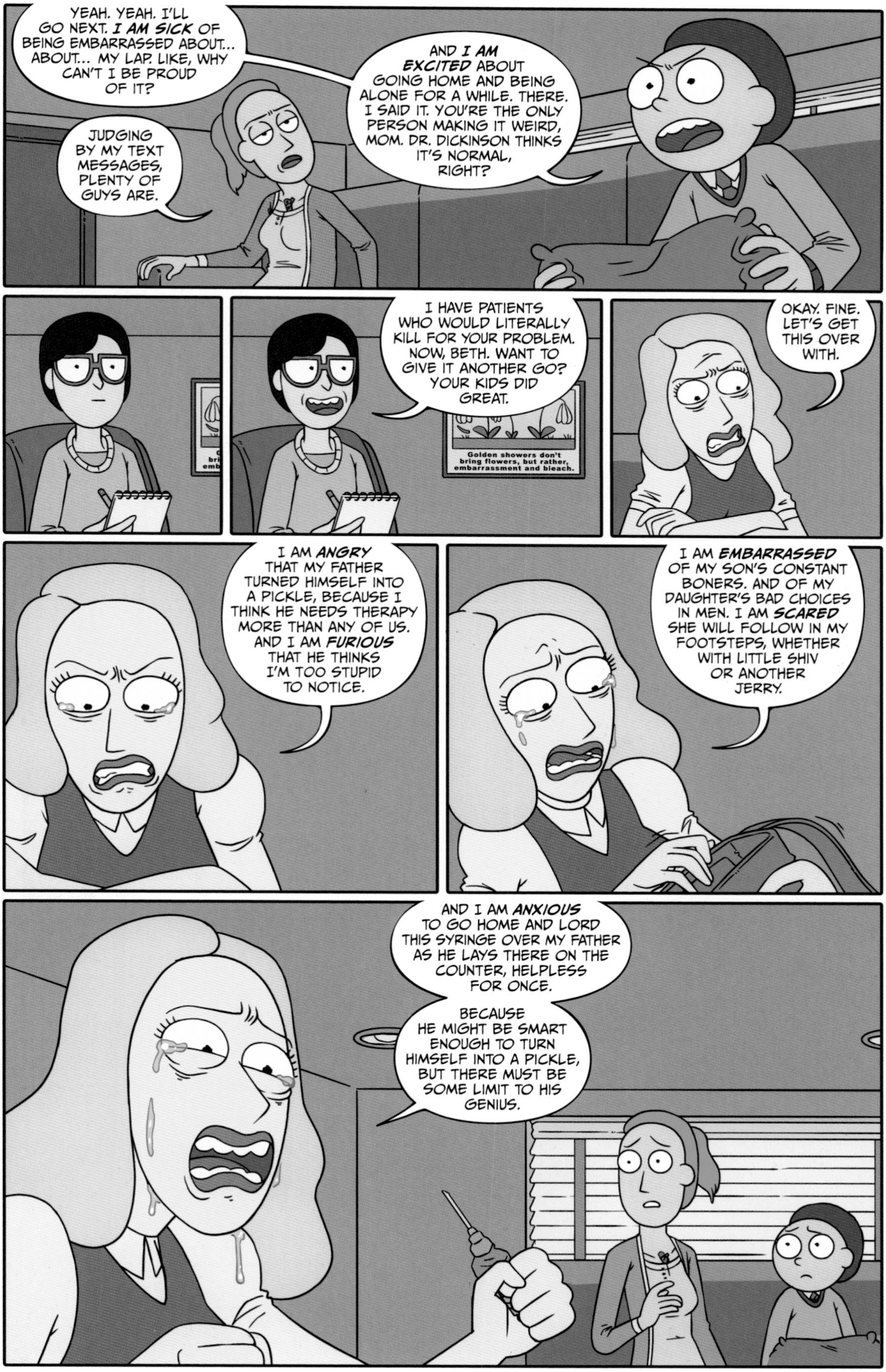
YEAH. YEAH. I'LL GO NEXT. I AM SICK OF BEING EMBARRASSED ABOUT... ABOUT... MY LAP. LIKE, WHY CAN'T I BE PROUD OF IT?
JUDGING BY MY TEXT MESSAGES, PLENTY OF GUYS ARE.
AND I AM EXCITED ABOUT GOING HOME AND BEING ALONE FOR A WHILE. THERE. I SAID IT. YOU'RE THE ONLY PERSON MAKING IT WEIRD, MOM. DR. DICKINSON THINKS IT'S NORMAL, RIGHT?
I HAVE PATIENTS WHO WOULD LITERALLY KILL FOR YOUR PROBLEM. NOW, BETH. WANT TO GIVE IT ANOTHER GO? YOUR KIDS DID GREAT.
Golden showers don't bring flowers, but rather, embarrassment and bleach.
OKAY. FINE. LET'S GET THIS OVER WITH.
I AM ANGRY THAT MY FATHER TURNED HIMSELF INTO A PICKLE, BECAUSE I THINK HE NEEDS THERAPY MORE THAN ANY OF US. AND I AM FURIOUS THAT HE THINKS I'M TOO STUPID TO NOTICE.
I AM EMBARRASSED OF MY SON'S CONSTANT BONERS. AND OF MY DAUGHTER'S BAD CHOICES IN MEN. I AM SCARED SHE WILL FOLLOW IN MY FOOTSTEPS, WHETHER WITH LITTLE SHIV OR ANOTHER JERRY.
AND I AM ANXIOUS TO GO HOME AND LORD THIS SYRINGE OVER MY FATHER AS HE LAYS THERE ON THE COUNTER, HELPLESS FOR ONCE.
BECAUSE HE MIGHT BE SMART ENOUGH TO TURN HIMSELF INTO A PICKLE, BUT THERE MUST BE SOME LIMIT TO HIS GENIUS.

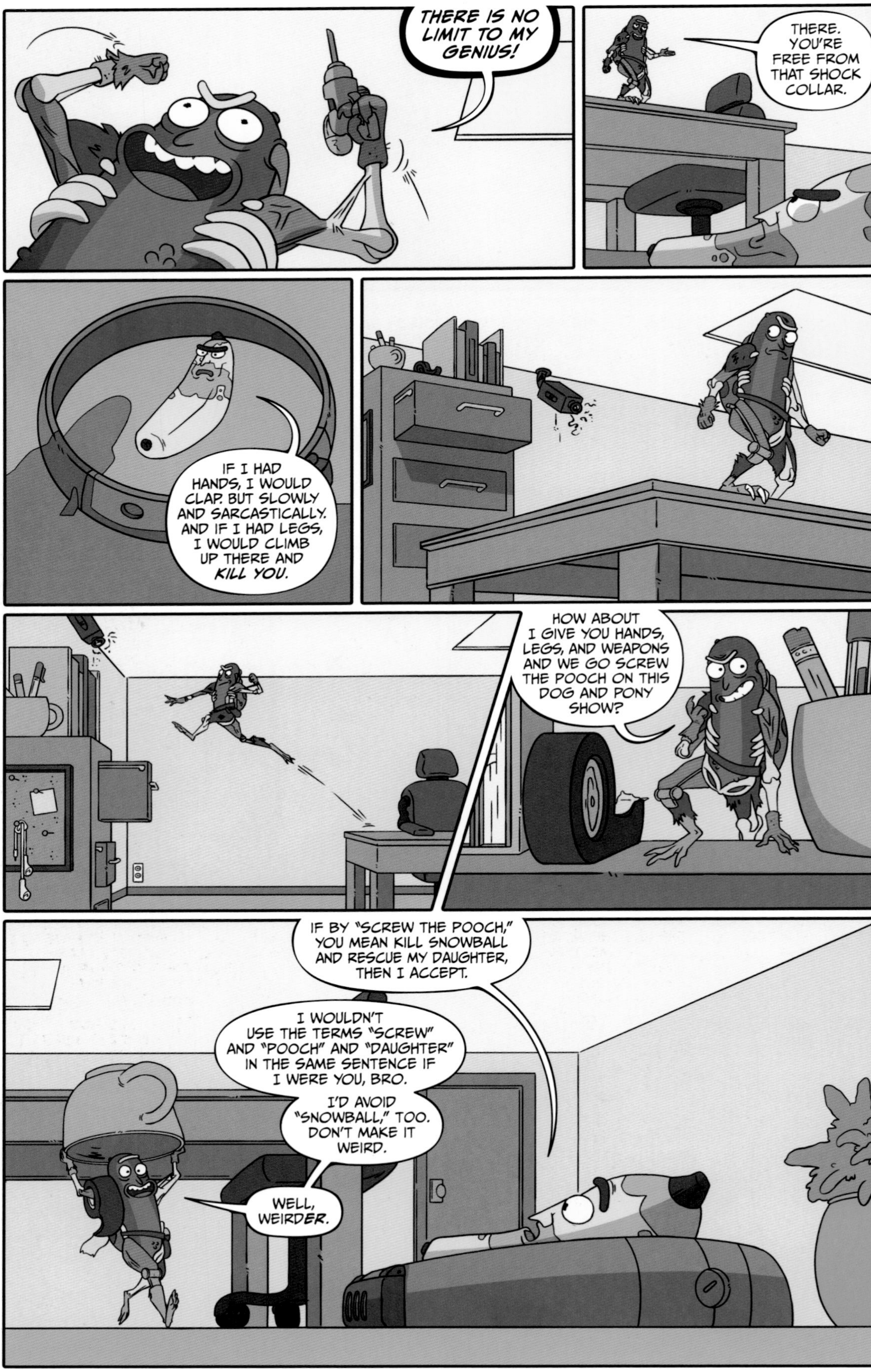

THERE IS NO LIMIT TO MY GENIUS!
THERE. YOU'RE FREE FROM THAT SHOCK COLLAR.
IF I HAD HANDS, I WOULD CLAP. BUT SLOWLY AND SARCASTICALLY. AND IF I HAD LEGS, I WOULD CLIMB UP THERE AND *KILL YOU.*
HOW ABOUT I GIVE YOU HANDS, LEGS, AND WEAPONS AND WE GO SCREW THE POOCH ON THIS DOG AND PONY SHOW?
IF BY "SCREW THE POOCH," YOU MEAN KILL SNOWBALL AND RESCUE MY DAUGHTER, THEN I ACCEPT.
I WOULDN'T USE THE TERMS "SCREW" AND "POOCH" AND "DAUGHTER" IN THE SAME SENTENCE IF I WERE YOU, BRO.
I'D AVOID "SNOWBALL," TOO. DON'T MAKE IT WEIRD.
WELL, WEIRD*ER*.

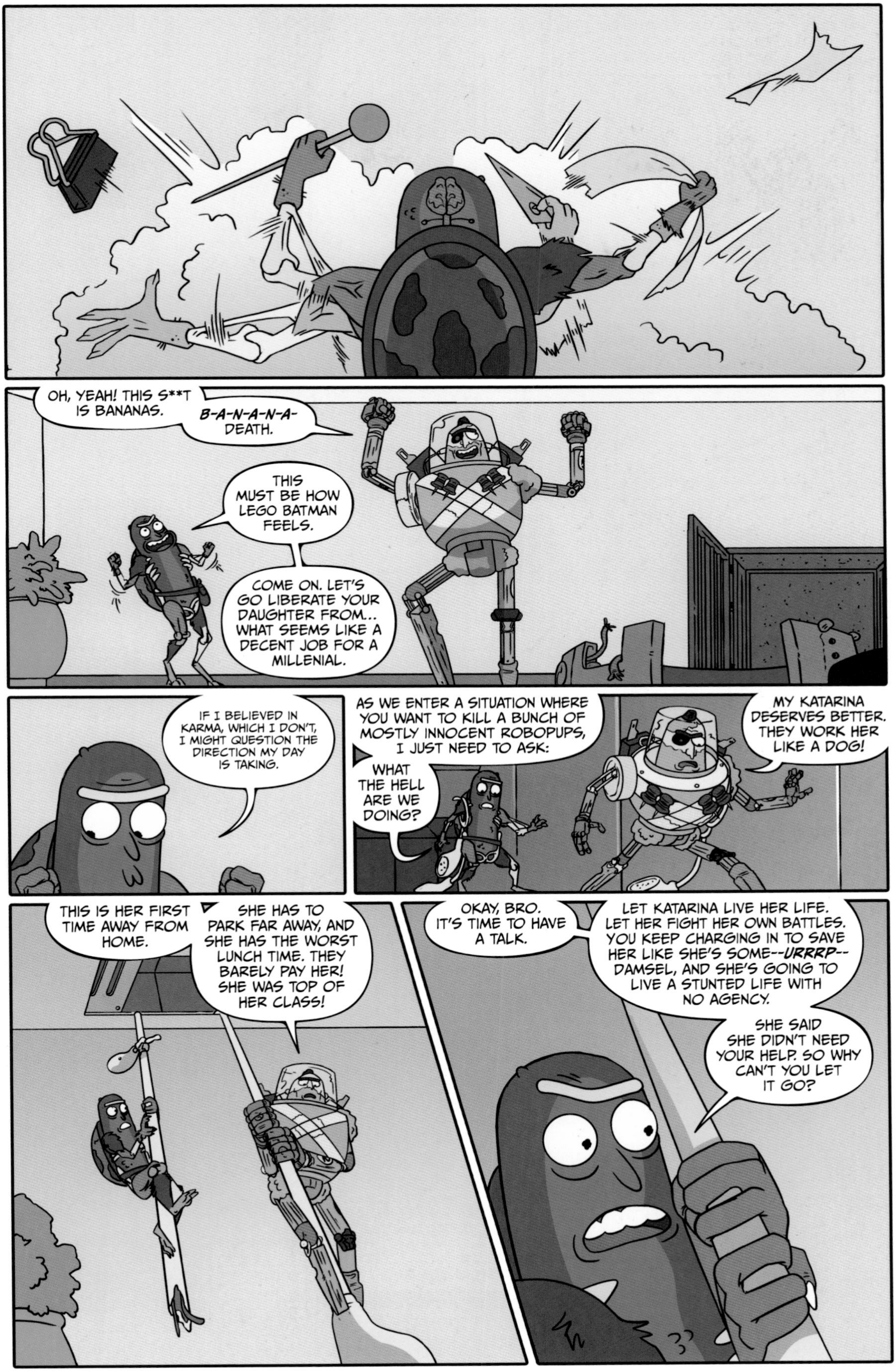

OH, YEAH! THIS S**T IS BANANAS.
B-A-N-A-N-A-DEATH.
THIS MUST BE HOW LEGO BATMAN FEELS.
COME ON. LET'S GO LIBERATE YOUR DAUGHTER FROM... WHAT SEEMS LIKE A DECENT JOB FOR A MILLENIAL.
IF I BELIEVED IN KARMA, WHICH I DON'T, I MIGHT QUESTION THE DIRECTION MY DAY IS TAKING.
AS WE ENTER A SITUATION WHERE YOU WANT TO KILL A BUNCH OF MOSTLY INNOCENT ROBOPUPS, I JUST NEED TO ASK:
WHAT THE HELL ARE WE DOING?
MY KATARINA DESERVES BETTER. THEY WORK HER LIKE A DOG!
THIS IS HER FIRST TIME AWAY FROM HOME.
SHE HAS TO PARK FAR AWAY, AND SHE HAS THE WORST LUNCH TIME. THEY BARELY PAY HER! SHE WAS TOP OF HER CLASS!
OKAY, BRO. IT'S TIME TO HAVE A TALK.
LET KATARINA LIVE HER LIFE. LET HER FIGHT HER OWN BATTLES. YOU KEEP CHARGING IN TO SAVE HER LIKE SHE'S SOME--URRRP--DAMSEL, AND SHE'S GOING TO LIVE A STUNTED LIFE WITH NO AGENCY.
SHE SAID SHE DIDN'T NEED YOUR HELP. SO WHY CAN'T YOU LET IT GO?

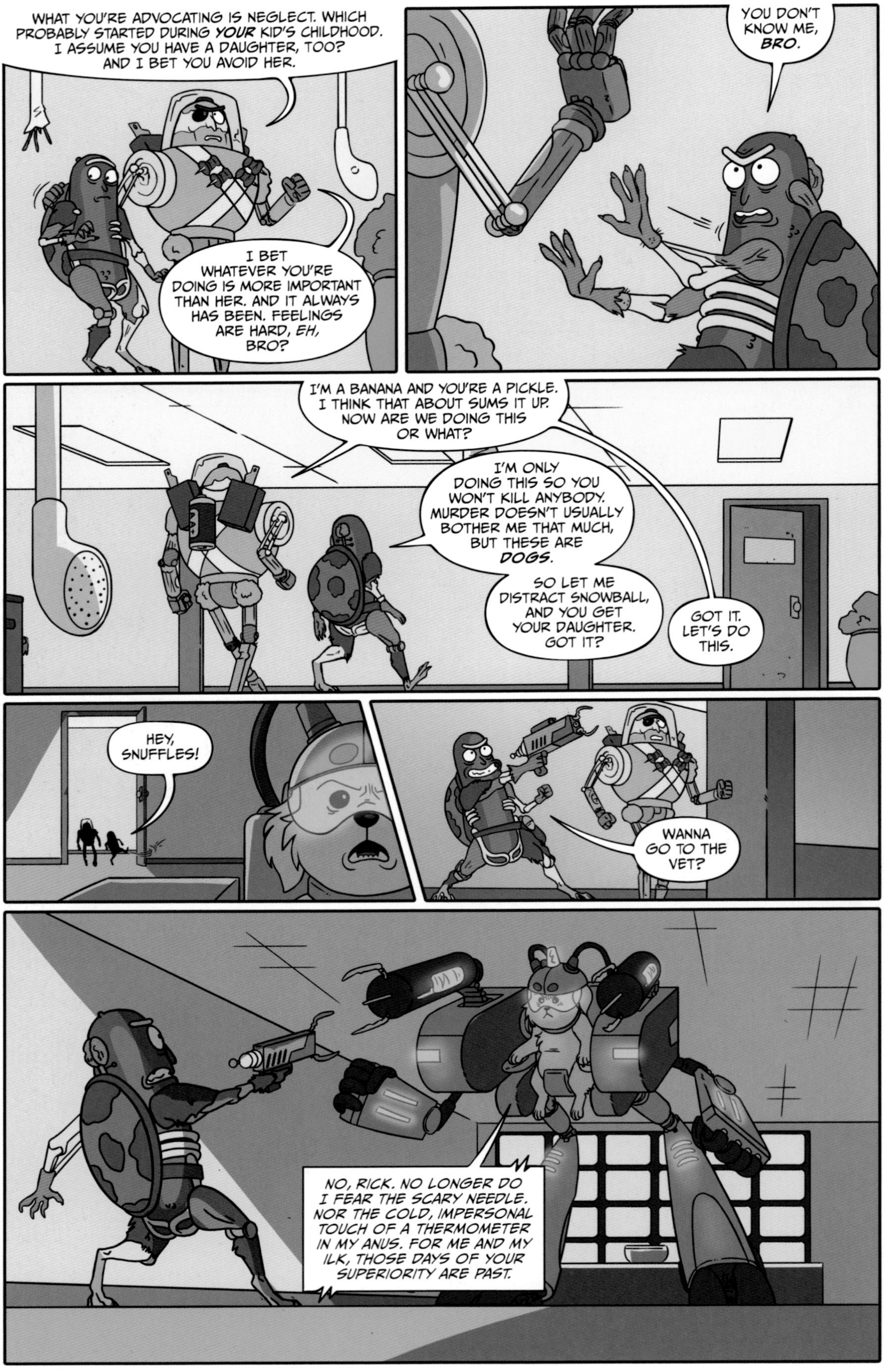
WHAT YOU'RE ADVOCATING IS NEGLECT. WHICH PROBABLY STARTED DURING YOUR KID'S CHILDHOOD. I ASSUME YOU HAVE A DAUGHTER, TOO? AND I BET YOU AVOID HER.
I BET WHATEVER YOU'RE DOING IS MORE IMPORTANT THAN HER. AND IT ALWAYS HAS BEEN. FEELINGS ARE HARD, EH, BRO?
YOU DON'T KNOW ME, BRO.
I'M A BANANA AND YOU'RE A PICKLE. I THINK THAT ABOUT SUMS IT UP. NOW ARE WE DOING THIS OR WHAT?
I'M ONLY DOING THIS SO YOU WON'T KILL ANYBODY. MURDER DOESN'T USUALLY BOTHER ME THAT MUCH, BUT THESE ARE DOGS.
SO LET ME DISTRACT SNOWBALL, AND YOU GET YOUR DAUGHTER. GOT IT?
GOT IT. LET'S DO THIS.
HEY, SNUFFLES!
WANNA GO TO THE VET?
NO, RICK. NO LONGER DO I FEAR THE SCARY NEEDLE. NOR THE COLD, IMPERSONAL TOUCH OF A THERMOMETER IN MY ANUS. FOR ME AND MY ILK, THOSE DAYS OF YOUR SUPERIORITY ARE PAST.

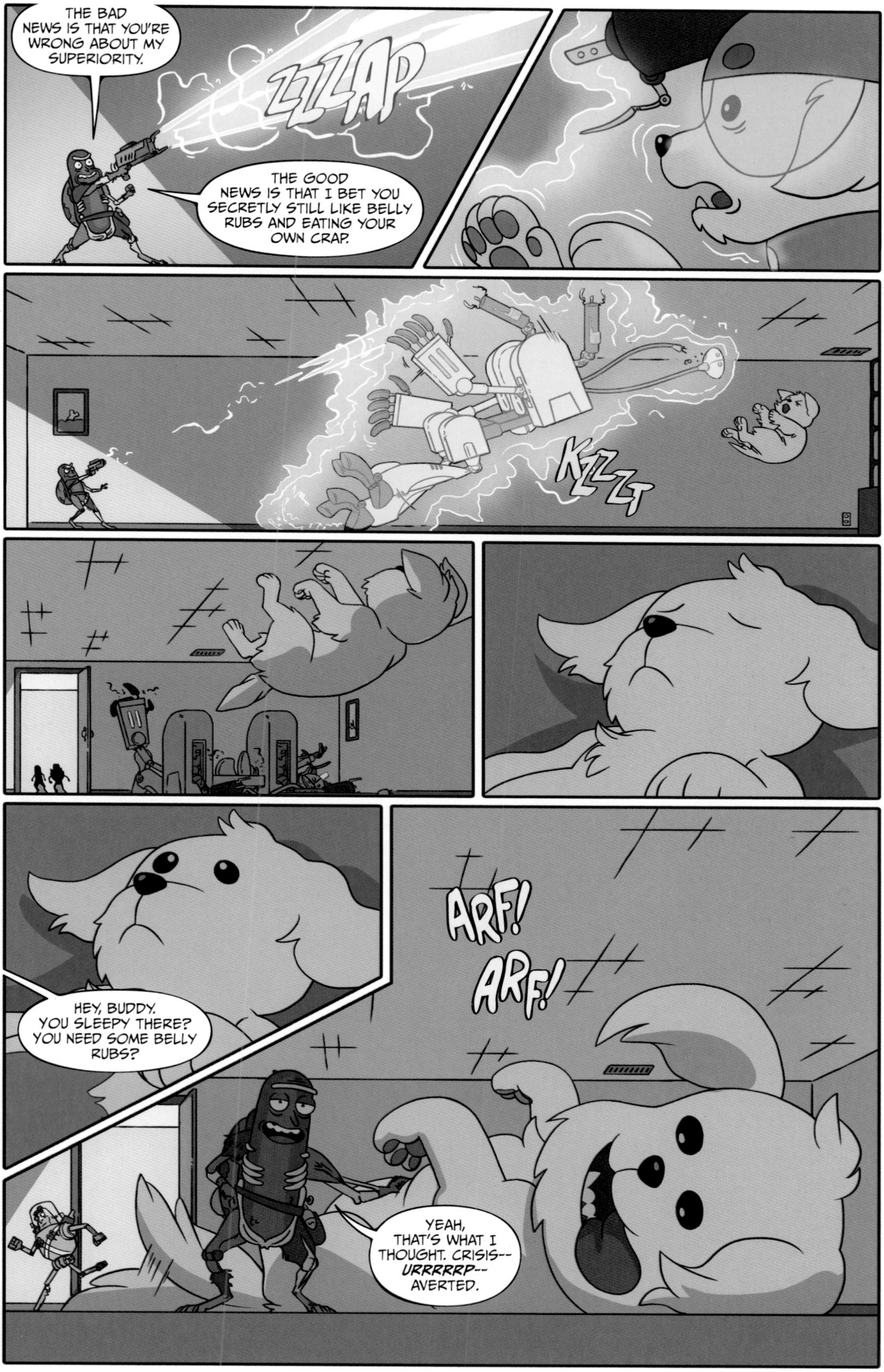
THE BAD NEWS IS THAT YOU'RE WRONG ABOUT MY SUPERIORITY.
ZZZAP
THE GOOD NEWS IS THAT I BET YOU SECRETLY STILL LIKE BELLY RUBS AND EATING YOUR OWN CRAP.
KZZZT
HEY, BUDDY. YOU SLEEPY THERE? YOU NEED SOME BELLY RUBS?
ARF!
ARF!
YEAH, THAT'S WHAT I THOUGHT. CRISIS-- *URRRRRP--* AVERTED.

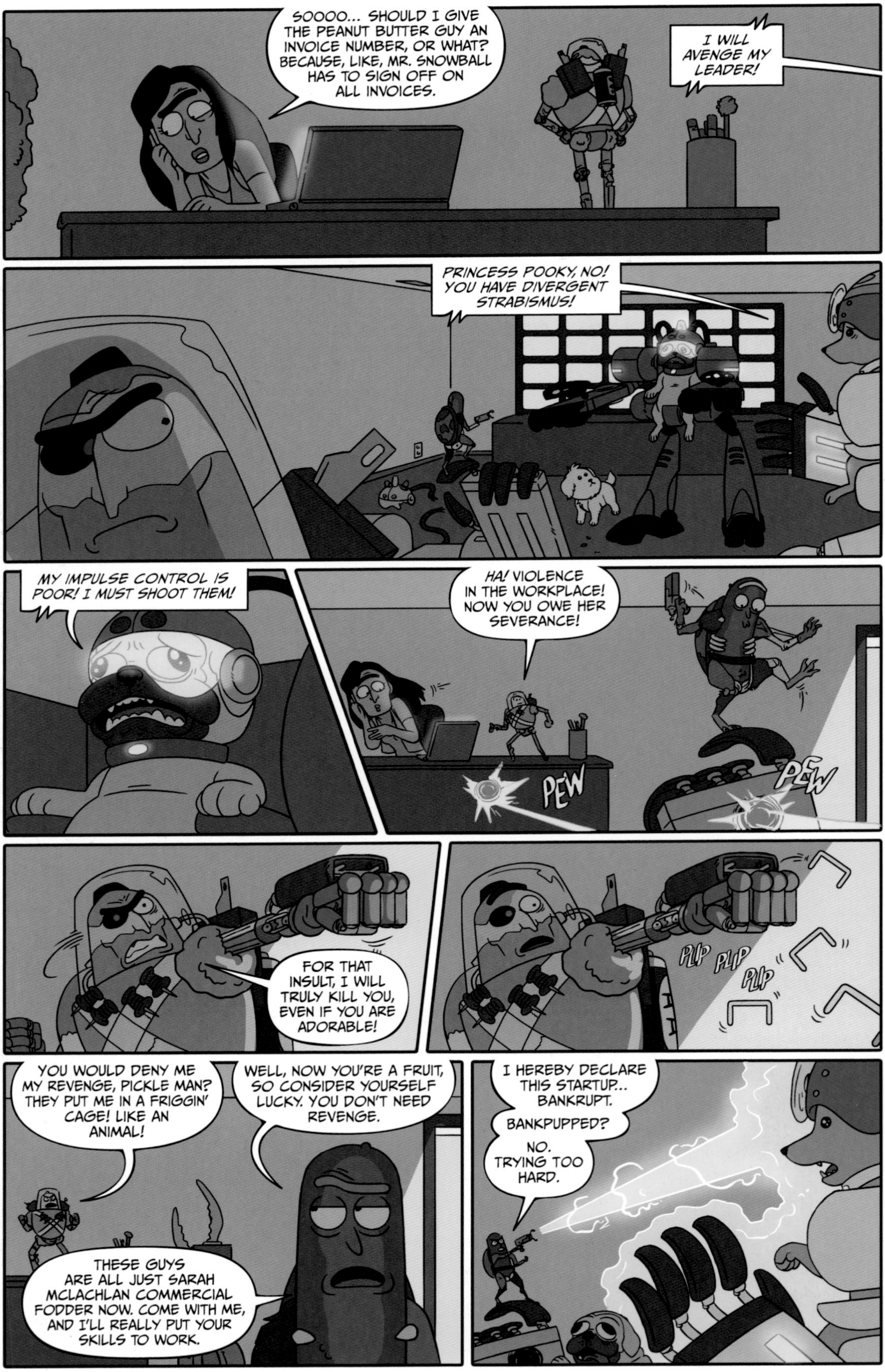
SOOOO... SHOULD I GIVE THE PEANUT BUTTER GUY AN INVOICE NUMBER, OR WHAT? BECAUSE, LIKE, MR. SNOWBALL HAS TO SIGN OFF ON ALL INVOICES.
I WILL AVENGE MY LEADER!
PRINCESS POOKY, NO! YOU HAVE DIVERGENT STRABISMUS!
MY IMPULSE CONTROL IS POOR! I MUST SHOOT THEM!
HA! VIOLENCE IN THE WORKPLACE! NOW YOU OWE HER SEVERANCE!
PEW
PEW
FOR THAT INSULT, I WILL TRULY KILL YOU, EVEN IF YOU ARE ADORABLE!
PLIP
PLIP
PLIP
YOU WOULD DENY ME MY REVENGE, PICKLE MAN? THEY PUT ME IN A FRIGGIN' CAGE! LIKE AN ANIMAL!
WELL, NOW YOU'RE A FRUIT, SO CONSIDER YOURSELF LUCKY. YOU DON'T NEED REVENGE.
THESE GUYS ARE ALL JUST SARAH MCLACHLAN COMMERCIAL FODDER NOW. COME WITH ME, AND I'LL REALLY PUT YOUR SKILLS TO WORK.
I HEREBY DECLARE THIS STARTUP... BANKRUPT.
BANKPUPPED?
NO. TRYING TOO HARD.

GO ON, DADDY. I NEED TO TAKE THESE LITTLE GUYS OUT TO WINKY TINK.

OKAY, HONEY. MAKE SURE YOU'RE HOME BEFORE DARK. AND DON'T TALK TO STRANGE MEN. OR BRING HOME THOSE DOGS.

SNORT SNURRG

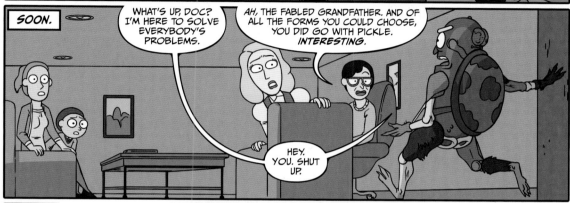

SOON.

WHAT'S UP, DOC? I'M HERE TO SOLVE EVERYBODY'S PROBLEMS.

AH, THE FABLED GRANDFATHER. AND OF ALL THE FORMS YOU COULD CHOOSE, YOU DID GO WITH PICKLE. *INTERESTING.*

HEY. YOU. SHUT UP.

MORTY, YOU'RE JUST LONELY BECAUSE HIGH SCHOOL IS A BORING HELL THAT MAKES EVERYONE AWARE OF HOW DEEPLY FLAWED AND UNLOVABLE THEY ARE. AND ALSO BECAUSE SIDE BOOB.

HERE'S YOUR F*****G DOG.

SNUFFLES!!

BETH, I LOVE YOU, BUT I HATE THERAPY. OKAY? SUMMER, YOU JUST WANT MALE ATTENTION. SO HERE I AM. LET'S, I DON'T KNOW, GO BACK TO THAT PLANET WHERE THEY LIKED YOUR DUMB SHIRT. DR. DICKINSON, THE MOTHERLODE OF PATIENTS IS IN YOUR WAITING ROOM. START BY ASKING HIM WHY HIS NAME IS JAGUAR.

NOW, HOW ABOUT THAT SYRINGE?

NO! I'VE HAD ENOUGH. YOU'RE MESSING UP THIS ENTIRE FAMILY, AND YOU NEVER TAKE RESPONSIBILITY.

I SHOULD BREAK THIS SYRINGE. YOU HAVE NO IDEA HOW HARD MY DAY HAS BEEN!

MOM, HE'S LITERALLY A PICKLE COVERED IN RAT GUTS.

...NOW YOU CAN SEE HOW HARD MY DAY HAS BEEN. ALL OF YOU.

GENIUS ISN'T-- *URRRP*--EASY.

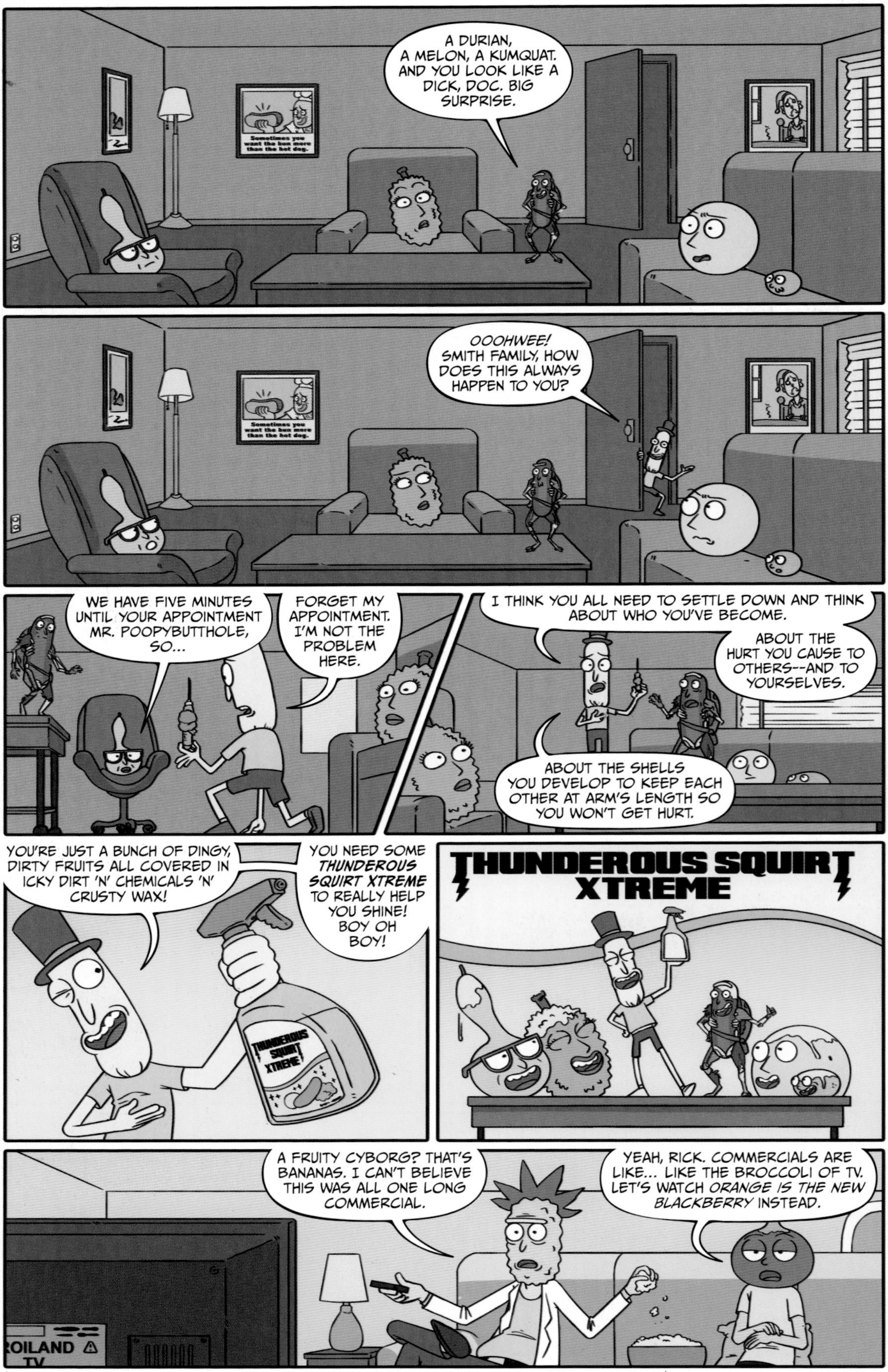
A DURIAN, A MELON, A KUMQUAT. AND YOU LOOK LIKE A DICK, DOC. BIG SURPRISE.
Sometimes you want the bun more than the hot dog.
OOOHWEE! SMITH FAMILY, HOW DOES THIS ALWAYS HAPPEN TO YOU?
Sometimes you want the bun more than the hot dog.
WE HAVE FIVE MINUTES UNTIL YOUR APPOINTMENT MR. POOPYBUTTHOLE, SO...
FORGET MY APPOINTMENT. I'M NOT THE PROBLEM HERE.
I THINK YOU ALL NEED TO SETTLE DOWN AND THINK ABOUT WHO YOU'VE BECOME.
ABOUT THE HURT YOU CAUSE TO OTHERS--AND TO YOURSELVES.
ABOUT THE SHELLS YOU DEVELOP TO KEEP EACH OTHER AT ARM'S LENGTH SO YOU WON'T GET HURT.
YOU'RE JUST A BUNCH OF DINGY, DIRTY FRUITS ALL COVERED IN ICKY DIRT 'N' CHEMICALS 'N' CRUSTY WAX!
YOU NEED SOME *THUNDEROUS SQUIRT XTREME* TO REALLY HELP YOU SHINE! BOY OH BOY!
THUNDEROUS SQUIRT XTREME
THUNDEROUS SQUIRT XTREME
A FRUITY CYBORG? THAT'S BANANAS. I CAN'T BELIEVE THIS WAS ALL ONE LONG COMMERCIAL.
YEAH, RICK. COMMERCIALS ARE LIKE... LIKE THE BROCCOLI OF TV. LET'S WATCH *ORANGE IS THE NEW BLACKBERRY* INSTEAD.
ROILAND TV

THE END.

DAN HARMON is the Emmy® winning creator/executive producer of the comedy series *Community* as well as the co-creator/executive producer of **[adult swim]** 's *Rick and Morty* ™.

Harmon's pursuit of minimal work for maximum reward took him from stand-up to improv to sketch comedy, then finally to Los Angeles, where he began writing feature screenplays with fellow Milwaukeean Rob Schrab. As part of his deal with Robert Zemeckis at Imagemovers, Harmon co-wrote the feature film *Monster House*. Following this, Harmon co-wrote the Ben Stiller-directed pilot *Heat Vision and Jack*, starring Jack Black and Owen Wilson.

Disillusioned by the legitimate industry, Harmon began attending classes at nearby Glendale Community College. At the same time, Harmon and Schrab founded Channel 101, an untelevised non-profit audience-controlled network for undiscovered filmmakers, many of whom used it to launch mainstream careers, including the boys behind SNL's Digital Shorts. Harmon, along with Schrab, partnered with Sarah Silverman to create her Comedy Central series, *The Sarah Silverman Program*, where he served as head writer for the first season.

Harmon went on to create, write, and perform in the short-lived VH1 sketch series *Acceptable TV* before eventually creating the critically acclaimed and fan-favorite comedy *Community*. The show originally aired on NBC for five seasons before being acquired by Yahoo, which premiered season six of the show in March 2015. In 2009, he won an Emmy for Outstanding Music and Lyrics for the opening number of the 81st Annual Academy Awards.

Along with Justin Roiland, Harmon created the breakout **[adult swim]** animated series *Rick and Morty* ™. The show premiered in December 2013 and quickly became a ratings hit. Harmon and Roiland have wrapped up season three, which premiered in 2017.

In 2014, Harmon was the star of the documentary *Harmontown*, which premiered at the SXSW Film Festival and chronicled his 20-city stand-up/podcast tour of the same name. The documentary was released theatrically in October 2014.

JUSTIN ROILAND grew up in Manteca, California, where he did the basic stuff children do. Later in life he traveled to Los Angeles. Once settled in, he created several popular online shorts for Channel 101. Justin is afraid of his mortality and hopes the things he creates will make lots of people happy. Then maybe when modern civilization collapses into chaos, people will remember him and they'll help him survive the bloodshed and violence. Global economic collapse is looming. It's going to be horrible, and honestly, a swift death might be preferable than living in the hell that awaits mankind.

Justin also really hates writing about himself in the third person. I hate this. That's right. It's me. I've been writing this whole thing. Hi. The cat's out of the bag. It's just you and me now. There never was a third person. If you want to know anything about me, just ask. Sorry this wasn't more informative.

J. TORRES is a comic book writer orbiting near Toronto, Canada. His other writing credits include *Do-Gooders, How to Spot a Sasquatch, BroBots, Teen Titans Go,* and *The Mighty Zodiac*. His favorite princesses are Disney's Snow White, Mononoke, The Paperbag Princess, Starfire, and Wonder Woman.

DANIEL MALLORY ORTBERG is the co-founder of *The Toast* and the current *Dear Prudence* at Slate. He is the author of *Texts From Jane Eyre* and *The Merry Spinster*. Follow him on Twitter @danielortberg.